*ROMANCING
SPAIN*

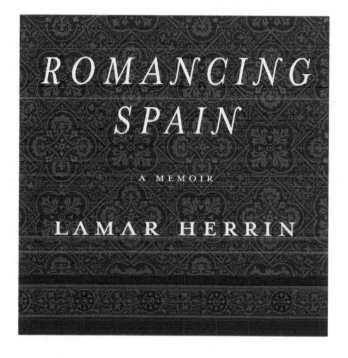

ROMANCING SPAIN

A MEMOIR

LAMAR HERRIN

UNBRIDLED
BOOKS

Unbridled Books
Denver, Colorado

Library of Congress Cataloging-in-Publication Data
Herrin, Lamar.
Romancing Spain : a memoir / Lamar Herrin.
p. cm.
ISBN 1-932961-22-4
1. Herrin, Lamar.   2. Authors, American—20th century—Biography.
3. Spain—Social life and customs—20th century.   I. Title.
PS3558.E754Z48   2006
813'.54—dc22
2006001548

1   3   5   7   9   10   8   6   4   2

Book Design by SH • CV

First Printing

For my wife, Amparo, who,
among all her other lovely gifts,
gave me this love story to write.

ONE

SAY TO MY WIFE, YOU PLAY SANCHO PANZA TO MY Don Quixote and one day I'll return the favor. She reminds me that Panza is a squat tubby little man who is finally a bigger dupe than Quixote himself, and doesn't really think she is suited for the part. My wife is considerably shorter than I am, this is true, not squat but not exactly willowy either, and she is Spanish. Not from La Mancha but Valencia, the region in Spain where the best fruit and vegetables are grown and the women are renowned for their beauty.

My wife is a dreamer but not a dupe. She likes to "fantasize," but she knows the ground she stands on. Old ground. The town in which she was raised had been founded by the Iberians. Then came the Phoenicians and Greeks. The Romans, with a single lovely arch, spanned the ravine, and the bridge still stands. The Visigoths ousted the Romans. Then the Moors took the town and built their citadel, their *alcázar,* on top of the hill. The Christians built their church within the walls of the *alcázar*. My wife used to dig lopsided coins out of the rubble of the old neighborhoods, *los barrios bajos*. These coins were embossed with Roman emperors' heads. Even as a child she knew she stood on three thousand years of Western history.

In the summer they hung a cloth across one side of the bullring and showed the movies the priests approved of. These were mostly American movies extolling the virtues of a small-town hero who saved his town from some intruder, some disaster or some disease. My wife's favorite was Jimmy Stewart, and she fantasized that one day a tall drawling American would come save her. From what? Three thousand years of history?

That bullring was carved out of the stone of the hillside on which it was built. Sure, she could dream, but she knew the stone she sat on. What exactly am I proposing?

There are towns like my wife's scattered all over Spain. Our children are gone, our daughter in college, our son out in his life. We have some time. Why don't we rent a car and travel the country . . .

In search of what?

I don't know. Perhaps a town that somehow transcends all the rest, the prototown that set the standard for those like my wife's.

Hers is named Bocairente. It is located in the hills of Valencia, sixty kilometers from the sea. It manufactures blankets. As picturesque and storied as it is, the town can be almost baroque in its small-minded malice, its class hatreds and its grudges that do not abate with time. In towns like hers, three, four generations sit around their *mesas camillas* at night, with the tablecloth draped over their laps and a coal brazier warming them from beneath, and they tell stories and they do not forget.

Some unflattering aspects of her town she wants me to remember— just in case my romantic nature is about to run away with me.

Surely Sancho Panza gave Don Quixote similar advice. That knight you've set your sights on is a goatherd. He'll kick you in the *cojones* before he'll fight you fair and square. His goats are more chivalrous. Those books are all moldy and those times are past.

She's slipped into her part.

But like Panza, she does not say no to traveling the country with an American who grew up believing that surely there was a city on a hill somewhere that did not glitter with the arches of a McDonald's but with the settled wealth of centuries.

Nevertheless, she offers a very practical suggestion. What would it take for me to make up the perfect town? Why don't we sit down and draw up a list of features?

For some reason I back off. I tell her I wouldn't know where to begin.

Sure, I would. For instance, just how attractive would I want a town to be before the tourists start piling in? A town too beautifully preserved might ensure its own destruction. What had been a modest little palace becomes a *hostal,* that *casa señorial* a gift shop of *cosas típicas.* Does there come a point where beauty and authenticity are mutually exclusive categories? At what point does the balance begin to tip?

This is my wife's least effusive side. She can be exclamatory in her enthusiasms. The Spanish are by nature an exclamatory people. Their rhetoric is such that they can repeat a word or phrase three, four, five times and never depart from the rhythms of common speech. *Pero hombre . . . pero hombre . . . pero hombre . . . Que* this and *que* that. Put them in the presence of an impressionable foreigner, though, and they sober up. They become measured, instructive, rarely begrudging, but in their tone they set up a distance and you know they are keeping something for themselves. You wonder what it is since they are the most obliging of hosts.

Twenty-eight years we've been married and there's a reserve in my wife I still haven't broken through to. Such a theatrical people—it stands to reason they're holding something back.

I think of those small round tables, the *mesas camillas,* three or four generations seated at that still center, that hard core.

Don't be such a Quixote. My wife shakes her head.

Which do you fall in love with first, the woman or the country?

She kisses me on the cheek. She smiles. I don't want to give the wrong impression. My wife is still very girlish. She had the run of that town in which she grew up. Her father was the town secretary, that is, the town's legal authority, and my wife, stunningly pretty as a child, was known as the *secretarieta,* or the little secretary, and everybody buttered her up. She became a gleeful consumer of what the town had to offer. Perhaps twenty years after she'd left the town, I happened to be walking alone in the old neighborhood, the *barrio medieval,* and I heard one woman whisper to another, *Es el marido de la secretarieta*—the husband of the *secretarieta.* Her currency had lasted that long.

Yet that mysterious reserve. And that poise. Everyone knows the Spanish have their reclusive side, their Santa Teresas and their San Juans de la Cruz. A cell into which they withdraw.

Más quixote que quixote, my wife, still smiling, delivers her judgment of me. But there comes a point when nobody would want to be married to one. A befuddled old fool whipping himself into a frenzy on the high desolate plain known as La Mancha. Only a Sancho Panza.

Let me jump ahead.

I am writing these words seated at a leather-topped table in a high-backed chair with my feet up off the floor on a footrest. The floor, par-quet now, would once have been laid with cold tiles. The room is nicely heated, spacious, with period furnishings. We thought we were coming to a monk's cell, for the room is located in the Real Monasterio de Guadalupe, and instead find ourselves in a Renaissance palace. The cur-tains are long velvet drapes. This is the same Virgin of Guadalupe who was taken to the New World and became the *virgen de las americas,* but she is as revered here as she is there. Pilgrims still make their way to her shrine, located high in the sierra along the eastern edge of Extremadura. Extremadura, a hard land, gave Spain most of its *conquistadores.* They exchanged the Virgin for New World gold. Every altarpiece in every church in Seville is coated with it.

My wife lies asleep. The town of Guadalupe is steeply sloped and after a morning of walking its medieval streets she has decided to extend the afternoon *siesta*. From my writing table I can see up the hill to the peak and a hermitage located there. We had planned to make our way up to that hermitage together. She whispers, You go.

I go to sleep instead. Then I wake and start up that hillside.

We are two weeks into this trip, but as I piece together shepherds' trails and the narrow diagonal paths left by the sheep, it's as if I'm trying to put an end to preliminaries. I am no pilgrim, no believer—in fact, the statue of the Virgin, a spare, expressionless piece of sculpture, crowned and lavishly gowned, leaves me cold—but something tells me the time to make an effort has come. There's a road you can drive to the hermitage now, and I see no one else walking this hillside. I come upon a flock of sheep that start, wobbly-legged, to each side and let me pass. I am afraid that night will catch me, not afraid of what might happen to me then, just that the darkness will roll down this hillside and make the piecing together of paths a matter of chance. For that reason, I don't spend much time looking back; when I do, the monastery and its church look like a massive bulwark around which the white chips of the houses are clustered, and the surrounding hills, a rich russet brown with tints of lavender, are deepening in their folds. I hear the sheep, the dull-clappered movements of the bellwether, and smell their droppings and the drifting smoke of someone burning the prunings of olive trees. Toward the top of the hill the path becomes better defined and is accompanied partway by a rock wall. You can begin to imagine yourself in the presence of other pilgrims, not a procession of the devout, but someone not out entirely for exercise either. I think of my wife. She would have resisted the arduous uphill climb but would have come to life here.

By the time I reach the hermitage there is just enough light left to make out the blue ceramic lettering of the sign set into one of its walls. It tells me that the hermitage was built in the fifteenth century at the request of Fray Fernando Yanez so that pilgrims to the shrine of the Virgin of Guadalupe might know they had almost arrived. The design is a Mozarabic gothic; there are gated doors on all four sides. Inside is a stone cross, and by positioning yourself just right you can superimpose that cross on Guadalupe's shine some four kilometers below. This is what pilgrims coming from afar saw. Those who struggled up the mountainside, as I have, as an act of penitence or in fulfillment of some vow, saw the hermitage silhouetted against the sky. The sign I am reading claims that Miguel de Cervantes once climbed the hill to leave the *grilletes de su cautivo* at the base of this cross. He, too, was a devotee of the Virgin. He had fought in the battle of Lepanto, then had been captured. While a prisoner in Onan he had made the Virgin a vow: If he ever got free he would take her his leg irons. He'd had to carry them around a good part of Spain before he bore them up this hill.

If I had known, I could have carried a weight of my own up this hill. I could have loaded my pockets with stones and left them not as an offering to the Virgin, not even to Miguel de Cervantes, but to his Don.

I can see my wife smiling in her sleep. At times when her dreams please her she'll chuckle through a good part of the night. I love listening in. At the bottom of her being she is so happy that she can chuckle with a sort of dove-soft purr about it. Educated by the nuns, she has a quiet and exacting sense of the way things should be done, but when I married her she was beset by self-doubt and I knew what I was marrying myself to: the pursuit of her happiness.

There is a luminous quality to her happiness; it sheds light on everyone around her. Similarly, her sadnesses cast a gloom and you feel deprived.

Then there are times when I get tired of thinking about my wife and prefer to think about the country instead. A countryman of hers, Cervantes, had stood here, a one-armed man carrying a brace of leg irons, to fulfill a vow he'd made to the Virgin. To keep in touch with that deep credulous part of himself, he had created a Quixote and set him loose on this land. It was the Quixote in him who had climbed this hill and the Sancho Panza he'd left behind, chuckling in his sleep.

That dupe's dupe. That squat and tubby little man.

· · ·

TWO WEEKS AGO, in a small rented Nissan, we started this trip. We had family to see in a town outside Alicante, on the *costa azul*. My wife's brother lives there with his adopted son, the son's Dominican wife and their two children. The brother, a painter, something of a dandy, I met on a boat crossing the Atlantic in 1969, and it's fair to say he is the reason I am in Spain now and not in Italy or, perhaps, Greece. He had what I've come to identify as a castle complex. When I met him he'd made some money selling his paintings in the States and proposed traveling southern Spain in search of a castle he could restore. In the spirit of the '60s, he'd wanted to house a utopian community of artists there. From castles he'd switched his sights to abandoned palaces and *casas señoriales* and was presently attempting to get the money together to restore the ruins of a mill.

We spent two days with my brother-in-law and his family and then another four days in Seville, where we had friends from the two years we had lived there. Even in February, tourists were everywhere. You had to know the city and its neighborhoods and little secluded plazas if you hoped to get away, and we did. A beautiful city, narcissistic in its self-regard, so attentive to detail and skillfully refurbished it was like a city behind glass. Around it were scattered the *pueblos blancos,* the white towns, quaint and Moorish, the stuff of which postcards are made.

We decided to explore the poorer and less visited towns of Extremadura. In search of one. *La cosa verdadera*. The real thing.

Let me jump all the way back.

In 1969, when I first set foot in Spain, I was not a man I much cared for, and, consequently, I did not have many real friends. With some justification, I could blame it on the times. I had participated in civil rights marches and in protests against the war in Vietnam; I had read perhaps too much Sartre and Camus and was fueled by disgust for most of what I saw around me, the duplicity and brutality and thrill-seeking of an almost reverential sort. There were thousands of others like me. Institutions were stifling, and that included the institution of marriage. Mine was a two-year marriage; my first wife and I parted friends (and later I would learn just how good a friend she could be), but with an almost angry sense of relief. How had we ever gotten trapped in that? But the alternative was to get caught up in the mad energy coursing through the world, to throw in with the kids and their middle-aged champions, the Norman O. Browns and Timothy Learys and Ken Keseys. Mockery was all the rage, when outrage wasn't, and the put-on was the art form of the day. I was drawn to the mockery, but only because what I saw around me were endless acts of bad faith. Most of the rock and folk music I heard seemed puerile; I listened to those few jazzmen willing to take their music to the very limit of sound and sense, genuine questers, I believed. But then Coltrane died and Davis began to flirt with rock. My twenties were the '60s, and by 1969 I was confused, gloomily self-absorbed and tired.

My parents had both come from the same small town in Georgia. I had never lived there, only made visits as a child, but I found myself going back and sitting at the feet of aunts and uncles and my surviving grandmother as if they were oracles. I was particularly fond of my Aunt Marie. She was the family's maiden aunt, who had cared for her parents until their deaths and put herself in charge of family reunions. When I was a child she used to send me letters with cut-out pictures of little bunnies and chicks pasted in the margins. In these letters she related the doings of all my many cousins. I did not go to the reunions; there was something too programmed, for my taste, about people showing up on a particular day to occupy their branch on the family tree. But I went to my Aunt Marie, and out of bottle-bottom glasses she would regard me sometimes as if I were insane, or, what for her might have been the same thing, as if I'd cut my link forever to the child I'd been. Then she'd get over it, and I would, and for a brief period I'd be the child and she the aunt who fixed me grits with redeye gravy for breakfast. There came a moment when the world split into my Aunt Marie and her grits versus LBJ and his bombing raids over Hanoi, and I knew I had to do something. "America, love it or leave it," was the bumper sticker of the day. I didn't love it. I loved some of the land—that red Georgia clay—and some vegetation—those aromatic Georgia pines—and I loved some people who, when they weren't transformed into rampaging consumers of everything the American war economy had to offer, could evoke for me moments of my youth. But the country had betrayed me.

In a letter to his daughter, F. Scott Fitzgerald once described America as a "willingness to believe," and without knowing it I must have been a real believer. In junior high school we read "The Man Without a Country," and were made to understand that such a man, cast adrift on the world's seven oceans, suffered a fate worse than death. We were taught to cleave to our country, when, I see now, we should have been taught Machiavelli's *The Prince* and the practices of realpolitik instead. I was left with a great capacity for belief, but drained dry and emitting a sour smell. I had friends, but at the depth at which I needed them—or at the depth at which I needed to be compensated for what I had lost—I had nothing and nobody. The uplift of sex and the abundance of it barely lasted the night. I knew people who believed there was an orgasm to be had that would blow all the shit away and usher in a new world. I was not one of them. I was not even a particularly lusty lover. I was too self-absorbed for that, too used to sampling my own emptiness and lashing out.

So I left it—the country, my family, my Aunt Marie. Thousands—maybe tens of thousands—of others did, too, but how many of them stepped off into Franco's Spain?

. . .

I KNEW NO ONE in Europe, was not carrying the name of anyone to see in London or Paris or Rome. It was a curious sort of tabula rasa I was setting up for myself. I had been in Mexico, visiting some American friends in San Miguel de Allende, but I was not going to Spain because I'd had a taste of it in Mexico. I was going because it was December and the first and warmest port of call in Europe was Malaga, and it seemed only logical to stick to the Mediterranean rim and move north when the weather warmed. I was taking a boat and not a plane for the drama of the thing. My first trip abroad; shouldn't I get a sense of what it must have been like to live in a world of water before making land? The '60s for me were like an exhilarating but ultimately enervating sea, a sea in up-heaval, and maybe I was telling myself to take the metaphor home, to weather the sea in fact.

I set sail on the Italian liner *Cristoforo Colombo* and, as I said, met my future brother-in-law on board. After we'd disembarked and begun to travel together, he told me that he'd been treated so well in the United States by the family he'd lived with that he'd made a vow: He would be-friend an American coming to Spain and return the favor. He'd seen me standing at the ship's stern, gazing at the wake as if I were being pulled home. I'd looked lonely. It was true, I was alone, and after the second day out, when the weather improved, I spent time back on the stern, not so I could gaze homeward but because that was where the most space was, and it was a hemisphere of water, wind and a few trailing gulls that held me there. Years before, traveling somewhere between San Antonio and Laredo, Texas, I'd had a similar reaction. I'd pulled off the untrafficked two-lane road and stood behind my car under a sky like an overturned bowl, the grassland flat from horizon to horizon, and thought: Those with a gift for transcendence can do it through the mind; the rest of us need the right geography. There was this perfectly shaped hemisphere of space, and there was me. Under those conditions, there was no reason not to blend in. But that was land I'd been standing on and this was water we were plowing through, which put an edge of uncertainty on the whole business. I suppose I did look lonely and maybe even a little scared standing there at the stern's rail. Although he's never said as much, it might have passed through my brother-in-law's mind that I was the sort who could jump.

Growing up, I'd wanted to be a baseball player and had the rangy build for it. Later, under the influence of Montgomery Clift and James Dean, I'd turned my attention to acting and talked myself into believing I had the talent and the looks for that—blond, boyish, a Kirk Douglas dimple in the chin, eyes not quite as blue as Paul Newman's. I'd actually performed small parts in movies, and in one of them, a submarine melodrama in which I played a sonar operator, I was on the set for eight weeks. It was during that tedious, idle time that I started to read seriously, and it's fair to say that that was when the balance began to shift. I would go back to school, study literature and become a writer. I did go back and study literature; for five years I even taught it in a couple of colleges. But a writer I had not become. I was carrying a small typewriter with me, and a plan for a novel, but had yet to write a page I would want held against my name.

Was I the sort who could jump? I don't know, and still don't. Since I first read it, Keats's line, "to cease upon the midnight with no pain," has never been far from my mind.

My brother-in-law-to-be walked out to the ship's stern dressed in a navy-blue Castilian cape (I believe the lining was red) and asked if I would like to join his group of friends. I had noticed him, small, dapper (a suit and vest beneath the cape), elegant but very animated, playing to an audience of six or seven, and here he was restricting himself to me. He had been buying champagne and may have brought a bottle and two glasses with him. I can't be sure what we talked about during that first meeting—probably something about his stay in the States and my plans to get off the boat in Spain rather than taking it all the way to some Italian port. But the sense of what we talked about would have been: Boats on the high seas are by necessity places where people get together. I've already gathered a group of friends around me. Come be one of them.

He was a great talker. He was educated—to please his father he'd taken a degree in law, but had never practiced. He was well read: from the ancients to the Church fathers to those modern writers who had no truck with existential nihilism. He was not afraid of seeming sentimental because he knew that with the fervor of his belief he could talk sentimentality up to a higher plane. Saint-Exupéry's *The Little Prince* and Hesse's *Siddhartha* were current favorites of his. He thought he had it in him to find that capacity for love under the toughest of hides. He'd walked the streets of New York, Washington and Philadelphia at night and never been bothered; he'd even turned a couple of would-be antagonists into friends. This was the '60s, that particular side of the '60s, a world of bounty (the United States had been bountiful to him) where napalm wasn't flaming over forests and rice paddies and Boss Conner wasn't turning his dogs loose on uppity black men, and he was asking me to leave that other world of the '60s behind me and come be one of his group.

If I was out to take the metaphor of the sea back to the fact, there was the wake, a stream of jade-white flowing out into green, and what were wakes for if not to let your garbage go? I should let mine go, and the gulls would take care of the rest.

I don't think he mentioned his sister that first time we talked. He looked Spanish—black hair, olive complexion, aquiline nose. The brown of his eyes, though, was a soft chocolate, and the definition broke down. I've seen him squint at a canvas with a stern sort of concentration, as if trying to summon a rigor into his vision that just wasn't there. What would it take to bore through? But he was a gay gesturer, he could turn sharply on his heel and he wore his cape well. He saved his sister for the next day out.

. . .

I HAVE HER NOW on my arm. The town we are in is called Zafra, still in Extremadura, and what distinguishes it from the other towns we've visited is that its *plaza mayor* and its *plaza menor* are linked. Both plazas are colonnaded. The columns are of stout stone, and the design of the capital and base vary from house to house, as do the dimensions of the arches. There are *plazas mayores* in Spain that are jewels of architectural uniformity—spacious and true to their design in the finest of detail. They have always produced in me conflicting effects. In their symmetry they center the town and hold it there, but because the opposing walls may be seen to mirror each other and, at every turn, offer you more of the same, these plazas can seem to hover. The best of them—I am thinking of Salamanca, with its rose-tinged stone—reconcile the effects and give a sort of privileged and time-honored lightness to every step you take within them. For that reason poets wax eloquent over them and frequently you find verses inscribed on their walls.

When my wife and I arrive in a town we come straight to the *plaza mayor*, stroll it once and allow it to give us a centrifugal push into the rest of the town. The spacious *plaza mayor* in Zafra, I'm convinced, grew out of the more tightly confined *plaza menor*. Palm trees grow at one end of the *mayor;* shops do business under the arcades. It is a cool day toward the end of February, but even so, a couple of bars have tables set out. At a corner of the plaza we pass through a low combination of arches into the *menor,* and at its center there is an iron cross, vaguely reminiscent of the ones that Franco's forces erected in town after town to commemorate those fallen fighting the Antichrist. But this cross is far older than those. Children are playing soccer around it, but in spite of their shouts and leaping feet, we can feel this plaza taking hold, and as we walk it the millennia pull at our steps.

My wife smiles and tugs on my arm. Charming plazas, both of them, but I'm not entirely off that boat where I met her brother, with that ashen blur of air and water at the horizon as our only boundary. Do you remember, I ask, what you said when your brother called from Malaga that day we landed and told you he had a surprise?

There's no reason not to give the names. The brother's is Antonio Ferri. His sister, the woman I married, is named Amparo. The word means "sheltering care." The Virgin of the Unsheltered, or *los desamparados,* is Valencia's *patrona.*

My wife has an amused and alerted expression on her face. Going back in time puts her on alert. But she's slept well. She's game for it.

I'll give you the hint Antonio gave you, I say. He told you the surprise wasn't a coat. You must have asked him for one.

He liked to dress me.

I know.

He always brought me clothes.

Maybe it was time he stopped.

He wouldn't have. You know that as well as I do.

My wife and I speak in a combination of Spanish and English, whichever is more emphatic or quicker to the tongue. "He wouldn't have" in Spanish is, to my ear, to *our* ear, a more tentative expression, *"No lo hubiera hecho,"* so she used English. But in Spanish "You know that as well as I do" is *"Lo sabes de sobra,"* which concludes with a punch that leaves no doubt.

But there is always doubt when it comes to Amparo and her brother, and she knows *that* as well as I do.

He said, I remind her, I've brought you an *americanito*. Did you ask him for one?

If he couldn't find me a nice coat. She laughs and squeezes my arm. After all that's happened to her, after all the medical tests and the batteries of drugs doctors have prescribed to defend her against various pains, after her three operations, she still has a laugh that rises on the air like a fountain spray, as pristine as the day I met her. In the *plaza menor* in Zafra it does something wonderful to this low-slung stone.

Then I got on the phone. Do you remember what I said?

Something I couldn't understand, she replies.

Practically the only Spanish I knew at the time were a number of expressions using the verb *tener*. *Tengo sueño*—I am sleepy. *Tengo sed*—I am thirsty. *Tengo hambre*—I am hungry. *Tengo ganas*—I am full of desire for something, whatever the verb is that follows. *Tengo ganas de conocerte*—I am dying to know you. I tell my wife I believe that was what I said.

And she tells me that whatever it was, she had to get Antonio to interpret. It wasn't just my accent. In 1969 the phones in Spain could crackle all the way down the line.

She tugs on my arm again and quickens her step. The children kick the ball around the iron cross, their voices within these four walls confused with their after-ring. The sky is clear, a rose mallow shading the blue. To live here within these walls, in one of the small cold *pisos* balanced on an arch, built over an arcade. In the presence of this stone. Even in the most grandiose of cathedrals, it is the stone itself I'm drawn to, as if the figures that have been carved there are as ephemeral as the figures in clouds. Only a fool would worship the cloud figures and not the stone.

Let's don't go back into all that, my wife requests, still in possession of her good humor, her fine spirits. Not now.

Fair enough. But that night, in a room looking out through the palm trees in the *plaza mayor,* I'm drawn back to that boat. The palm fronds scraping in the breeze may have brought to mind the *Cristoforo Colombo* as it rose and fell on the waves. But more likely it was because the better part of me was still on board.

How much of the past do we remember anyway? Events stand out, moments kept alive by a luminosity that will be within us till the day we die, but other than that, how much of our lives is really left? The dailiness is gone. At a certain stage in your life, who remembers the uneventful anymore? Something got us from event A to event B, but try to bring it back and you know at once what a flagrant act of imagination you're involved in, and if you're in a certain mood, where all you want is your life, this life you've lived, never mind an eternal hereafter, you can despair.

My wife did not want to go back into all that. But the quixotic act does not consist entirely in sallying forth. You sally back, too; you sally forth and you sally back so that you don't leave large parts of yourself behind, and if your Sancho Panza doesn't desert you, you eventually get to . . . I'm not sure where. At the end of the second book, Quixote gets to his deathbed just in time to recant his mad attachment to the books of chivalry, but by then the powers that be, the Church and the State, have him in their grip, and it's a case of the Establishment sweeping one more rebel into its fold.

My wife has signed on for the sallying forth half of the quixotic act. We will travel Spain—from Zafra to Trujillo, where the Pizarros lived, and from there to the valley of the Vera—and while she sleeps and while she summons her forces each morning to do justice to the day ahead, I will sally back.

. . .

SHE WAS A CHILD OF TEN. She had large eyes, a delicately arched nose, lovely lips, wind-chapped, already womanly in their line. She wore a prim blouse and sweater of dark wool. It was cool in her town in the mountains. Her mother dressed her well. But she ran the streets with her friends, and even then there were those among them who must have asked: How can such a privileged being be such a primitive force? But children live with contradictions far better than adults. She led her group of adventurers down beside the stream where the old blanket factories had been located. The new factories were up on the hill. The children played down by the stream, then strayed under the bridge where trash had been thrown. This was the new bridge, built after the civil war to supplement the one the Romans had left. She was playing there with her friends, picking through the trash—somebody's rusted baby stroller, old sweat-stiffened shoes—when a woman from the town saw her, made her way down the path and, with an imperiousness that certain *solteras* earned, singled out my wife-to-be. She forced Amparo to leave her playmates behind and led her back up the path. Up top, on the bridge, precisely where in the summer evenings the woman and her other un-married friends gathered to catch a breeze, she gripped the child before her by the shoulders. Not you! she pleaded and hissed in Amparo's face. She directed Amparo's attention to where a number of anonymous children climbed over the trash below. They can play down there! Not you!

. . .

AMPARO WAS A YOUNG WOMAN in another town, in other mountains, where the family had gone to spend a month in the summer. The stream there was suitable for swimming. She had been swimming. The sun was in her skin, the warmth of the rock she'd lain on. The Spanish have a word—*rebosante*. She was brimming over with the day's bounty and her own good health. She'd returned home to share a tin of mussels with her mother as an *aperitivo* before lunch. First her mother felt queasy—but she had eaten only a few. Then my wife-to-be went under. Terrible pains. Seizures. She lost consciousness. The young doctor in the town, who was really only an intern on a sort of field duty, diagnosed food poisoning but was unable to induce vomiting. The mother was forced to lie down, but somebody, perhaps the father or the powerless doctor, called the priest, because the doctor and the priest were both there when my wife-to-be, still in her bathing suit, recovered on her own. The way it was described, or the way it would remain forever in my mind's eye, was that she swam up from that deep bottom and broke the surface with a rousing hunger for a food that wouldn't poison her. She was gasping for breath, and she was laughing. She might have her down times, but she has always come back from them with laughter in her mouth.

· · ·

THESE WERE JUST TWO of the stories Antonio told me about his sister. He was an indefatigable talker. He also had photos. He had photographs from Amparo's childhood, and photographs of her as a radiant and breathless young woman of twenty, and he had photographs of that gawky age in between when she seemed long-nosed and long-chinned and barely recognizable. He insisted I see them all, as if only in that way could I chart her progress toward some sort of apotheosis of beauty and goodness. Hers, he insisted, was beauty that could only improve with age.

He was right. He had an eye for bone structure and skin quality and a keen sense of how a woman bore herself. My wife's beauty has kept her company every year of her life.

Day after day we looked through the pictures and he told me the stories, until finally I had to tell him it was time to shut up about his sister and put the pictures away. Not another word, not another peek. I was half in love with her already.

. . .

MY FIRST LOOK at Europe was not at Malaga but up the Tagus at Lisbon, at dawn. The *Cristoforo Colombo* was to dock there briefly before continuing on into the Mediterranean. Set within its hills, the city was an orange-brown, the color of an old backlit parchment. There must have been smoke on the air contributing to the effect, but my first impression of the Old World was of a decrepit glow within which buildings, whole neighborhoods, instead of collapsing somehow remained intact. Antonio was with me on deck. Almost certainly it was he who had gotten me up for this sight, or perhaps we had never gone to sleep and had to add the effect of our tiredness to what we saw. I remember no sounds, no harbor horns or bells. Just the slow silent advance of our ship into that aging orangeness, and a dawn, a sense of dawn, that spoke of how long things had lasted, not how freshly created they could be made to seem.

In Malaga Antonio and I spent one day and night. It was in Malaga that he made the phone call. We walked the streets. In December the weather was shirt-sleeve, then quickly cool as you passed into shadow. This is a church; that was once a monastery with its cloister, where the monks lived; late-gothic, *renacintista*, early baroque, a fine example of the *plateresco*, full blown. Look there: that old escutcheon carved into the stone. Some nobleman's palace. A courtyard inside, slender columns, Mozarabic fretwork around the horseshoe-shaped arches; a fountain with its *azulejos* tiles. A Spain of the Moors, sensuous and serene. We ate large shrimp, *langostinos*, cracking their backs, peeling back the armored plating. *Tapa* time, late afternoon: Try this, try that. *Sepia* in its ink, mussels in a lemon sauce. Sip the sauce out of the shell. Sip the sherry from Jerez cool. Learn, observe: a people animated, instinctive, but with a sort of generational assurance in their bones. There was a right way to do everything. And there was only one right way. Sample it all, feel free, but don't groan with satisfaction, don't stretch.

The Christians had swept down from the north, fair-faced and square-chinned, carrying a Celtic light in the eyes. They'd met the olive-tinged Moors, whose features were refined. Look at the beauty— it's everywhere. In the women and men. That's rose and honey mixing in their skin. There's a music in their movement. See if you can hear it.

Look and listen.

On to Córdoba.

We woke in a *hostal* in the old *barrio*. Dawn. On the street below someone was playing a flamenco guitar in muted chords; someone was clapping in a strange syncopation; someone, a young boy with an aged hoarseness in his voice, was singing a lament, the sleeplessness of his love. Antonio, from the other bed, was smiling, sly and proud, as if he'd staged it all.

On to Granada, and in Granada the Alhambra, a fortress housing a palace meant to instruct every sense and then to please it, no end. Beyond the fortress walls rose the Sierra Nevada. Within the walls, mountain water flowed from patio to patio. There was the smell of water-freshened herbs. A microscopic fineness to the molding on the ceilings, over the doors. A tracery of design that lured the eye as lines of music lure the ear, design so pure you could stand in it and, if you were properly instructed and not unworthy of the role you were being called on to play, could feel on your skin. You bathed in the Alhambra; you were submerged but in an element, Antonio claimed, we had only the rarest of contact with today.

I felt it, didn't I? Heightened in each of my senses, cleansed, aroused? Prepared.

Which do you fall in love with first, the country or the woman?

I was a conduit for him. I was the one who happened to be standing at the stern of the *Cristoforo Colombo* when after a homesick stay abroad he was about to return to his country and needed a way to experience it afresh. And that suited me fine. He was an exacting and sometimes fussy but highly qualified teacher. If that was what he wanted, I would give him Spain.

Riding the train through the rice fields and the citrus-growing basin of Valencia. Coming out of the arid coastal hills onto the great littoral of the Levante, and the orchards of orange trees. Not the oranges, not the fruit itself, but the packed foliage and the deepening tints of green in the leaves. The green was lush and womanly, paling at the leaf-tip to a sort of springtime tease. Row after row of these trees as the train cruised by, some already hung with orange globes. A sense of settled wealth and exuberant fecundity. A memorable moment, and I remember what I said: You're not prepared. After all that chalky dryness up in the hills, you swing down and the orange orchards are almost too rich for the eyes.

I could make out stone irrigation troughs flanking the plots, troughs that dated to the Moors, who loved water more than the dusty battlegrounds the Christians drove them onto.

I remember what Antonio said. His tone became reflective, sober and almost resentful. It was not a characteristic tone of his. They say we're a country of extremes. It's what Franco says. We need a strong hand. How else do you expect me to govern a country that contains *andaluzes* and *cataláns?*

At the time I knew little of Francisco Franco. He had been the youngest general of any European army—I had read that. When he rose against Spain's Republican government he was still a young man. That was in 1936, and we were nearing the end of 1969, so he had ruled Spain for thirty-three years. That might very well have made him the longest-serving dictator in the world. And he was one of ours—I knew that. The United States had air and naval bases in Spain. But from the tourist's point of view, outward signs of Franco's dictatorship were hard to find. Perhaps only the *guardia civil,* with their marching boots and leather belts and those mouse-eared, patent-leather hats, gave the country a fascist stamp. They policed the country's coasts and its small interior towns, and they always patrolled in pairs. Spaniards made countless jokes about them, but the *guardia civil* were known to be the most humorless people in the world.

That's politics, I said. I'm talking about the orange trees, the changes in vegetation.

You're talking about Spain. We're a melodramatic country. Who can take us seriously?

His tone continued to take a plunge, and I felt a certain relief, if only from his nonstop proselytizing for everything under the Spanish sun.

I believe I cuffed him lightly on the shoulder—a gesture of affection I have never seen a Spaniard perform. I quoted the title of one of Thomas Wolfe's novels, which had been reduced to a cliché.

The words were clear enough, but he frowned at me, puzzled, then drew back, as if marking off the distance between us. You can't go home again? *Que tontería!* You can never leave in the first place. A Spaniard could travel to the North Pole, build an igloo, and within it he'd find the Alhambra and the orange trees and a *plaza mayor* for the evening's promenade.

We left it at that. By the time we pulled into the Valencia station he was back to being himself, and a great enigma for me. It was then that he told me his plan. I was to get a room in a downtown hotel—he would take me there—and he would visit his family alone. When he judged it opportune, he would invite me over. And if the opportunity did not present itself, he would arrange a meeting downtown.

It was nearly Christmas. I understood he'd want some time alone with his family first. But why bring them all downtown since they lived a good way out? Wouldn't it be easier if I got some flowers, or whatever one took (most commonly, little pastries, it turned out), and paid them a brief visit?

But he didn't mean the whole family. His father and mother would become formidable figures, gracious and intriguing and cursed by their roles of host and hostess into giving what they couldn't afford to lose. He meant his sister, of course.

.   .   .

MY TRAVELING COMPANION, who didn't particularly want to stop in Trujillo—perhaps because Pizarro is not one of her favorite conquistadors—but who, once she's here, wants to stay. The plain above which the town rises is strewn with boulders the size of the car, and the narrow roads over it are lined with rock walls. Most of the castle walls are intact, from the outer perimeter in, and standing on the top you look out over a hard, gray, bare and intractable world, which, from the start, must have had the conquistadors thinking of lush vegetation and gold. But my wife turns her attention downward to the town, where the conquistadors' fortunes were converted into palaces, whose pale brown sandstone has weathered into an even finer paleness and whose streets are quiet. A number of these palaces are situated around the *plaza mayor,* which is spacious and very active at this time of the day. It is early evening. Storks are nesting on the church tower and other eminences, their nests ragged and disproportionately large.

She tries to clarify her reaction for me. It's the busyness, she believes. It's the quietness of the streets, and the busyness of the plaza, and the sense of past wealth weathering down to whatever use it has in the present day. The people are unpretentious, friendly; they don't know what they have. On a larger scale it all reminds her of that town where she grew up, Bocairente. She could live here, she says.

Are we looking for a place to live? Is that the ultimate purpose behind this trip?

Trujillo is a bit too big for me; this very plaza, as impressive as it is, with its multiple levels and geometrical quirks and its assortment of arcades, is too monumental for my taste. Pizarro sits on his horse at one end of it. There's a bus, a tour bus I fear, parked just inside one of the arches leading up out of the streets. I don't quite see how that bus passed through that arch, but one tour bus will surely bring another. The government has just completed its expressway through Extremadura, and it passes within five kilometers of this town. In less than two hours you can be here from Madrid; on a Sunday you can spend the day in a *pueblo típico,* have a late lunch and be back in Madrid for the evening's entertainment.

Madrid is the hub of the country, built from scratch (or a tiny town) to be a capital for all of Spain. The newly finished expressways are the spokes. In the regions that compose the country—Galicia, the Austurias, Cantabria, the Basque Country, Navarra, Rioja, Aragón, Cataluna, Valencia, Murcia, Andalucia, Extremadura, La Mancha, Castile and León— there are those who consider those expressways to be more like tentacles. What Franco achieved by coercion with his police, capital-dwelling sightseers can do now with their cars. Spain will be one Spain: Madrid's.

Yet Trujillo reminds my wife of her hometown in the mountains of Valencia, four regions away. She could live here. A *piso* located over a bakery is for sale. On the sign is a phone number, which she jots down and would have called if she'd had the twenty-five-peseta coin it took and if I hadn't talked her out of it. She informs me, as if I didn't know, that as a child she lived over a bakery. Ever since we decided to make this trip she's been dreaming of that childhood town. She's been dreaming of her run of it and the fresh sensations it provided every minute of the day. And I assume you'd have to live with the Moors, Romans, Phoenicians and Greeks in your history to know what freshness really is.

Every night at dusk, she tells me, the men came down from the sierra with their burros and mules. They'd go out during the day to work their plots, or their carob and olive trees, and then at night they came back into the town. They came from various directions, and since the town was hilly and cobbled, at just the right hour you could hear their animals' hooves striking sparks out of the rock. It was all over town, that sound of their trot. Then they stopped at the old stone watering troughs and what you heard was the animals lapping. The men would talk if they came together at the same trough, tired voices, but since they'd been talking to themselves or their animals all day, they'd keep it up. There was something like a long summer twilight in those voices and the thirsty lapping of those burros and mules. And the smell. The town smelled like animals again, but since the animals had been up in the sierra they smelled like the thyme and rosemary and sage that grew there. Sometimes the men brought sacks of it back. Herbs that smelled like burros and mules.

I was just a little girl, she says, but I loved those hours at dusk. I stopped playing then. There was a spot just down from the church where the sounds and the smells all came together and I sat there, by myself. I was the *secretarieta,* so I could do things like that.

I love that image of her there, so pretty and so pure, a child sitting by herself. At other times she would go to the bullring to see the movies and dream of fearless and easygoing American men, but not then.

Still, I remind her, there's nothing of that here in Trujillo. A lot of cars and a tour bus. There's a fountain, but I can't hear it from here. Too many people trying to make a buck.

It's the hour of the day, she answers, with something suspended in her tone that, if I'm being honest, both scares me and eggs me on.

It's what happens when she returns to herself as a child. Almost all our friends know her as an accomplished woman, stylish and poised, at home in her beauty as few women are, extraordinarily thoughtful of others' needs, but at that vital center where she lives, she's always going back to start again. Sooner or later she will take a path out of her childhood that won't include me. It scares me. But I also want to be there to see her off.

You can't hear it, she goes on, and she means the fountain here in Trujillo, because it's not a sound you grew up with. So it has to compete with the buses and cars.

There's a keen but wistful expression on her face. Keen wistfulness—it's an emotion I can barely entertain.

. . .

I HAD A CHANCE TO LEAVE. For three days I didn't hear a word from Antonio. I don't think it was simply the prospect of meeting his sister that kept me there. I had stepped into a world—or I'd been ushered into a world and left there. I was twenty-nine, divorced, no kid. If I was a '60s casualty it was not from an overdose of drugs and rock music and polymorphous perversity. I had my wits about me. There was this crazy Spanish artist who wanted to go traveling through the southern half of Spain looking for a castle—and I said, Sure, okay. A utopian gathering of artists? Why not? Those were times when everybody led a fictitious life. He had a gorgeous sister he wouldn't shut up about, and I said, Sure, I'd meet her and even behave, if that would make him happy. He could visit with his family and I'd hang out in a hotel. In the meantime, I'd step out and take a look around.

For years I've been trying to get into words the effect that those three days of looking around had on me. As I said, I'd been in Mexico for a period, but Mexico was a slapped-together place, and even though it struck deep into the native American soul, it finally had the effect on me that other more prosperous but just as garish places did, places such as L.A. As though newly created each morning, it blossomed in a hectic rush, and by night it was done. Stepping out into Valencia by myself, without Antonio at my side, I became aware of history of the most incidental kind and sensed at once that a certain capacity in me was lacking. A cathedral or palace belongs to another age; you can stand back from it, amazed, and then go on with your life. But when the railing you lean against, the bench you sit on, the flagstones at your feet, the pigeons that wheel down for a crust of bread from their perches in the cornice of the building at your back—a building of doors and windows, small shops and humble *pisos*—when all of that seems imbued with a longevity that puts your mortal span to shame, what do you do?

I believe I must have felt the force of history as an alternative to the guru-wisdom of the times. If you caught the rhythms of the historical life just right, you could live in this world in a transcendent state and never miss a minute of it.

If you had the knack, the *don,* that is.

That was the condition I was in when Antonio made good on his promise and brought his sister into town to meet me.

He brought his *novia,* too, a quiet, lisping, pretty woman named Concha, self-effacing to a fault, but who was, Antonio claimed, a fine poet. Other than the fact that they were the same size, it was hard to see her at Antonio's side. Antonio performed and she wrote her poems, which somehow seemed antithetical acts. I liked her, and we got along, but I think Antonio brought her that first afternoon not so we could meet but so his sister and I could go off alone.

Amparo wore an elegant blue dress. Celestial blue, she's told me many times. It was midafternoon on a sidewalk of the city and she wore a dress better suited for a nightclub. She wore it as if she were about to jump out of it and climb a tree. Her eyes were enormous, dark and bright as a buckeye and full of eager animation. The photographs Antonio had shown me could, depending on the angle, trim the nose, nip off a corner of the mouth, but face to face she couldn't be doctored or prettied up. Was she pretty? She didn't want to stand still long enough for me to decide. She was powerfully built, and her flesh seemed to be

streaming with vitality. She had a lovely broad forehead without a trace
of a wrinkle. It was a glistening honey-rose. Had she run there and
raised a sweat? The day was warm. But neither Antonio nor Concha
seemed affected by the weather, and I decided the perspiration on Amparo's face was the result of some internal activity.

She had no English, and her voice—which had been roughened over
the phone—was a girl's, almost prepubescent, high and tuneful and extraordinarily clear. I knew at once that I could learn Spanish from her.
We shook hands, and hers was damp. She shared a laugh with Antonio
and Concha and then, as though declaring the formality of the handshake
a thing of the past, stretched up to kiss me on each cheek. I felt her hu-
mid warmth, detected a scent of orange blossoms. Or perhaps an orange
tree was blooming nearby. I know there was a palm tree overhead. I was
bent over—at the angle of the palm—a head taller than anyone there.

There was an instant when I felt conspicuous on the sidewalk and
they looked me over. She wouldn't believe it, but looking back now, it
seems a decisive moment when they could have thought better of it,
turned on their heels and left me there. Or when I could have interpreted
my hulking out-of-placeness as a sign to get out of town on my own. But
I laughed at myself instead, made a palms-up, empty-handed gesture of
surrender, and this girl named Amparo—because she offered shelter—
took my hand and took her brother's place. She became my guide. She
showed me the city.

A city I had already seen. She quickly dropped my hand, rushed
ahead, then urged me to catch up. The market, the old stock market
called the Lonja; a baroque palace, the Marqués de Dos Aguas. The
gothic cathedral and beside it the Basilica, where the statue of the *virgen
de los desamparados* was enshrined. The Virgin was dressed in the jewels
she'd inherited from the widows of the city; she had a no-nonsense expression and a piercing-thin nose; from beneath her sheltering skirts

cherubs peeked out. Outside, on a street called Calle de los Caballeros, was a string of palaces, and even though they were private residences, Amparo led me inside. Patios. A fountain, a stone well. She took the liberty of running halfway up a stone staircase and I shouted to her to stop. Shouldn't we leave this to the people who live here? Shouldn't we draw the line? But I couldn't say this, and Antonio was not there to translate. I could say, *Espera!*—wait.

It's the other clear picture I have of her from that day, to go with the one on the sidewalk. And it was another moment when I could have turned around and left her there, trespassing halfway up someone's gothic-traced flight of stairs. That blue dress against that gray stone, the blue of the sky that shone in the opening above her. Her hair was brown, not black, with traces of auburn. She'd stopped at the sound of my voice and the hair had fanned out. Her lips were parted. I had nothing to compare her to. She was extraordinarily beautiful and she reminded me of a bounding goat.

I understood her brother's fascination. From those three days of observation I had a sense of what the women of the city were like. They were dressers, but strictly in line with the fashion of the day; they moved with a confident clip in their heels; they employed identical theatrical gestures; they spoke in quick pulses whose rhythms, if not the words, I'd come to understand. They were enthusiastic, never unsophisticated, and they shielded themselves with an airy disdain. They belonged to the same club.

She didn't. Not one of them would have worn that dress to bound up that staircase and then stop with just that startled and eager look on her face.

She came back down the stairs and took my hand. Her hand was still damp and it was trembling with thwarted animation. She said something reassuring to me, probably *No te preocupes,* not to worry, she knew what she was doing. Later she'd tell me stories of her childhood, when she'd had the run of that town where she'd been brought up, and I'd understand. She was favored.

The next time I saw her she had called the hotel in advance. Actually, Antonio had called to invite me to dinner at his parents' house the day after Christmas, and before he hung up she'd gotten on the phone. I come there, she said in a halting English that still sparkled. Antonio got back on and said they would both come by that afternoon.

It was Christmas Eve. I ran out to find them gifts. I had already told Antonio about Miles Davis's recording of the *Concierto de Aranjuez* on his album *Sketches of Spain*, Davis's trumpet instead of Segovia's guitar, and luckily I found that right off. For his sister I sensed I could get anything, and consequently, nothing I could find seemed right. Finally, in the gift shop beside the hotel, I bought her a long gold-and-black cigarette holder even though I hadn't seen her smoke.

I could see her striking a pose.

But she was not the same girl.

Antonio brought me a copy of *The Little Prince* and in the inscription referred me to a certain page where his feelings about the goodness hiding in the worst of man were best expressed. His sister gave me a silk cravat, beige-tan with flecks of gold. She tied it for me—she showed me how. I had on a checked wool shirt it didn't go with, but I wore it to the café where we sat and had drinks. She was subdued, a little withdrawn; she was attentive, but it was as if all that life in her eyes had been forbidden to speak. I gave her the cigarette holder, and the pose she struck with it seemed forced. Antonio set his record aside and, with the flair he'd shown on the boat when he'd worn his cape and bought champagne, used the cigarette holder himself.

His sister was not sad—she was restrained, which seemed like a form of sadness coming from her. I imagined that her wary parents had sworn her to a code of behavior with this untrustworthy foreigner on the scene, and I believe now, of course, that I was wrong. Her parents were wary, and there were bitter battles ahead, but that second day I saw her I simply met a second Amparo, attentive, subdued and a little withdrawn, as if she'd receded into an upbringing that would include a stint with the nuns and, with all the naturalness in the world, had achieved a fit.

Or perhaps she simply felt sorry for me, having to spend Christmas alone. She wore a pantsuit of pearl gray, which for all I knew might have been a form of mourning for her. *Pobre chico.* She wished me a Merry Christmas and kissed me on each cheek. That was really the first time I felt anything like a surge of desire for her, for that body that was being withheld. She walked off arm in arm with her brother, and I stood aching with it. But it was brief. And conditioned, in a sense, by everything I saw around me. A brief, powerful and conditional desire.

. . .

IT TURNED OUT Antonio was always bringing friends home and had been warned not to keep doing it. His mother was a fabulous cook, but one day his little sister would grow up and his friends' appetites would turn toward the forbidden. He had to stop. But he hadn't. He knew people from all over Spain—he had brought famous actors and actresses to sample his mother's paella—and every single one had remarked on what a beautiful young sister he had.

Except "beautiful" wasn't the word. Something like a rare dish that one must taste to discover its real worth—or if it is even real.

But this time he had done the unthinkable. He'd brought a foreigner home. And not just a foreigner—an American. Americans, at that stage of Franco's reign, were provocative figures. The movies Spaniards saw were almost entirely American. Censorship, both from the Church and State, could be strict, but it was famously irregular, and in addition to Jimmy Stewart and Gary Cooper, less reputable figures such as Marlon

Brando could slip through. Years later, when the Franco lid had been lifted and Spain had a belated but accelerated '60s of its own, a Spanish woman told me that during her teens all she had known about sexuality she'd learned from Elvis Presley. Spaniards turned to Americans for their wholesomeness and their rawness and their indifference toward anything more remote than the day before yesterday. So bringing an American home was like seizing some turbulent and contradictory figure out of your dreams and plunking him down in the presence of your virginal sister.

This was what Antonio had done. And his sister hurt because she thought I hurt. Why should I be distrusted? It was painfully unfair.

Her father was named Antonio Ferri Girones, her mother Delia Martín Marco. Antonio and Amparo took the Ferri from their father, the Martín from their mother. The Ferris had their origin in Florence, Italy, where before emigrating to Spain in the eighteenth century they'd belonged to the silk-trading and banking world. But more recently her father's family had been farmers, while her mother had been raised in the capital of Valencia, in a *piso* beside a convent and one of the two remaining city gates, Los Torres de Quarte. The towers had been shelled by Napoleon's troops when they'd tried to take the city, and the shell craters still showed. Amparo's father's father had fought in the Spanish-American War and vowed vengeance against any American who set foot on his land. But that grandfather was dead and Señor Ferri, with his farm upbringing, insisted on setting a table with everything the market had to offer.

An accident early in his youth had cost him a leg. He used a crutch. He compensated psychologically with a sort of goodwilled profligacy. An *aperitivo* of mussels in paprika sauce. A first course of artichokes baked to a crisp in olive oil. Then an enormous seafood rice dish garnished with all the Mediterranean had to offer. I was shocked and then sobered to discover there was a platter of meat still to come—beef in a thick wine sauce that included an enlivening touch of rosemary. Fruit for dessert—oranges, pears, and an achingly sweet melon. Then *flan* made with flecks of orange peel. I thought I was done. Then the coffee—dark and thick enough to sip with a spoon. Señor Ferri swung up to his bureau and came back with a box featuring the portrait of some Renaissance nobleman on the front. He made the presentation. Every dish in Spain was presented for admiring inspection before it was served. I admired the bottle of Duque de Alba cognac fitted inside its felt-lined box. It was a fine-tempered fire going down my throat and a fine-tempered fume rising into my head. I couldn't move. The talk had been about the things I had seen and still must see in Spain, with Antonio serving as translator. Nothing about the United States or who I had been. But the talk soon turned to the topic of, it seemed, every meal served in Valencia—other meals that exceeded or fell short of the one you were presently eating. So this shellfish rice came on top of five others and that artichoke heart you were approaching with such incredulous delight had its antecedents. You ate them all—past and present.

Amparo's mother watched me with a gracious smile fixed on her face and her head held at an imperious tilt. I remembered that she'd been brought up beside a convent and a city gate and would have an inbred sense of who should be let in and who should be kept out. I thanked her. I thanked them both. If it had been within my verbal command I would have told them I had no designs on their daughter; a single course more, however enticing, and I was dead. Instead I closed my eyes and Señor Ferri held up that last course beneath my nose. Puros from Havana. He lit one for me. I saw Antonio smiling through the smoke. I put any last expectation aside and decided to let myself go with the flow. It was a poor choice of metaphor; I was already submerged.

It turned out that a bed had been prepared for me, and it was Amparo's role to lead me to my siesta. She would not be gone long, but she should be the one to plump my pillow and make sure the sheet was turned back at the proper angle. I let her lay me down. She was dressed in a stunning black dress with embroidery as bright as the plumage of a jungle bird up both sleeves. I closed my eyes and saw her in the dark. When she had performed her duties she tousled my hair as she would a child's. She was back in the dining room before suspicions could be aroused.

As if they hadn't been already.

. . .

I WAS TWENTY-NINE, she was twenty-two. I had survived a broken marriage and the sexual chaos of the '60s. But barely. My country's political and military behavior had been a daily aggravation. There was the great engulfing Establishment and there was the counterculture, a beleaguered establishment of its own. The clothes you wore, your grooming, the expressions you used, your gestures, how you moved, what you ate and the newspaper you read, the car you drove and the gas station where you filled it up, everything, your toothpaste, your favorite sports team—name it, and it placed you in one camp or another. It was all too confining. And dully predictable. So I busted out and ended up in Franco's Spain. And not just in Spain but in a family that subscribed to a code of behavior that took us centuries into that country's past. In some neighborhoods, and especially in the towns, I would see tall, darkly grilled windows projecting over the sidewalks. They looked like handsome cages. That was where, not too long ago, unmarried women would sit and talk to prospective *novios*. It was as far into the world as they'd been permitted to go.

Amparo and I could not date unless we were chaperoned. Meeting for an early-evening drink or *aperitivo* was one thing, but a date, which meant after supper you went out together into the night, was forbidden unless you had a *carabina*—a rifleman—at your side. I thought of stagecoaches in the Old West and could never quite understand in which direction that rifle might be aimed. For our first date we went to see a movie, *The Lion in Winter*, with Peter O'Toole and Katharine Hepburn fulminating back and forth in dubbed Spanish, and Amparo's mother went with us. Henry II and Eleanor of Aquitaine—one of the world's great embattled marriages, and we sat there, trying to behave. Later the Ferris would relent and allow Antonio to go with us, and Antonio would conveniently disappear. But that was later, and by then I had become used to the supervision and in some way had surrendered myself to it.

This was not easy for me to understand, and I didn't at the time. In Franco's Spain it seemed there was a prescribed way for doing everything, and yet within those prescribed ways the Spanish led rich, expressive lives. How could that be? I was used to the Establishment back home, which was about as expressive as settling concrete, and to keep ahead of settling concrete you had to be on the move. I was worn out. I didn't know how worn out at the time, but enough, it seemed, even as I complained, to allow the Spanish to take care of me for a while. This was how it was done? This was how Franco and his friends demanded I do it? Well, I'd be damned!—even as I went ahead and did it their way.

It occurred to me that there could be no such thing as a Spanish renegade, as I understood the term. An American can repudiate his land, step off the edge, and it's a free fall with nothing to catch him in the end. At every turn and tumble a Spaniard's fall will be broken by the history of who he's been, by the customs and traditions and ceremonies of the region, town and *barrio* in which he's lived. Did I have anything comparable? Only, I realized with a rueful smile, my Aunt Marie. Whom I loved but who was no safety net.

There were these ancient ways? Grumbling, making great howling protests of disbelief, I gave in to them and savored the relief.

While Amparo fought them, and that was the irony that underlay our love from the start. She was thoroughly Spanish, as nourished by her country's traditional life as anyone, perhaps more so since she was in such close touch with the child in her. But the child wanted alternative ways, and then the woman did. In good faith I couldn't offer them to her. I loved who she'd been, and I came to love the vibrant young woman who stood before me. But not necessarily who she wanted to become. I didn't know who she wanted to become, not an American, for god's sake, who lived in a small town and whose husband (or daddy) saved the town from some disaster, some intruder, some disease. Not that!

The tension got to her first, and I was no hero.

Below the *pensión* I moved to was the church of San Agustín. Beside it was a small park with orange trees, where, in the afternoons, before she took the bus back home for supper, we would sit and she would teach me Spanish. I had to get past my Spanish of straight-ahead urges into the more elusive world of the reflexive verbs and the various conditional tenses. In Spanish you do not say, I dropped the glass and it broke. You say, depending on just how self-exculpating you wanted to be, *Se me ha caido el vaso; se me ha roto el vaso.* Meaning, the glass fell in my presence; it broke in my presence, but don't blame me. Before I left her side and strayed into Spain I would need to know some of the things the language could do. I managed to convey to her that during our castle search, at least, I would have Antonio to translate. She smiled. At first I thought she was smiling at her brother's fanciful notions, but I came to realize she was smiling at my naïveté. Antonio could talk castles out of clouds, but they vanished and something else took their place—didn't I know that by now? *Aayyy, niño,* somebody needed to help me—I think that was what she said; it was certainly what she meant. She took my hand with a reproving sort of fondness, and squeezed. These little seizures of affection she called *arrebatos.*

Then, with no warning, the strength seemed to drain out of her hand, and although she didn't stop smiling the presence in her eyes went with it, and she was offering me a blank. She had lost none of her color; she was healthy and glowing and just not there. These debilitated spells might come on her that quickly, and I soon came to catch that unmoored look in her eyes as something essential in her drifted away. But not then.

Que te pasa? I asked her. *Estás bien?* Yes, she would answer. Her voice was distracted and tinny—without its usual timbre. *Déjame,* leave me alone, for a moment. She settled against the iron back of the bench and seemed to go to sleep. I did as she asked. I left her alone. She was perfectly still, eyes rolled down in their sockets and closed. I could barely see her breathe.

I remember looking above me and noticing an orange that was hard, green and perfectly round, somewhere in size between a shooter marble and a golf ball. I gave my attention to that orange until I couldn't anymore, then I took her hand and whispered her name. Soundlessly, and without a quiver in her face, a tear slipped out of the corner of one eye and down her cheek. Only that one. *Tengo que ir,* she said. She wanted to go. I said she wouldn't be able. *Si, que puedo,* she insisted she had it in her. That weakness had come on her suddenly, but clearly it had not taken her by surprise. I didn't know what to do. She walked out of the park and caught a taxi to her bus stop, and I sat there staring at that orange above me, young and green and packed with a life force that might blow this city away, a lovely roundness and a hard rind.

In her absence I had begun to see her in the things she wasn't, and from that moment on I should have known.

I tried to talk to Antonio, but when it came to his sister it was not easy to pin him down on the specifics of what doctors might have said. Yes, they had seen one, but the diagnosis had been vague and unalarming and the prognosis was that future womanhood would set things right. Childbearing seemed to be the answer. Later he would tell me of a neurologist they had consulted in Pamplona, who had uttered the word "epilepsy," but hypothetically, with no evidence to back it up, and the only thing the doctor had advised was for her not to take up driving.

I didn't push Antonio any further. I went with him to the small city in the mountains, Onteniente, where his uncles and cousins ran a blanket factory and he was helping to design a line of tapestries. There I saw his paintings. I had seen a few in his parents' apartment, but they were mostly landscapes of the grasslands and wheat fields of Castile under a low, leaden sky. In his apartment I saw his women, set before a florid but strangely arid background, dressed in medieval gowns with their hair side-coiffed, as if in a snaking wind. His painting was heavily textured and these women seemed to emerge from its creases and folds. None was fully formed. They did not look like his sister, except in one respect: More than a few wore that expression she did when she was suddenly stilled and forced to stand back from herself, seemingly bereft.

I was back in Valencia within a week. The time seems short, but I remember being in my *pensión,* then out on the streets when the parade of the Three Kings came down Calle de la Paz, Valencia's most ornate street. The Kings and their helpers were throwing hard candy to the kids and a piece somehow flew into my hand. I tried to make a gift of it to Amparo, who was standing at my side. I unwrapped it and held it before her mouth and waited for her to stick out her tongue. She shook her head and pointed at my mouth instead. There was something vaguely sacramental about the way I put it into my mouth and let its mentholated sweetness dissolve. That would have been January 5, the day of the Epiphany.

Amparo showed me the port, the fishermen out mending their nets, which lay in large fluffy mounds up and down the pier. Botanical gardens. Roman ruins. Medieval bridges across the nearly dried-up river, under which gypsies camped. The city museum where I saw my first Sorolla painting, a beach scene, a trio of young girls, dressed diaphanously, in a light that glowed rose-orange. It was, she said, Valencia's light at a certain hour of the late afternoon, and it could spread through the city like a balm.

She attended her classes in design, and I met her in the little Plaza del Carmen when she came out. Frequently she was with her girlfriends. She introduced me to one, and I thought I caught a mix of envy and condescension in the girlfriend's eyes, but it was hard to be sure, all their eyes were so lively, so capable, it seemed, of entertaining numerous emotions at once. Amparo sometimes had trouble with her girlfriends, and it was usually when they were in a group and their boyfriends were around. I don't think my wife has ever quite understood the effect she can have on men, or has believed me when I've told her. I do think she sensed the effect she had on me, and it frightened her some, even as she took a sneaking delight in provoking it.

I don't think she had ever been kissed on the lips. She'd had boyfriends and she'd had suitors, but I don't think that she ever had.

The next time she suffered a weak spell she didn't just seem to go to sleep, she actually did. I was with her at Mass, and I had noticed an air of distractedness about her before we'd gone in. Soon I would come to read that distractedness for what it was: a sense of being estranged from the place where she belonged and an anxious casting around in her new surroundings. But not then. We were sitting in church, and during the Mass itself, when the bread and the wine were being consecrated, she quietly slumped against me. This time her head fell. I shook her quietly and lifted her chin. I could not wake her. There was a fluttering in the eyelids and there was that single tear slipping down her cheek, but she was gone. I set her back against my shoulder and left her there until the priest had concluded and his parishioners had taken communion and left. Then she woke up.

What is it? I said. What's happening to you?

She shook her head. She said it was time for her to leave, and I'm not sure she knew that she'd been gone.

I couldn't wake you up.

She whispered, *Está bien,* which meant, It's all right, but could also mean, That's enough.

I rode the bus with her back home.

I didn't know what I thought—I thought she needed to be reassured.

The next time I saw her we were walking beside the river. We had just passed through a small amusement park with rides for children. The gaiety in her eyes as we watched the children on the merry-go-round was offset by a puzzled self-questioning, and even though she'd continued to lead me on these walks I took her by the elbow and led her to a bench and forced her to sit there. The time had come to tell her something I wanted her to know. Somehow I thought it would do her good.

I wanted to say, I like you, you know. I like you just the way you are. I knew with my Spanish I couldn't get close to telling her that it was precisely the things that distinguished her from her more "normal" girlfriends that I liked the most, the things I suspected brought that self-questioning into her eyes and stranded her in moments of doubt, but I could tell her I liked her just the way she was. I thought I could.

The verb for "like" is *gustar,* but it's a tricky reflexive verb that in translation always seemed archaic. "I like you" became "You please me." I knew the verb for "love" was *amar,* and it was far too early to say that. So I chose a verb I could master and assumed meant no more than "I like you," or perhaps "I really like you," or "I'm fond of you know, you know." I said, *Sabes que te quiero mucho exactamente como eres.*

Her mouth dropped open and her eyes took off in a wild and panicky flight. I had just told her I loved her, loved the hell out of her, exactly as a Spaniard would who had dropped to his knee in his abject need to plead his case.

A Quixote before his Dulcinea.

An instant later she recovered and deduced that my Spanish had betrayed me. But there had been that dropped mouth and flaring eye. Much later she would refuse to admit having been taken by surprise by that miscommunication. She'd chalked it up to my poor Spanish from the start.

But with that mouth and that eye.

. . .

SHE SITS ACROSS FROM ME NOW, her mouth set in a musing line and her eyes quiet, a little tired. We're in the Valley of the Vera, at the northern edge of Extremadura, and tomorrow we'll be traveling into Galicia, toward the sea, where she can get fresh fish after so much lamb and pork. The valley is lovely with rocky streams pouring down out of the mountains—*gargantas*, they're called here—streams narrowing into "throats." We've been told the town of Valverde de la Vera, where we've just eaten lunch, has only six or eight kids left in the school. When they're gone there will be none left to take their place. The town has slumping adobe houses, water-troughed streets, tiny plazas that make the ones we've seen in towns up to then seem grand. Half the houses are for sale. The only possible buyers would be *madrileños* looking for a quaint place to fix up to spend a couple of weeks during the summer.

Tell me the truth, I say. Back when I didn't know what to say and said "I love you" instead of "I like you" and your mouth dropped and your eyes flew open, just what was it you were thinking?

She protests that her mouth didn't fall open (she has a large mouth and doesn't like to think of it that way), but she's curious about why I've gone back to that moment, and a little pleased.

I can close my eyes and still see your face, I tell her. Why would my mind's eye lie?

She doesn't know. Maybe it has a guilty conscience.

Admit it. I scared you, didn't I?

Americans are always in such a hurry.

Even slow-drawling Jimmy Stewart?

Maybe I thought, he wants to get through with me before he moves on to someone else.

Spain, I remind her, is the land of Don Juan.

But Don Juan seduced his women. That's not what you were doing, was it?

I laugh, and protest, and shake my head. We're sitting over lunch, but really where we are is out in the town, where everything is buckling and bowed and there's not a right angle left. Water is running down the center of every street, a mysterious effect, that coursing of water and this dilapidated age.

I adored you, I confess. It was adoration, pure and simple, from the start.

But you left. Right after that is when you went to Tarragona to think things over. Maybe *I* scared *you*. Maybe . . . she teases it out.

But I'm not sure if behind the teasing there isn't a hint of dread. Perhaps she isn't pleased at all. We had to get through so much to get here, why in the world would anyone want to go back?

All I remember from Tarragona, I tell her, is seeing a plaque in one of the neighborhoods thanking Francisco Franco for twenty-five years without war. Something to be thankful for, I guess.

They put those plaques up all over Spain, she replies with an air of distraction, dismissing it as a historical quirk.

And I remember thinking that the Mediterranean could rise out of its bed and wash all this away and one of the few things left after the water had receded would be this plaque, to chart a new beginning.

Thank you, Generalísimo Franco.

.   .   .

EARLY IN FEBRUARY Antonio summoned me back to that town in the mountains, Onteniente. I thought he was ready to begin his search for a castle to buy and convert into an arts center for his friends. He claimed he hadn't given up on that project, but he had something else in mind.

The festival of *moros y cristianos* was about to begin, precisely in the town of Bocairente, where he and his sister had been brought up. That town was ten kilometers away. Then he summoned his sister, and since it was Antonio doing the summoning her parents had no choice but to let her come. She slept in a small guest bedroom; I slept in the twin bed beside her brother's. On most of the walls in his house, patient, pining women emerged out of rock. They took their patience from the rock.

But there really was a festival of *moros y cristianos* and a town where Antonio and his sister had been raised.

On first impression the houses seemed like the natural outgrowth of the rock on which they were built. They were set at angles to each other, like faceted stone, and on the tessellated tiled roofs lichens grew in patches of black and yellowing gold. The colors were Picasso's, and the facets and planes of his cubism must have come from his memory of towns like this one.

The church rode the top of the rock like some outsized galleon, and the hill behind the town rose along the zigs and zags of a *via crucis,* its stations marked with cypresses.

The townspeople took sides. Bands of Moors marched through the streets, black-faced and dressed in long silken robes, followed by the pursuing Christians, whose robes and tunics were more tightly cinched. The Christians marched to martial rhythms, while the Moors swayed by to a music that sounded like a long sensuous plaint. At the end of three days a mock battle was staged on the parapets of a castle erected in the *plaza mayor,* and the Christian reconquest of Spain was complete. Then the lines broke down. The Moors didn't really get run out of town, they mingled with the Christians and bought each other drinks.

During those days of fiesta I looked for but didn't see the *guardia civil.* I did see in one of the smaller plazas a wrought-iron cross, mounted on rock, honoring Franco's fallen, and was left to conclude that a town ruled by its Christian traditions was exempt from the day-to-day enforcement of the law. As in Onteniente, the town manufactured blankets, and traditionally during this time, everybody wore a blanket thrown over his shoulders. Someone had thrown a blanket over mine. I felt an extraordinary warmth (these were cold February nights). Because I was with Antonio and Amparo and because Amparo was still *la secretarieta,* I was included.

They drank a liqueur there called *herbero,* anise steeped in seven herbs that grew on the hillsides. And the *mesas camillas* they sat around were warmed from underneath by coal braziers. You sat with the cloth draped on your lap. The rooms were small. The sense of intimacy was powerful, a little dizzying. The streets that wound down to the old Roman bridge were wonderfully convoluted, and frequently ended in quaint cul-de-sacs.

I felt exhilarated, uplifted, then quickly depressed. What could I offer Amparo as an alternative to this? I could offer its absence, that was all. But she loved showing it all to me. She was the town's favorite still, so I became licensed to partake of the town in ways I didn't deserve. We ate in a number of houses. We ate red peppers stuffed with rice and chunks of pork, and we ate the pastries that the nuns made in the local convent. In one of the houses were three little girls, ages nine, eight and five. I think we dazzled them. It was through their eyes that I first saw how the town was seeing us, Amparo and me. Word of the sensation we caused would have quickly gotten back to Amparo's father, whose tenure here as town secretary was much admired. His daughter and I were being accorded a semidivine status. You could see it all in those three little girls' eyes, which glittered in a starry, disbelieving way. For a while the girls wouldn't come near us, but once they did it was nearly impossible to get rid of them. We had to escape into the hills. It was under an olive tree up there that I first kissed her. I seem to remember that there were daisies, *margaritas,* scattered around, but it was early in the year and I may be confusing those *margaritas* with others that always seemed to grow beneath olive trees, where we continued to kiss until we could make up our minds what to do.

I thought her lips tasted of olives—it was the smell that hung in the air. It was the smell that spread through the town, not olive oil sizzling on a stove but olives piled and pressed and sweating out a scent that wasn't sweet at all but rich with the oils of life. An elixir of some sort. She kissed me back, then pulled away, a little startled, and fixed a look on me that was not questioning so much as intent on placing me where I belonged in that world that had originated with the town at our backs. It was with that need to know that she kissed me the second time. An investigative kiss—what is this? who are you? where do we go from here? what other novelties lie in store?

.   .   .

THAT WAS YOUR FIRST KISS, wasn't it?

I told you it was, she says. Many times. I told you then.

Then? Up on that hillside, looking over the town?

Yes.

That was where you first told me you'd first been kissed?

Yes. Two firsts. You're playing with words.

I know. But it *was* under an olive tree, on a terrace looking over the town?

Yes. I don't know about the *margaritas,* though. I'm not sure about them either.

Do you remember what you were wearing? I ask her because I don't and she almost always does.

Yes. Don't you?

No. Tell me.

You should remember that. I should have been an unforgettable sight.

My memory, *vida*. Forgive me.

Maybe. Not yet.

We are driving through one of the few areas in Spain where olive trees don't grow. The valley of Jerte, on the way to Galicia. Cherry trees grow there instead, on both slopes. We are rising into the sierra of Gredos, and only a few of the trees are in bloom. I pull off the road and entice her out of the car and up to a tree whose bark is glowing with that mahogany sheen and whose red buds are packed and about to explode. I kiss her there, squatting a little to get under the branches. She fits without having to squat.

She's wearing a leopard-spotted sweater with black velvet slacks. She's lovelier than she was as a girl.

What's next? she's saying.

On to Galicia.

. . .

WHEN WE CAME DOWN from that terrace of olive trees in Bocairente we met a man who claimed to have seen a certain light in our faces and went on and on drunkenly discoursing about the nature of love. Spaniards drank to excess only during their towns' fiestas, which occurred once a year and might last a week. Toward the beginning of fiestas they tended to be poets who laughed a lot and celebrated everything under the sun, but by the end they became philosophers and that was when they could go on. This man had been an admirer of my wife's since she was a little girl. Like many others, he had been keeping an eye on her. He had a red inflamed face over the gray of no sleep, a small face with a big gaping smile and small eyes under bristling brows. He was dressed in a long robe, which hung open like a bathrobe, but not of silk: some rough-textured material, which meant he had been marching as a Christian and not a Moor. Still, he discoursed about that moment of love's awakening as a divine moment, which made him sound like a Moor.

He took us aside. That look—*aquella mirada divina*—he'd been waiting to see it on my wife's face since she was a little girl. The *secretarieta* had grown up. He took me aside, stage-whispering to the table at large: She was in love with me. *Hombre!* Then he wrapped us in two stout arms and wouldn't let go. He didn't expect us to believe him but it was the culmination of his life. Now he could die in peace. *Salud!*

Finally somebody unwrapped us and somebody shut him up.

Pesado is the word the Spanish use—someone is tiresome, a tiresome weight. I remember Antonio describing that man in that way, and since everybody in the town went by their nicknames he called him by his: Flor. He didn't explain why the man was nicknamed "Flower," he just said, *Que pesado es ese* Flor, *verdad?*

What a great crushing tiresome weight of a flower that man is.

But even as Antonio was expressing his annoyance, I thought he was pleased. Perhaps he was pleased because some kind of great crushing tiresome weight had been lifted off him.

"Pleased" is not the word. I'm not even sure "relieved" is.

Clearly, Antonio was attracted to his sister, but so, then, was everybody else: As a girl, as a young woman, she was someone to be prized. The only difference was that Antonio's had been the shaping hand. I ask myself: Was the fastest way for him to get her where he couldn't get his hands on her to hand her to someone else? Someone else he could shape? He had already taken me to his tailor in Valencia and had me measured for a suit whose cut he approved. He had never stopped instructing me in the small matters that take a Spaniard through his ceremonial day. I had to learn the code of *detalles*. The word meant "details," but really they were little acts of courtesy or kindness calculated to a fine degree. The finer the degree, the better the *detalle*. You took note if your friend expressed an interest in a tie you wore or a wine you drank or a *dulce típico* you'd described to him (the little pastries the nuns made in Bocairente, for instance), and not the next day but sometime later so that it could seem no more than a casual afterthought emerging from your own generous nature, you made him a gift of one. You scored a point; a *detalle* was credited to your account. Those not born with a sense of *detalle* in their bones had to work at it, but sooner or later, if you heard someone say, *Que detalle más bonito has tenido,* you knew you were on your way.

I resisted what seemed to me the patent falsity of it all, even as I understood that in a culture as highly wrought as the Spanish, "working at it" was something you did every day. Just as Antonio was working on me, making me into an artifact suitable for his sister, even as she was beginning to suffer the confinements of a culture that would allow a brother to do just that and might have been looking to me as a way to escape?

It was all too baroque for my taste, and I gave myself to it.

.   .   .

I HAD BROUGHT WITH ME a small Olympia manual typewriter. I had meant to write a novel about a little girl with an incurable disease who rode her horse into a lather every day in some woods. By chance the narrator observed this mad ritual and kept going back. I mention this not because of any light it might shed on my courtship of my wife, but because it gave Señor and Señora Ferri an opportunity to be true to their nature and get rid of me at the same time. They kept a house in a small mountain town, the very town where their daughter had nearly died from food poisoning. If I wanted to be a writer, why didn't I go there and write? They rented the house year-round. I could set up shop in the kitchen, where there was a fireplace and a rustic pantry and cane lathing on the ceiling. I would have my choice of bedrooms. The Ferris themselves would not show up until the summer, and by then . . . They were being hospitable and generous and, cannily, they were getting me out of the way. Even if I rode the bus back to Valencia during the weekends, that gave Amparo five days to come to her senses. And what was more, it gave her other suitors an open field.

I went to this town, Sot de Chera. I stayed there by myself for almost four months. It was there that I turned thirty. Almost every weekend I took a winding two-hour bus ride into Valencia where I reoccupied my old *pensión* room and spent the hours we had frantically trying to reassure Amparo that everything would be all right. Three times that I remember she rode the bus to visit me in Sot de Chera, twice with Antonio and once, I believe, with his *novia*, Concha. On one of those occasions, sitting on some boulders by the creek, I proposed to her. She didn't answer me then, I thought because she was elated and stunned, not because she might refuse me. That must have been in April. The almond trees had blossomed. *Margaritas* were certainly out beneath the olive trees. The orange trees were so dense a green that they made the surrounding hills seem chalkier than they were. But the water came down out of those hills, and it was a clean rushing green over the white of the rocks.

By then we had been through too much for her to refuse me. She had given up and come back too many times to give up now. We joined all the other couples in Franco's Spain with no place to go and hid away in the back booths of *cafeterías,* in parks, in botanical gardens, at the ends of piers in the port, in the ruins of palaces, in doorways, with the gypsies under bridges, even with no hint of sacrilege in church, kissing in long famished drafts. She was very strong and her flesh had a supple sort of density that made other women I might have held in my arms seem frothy by comparison. But I didn't let my hands stray. I held her. I cupped the lovely round of her shoulders; I stroked her face, the honey-rose of her cheeks; I passed my hand over her broad forehead and let it linger there as though I were taking her temperature. My Spanish improved, but never enough to tell her the effect that a being like hers was having on a being like mine. Then I took the bus back to Sot de Chera and, in English, tried to write that novel about a little girl racing death on her Arabian stallion.

I am getting ahead of myself.

.   .   .

IT IS THE GREEN of Galicia she loves. I have been in Ireland and she hasn't and she wonders if this is the sort of green you'd find there. I remember spongy green bog land. Galicia is a maze of curving valleys where the mimosa trees are in bloom in a bright chamomile yellow. The towns are very small, *aldeas,* clusters of free-standing houses. The dominant stone is granite. The closer you get to the coast the more granite you see, until they use granite for something as incidental as the stakes for their vineyards. Set up on granite pedestals, which give the impression of stubby legs, are oblong vented enclosures, made of wood, used to keep the grain for the animals dry. These granaries are called *horreos.* They are everywhere, and since not that many families keep animals anymore, I think of them as shrines. Some are quite ornate, but they are somber structures nonetheless, with their heavy vented walls and stone legs. There is always a cross at one gable point; many have two.

There is a shaggy cross of gray granite at the entrance to each of these *aldeas,* and in each of the tiny plazas a Romanesque Christ is weathering into the very cross he hangs on, while a Virgin carved at his back is eroding in tears.

I spend some time looking at these Christs. An expression of wide-eyed innocence is left on some of their faces, even of good cheer. The wounds don't show. The various roads to Santiago de Compostela pass through these hills and *aldeas,* and it occurs to me that these Christs are well suited for pilgrims who don't need to be flagellating themselves over hill and dale. In each little village there's a Christ happily making himself one with the granite out of which he's carved.

But my wife likes it here because it's green.

It is in Galicia that I realize in one little corner of my brain that I am perfectly serious about this search for the ideal town. I'll find it and live there with more of my kind. I'll give up the fight. A windmill is a windmill, a goatherd a goatherd. I'll say hello to my granite Christ every morning. I'll clear my head.

I don't know about my wife.

. . .

EARLY ON I had told Antonio about my brief marriage. I had told Amparo. It had been a youthful mistake. "A divorced man" was the last phrase I'd use to describe myself. Americans believed in fresh starts. You could carry it to extremes and say that Americans believed in tabulae rasae. The weight of history was too much to ask any one man to bear. You're history, as the expression went, and you're done.

A clean slate.

That was not how I felt about it. I said that my ex-wife and I had shaken hands and parted as friends. Actually, I think that last time we had slept together to see if, well past the eleventh hour, we could make it work. We did not love each other. If we could have genuinely consoled each other for how badly we had failed, something might have come of that. But we were too self-absorbed to console anyone except ourselves.

Without saying a word we'd concluded a mutual pact: I would keep her secrets if she would keep mine. We'd parted on friendly terms.

I told Amparo I was single and a lot wiser than I might have been. I told Antonio that I had make the kind of mistake that a few years later, when the '60s really kicked in, would never have been held against me. My first wife and I would have lived together a couple of months and that would have been that. I asked him to treat this information as a confidence, but perhaps that was unfair. Antonio was responsible for putting me in his sister's presence. When it seemed that Amparo and I were not going to be easily parted he took it on himself to "prepare" his parents, as he put it. It was for my own good.

He told his parents about my marriage. His father blew up and forbade me to set foot in his house. Curiously, but, I see now, squarely within his nature, Señor Ferri did not take that house in the little town of Sot de Chera away from me. I could keep my distance, stay there and write.

Antonio assured me that the storm would pass. I should take his father at his word. Write my novel. Come visit his daughter on the weekends. Stay clear of his house until Antonio gave me the okay.

Señor Ferri was a highly emotional and very sentimental man. His lack of a leg perhaps led him to be more generous than he might have been, and when he felt betrayed, with one less leg to stand on, he fell harder than the rest. He was very Spanish. If part of Franco's success consisted in keeping much of Spain in the dark, you can imagine what happened when the light burst in. I thought of Yeats's phrase, "A terrible beauty is born." Señor Ferri stood on his crutch and his one leg and weathered the blast. But the shock to his system was severe.

His wife could hold a grudge much longer, and did.

For six weeks he couldn't be approached on the subject of his daughter and me. Perhaps he was testing me, trying to see how steadfast I could really be. I stayed in Sot de Chera and made friends. The man whose house the Ferris rented had been a fighter pilot for the Republicans during the war. I knew him as Don José. He had a weather-squinted face, wore a beret and came to sit with me some evenings before my fire in the kitchen. Maybe he just wanted to keep an eye on the house, but in the process he told me his war stories with a good-natured equanimity that I came to marvel at and somehow to attribute to his life in the *campo* and in the mountains that surrounded the town. I took walks into those mountains, pulling myself up steep trails by grabbing hold of small bushes, which more than once turned out to be *romero* and *tomillo,* rosemary and thyme, and which left an inspiriting scent on my hand. But I also walked them with the priest of the town, Father Enrique, who was no older than I and was so short that the two of us together provoked laughter everywhere we went. Sot de Chera had been his first parish, and the stories he told me were stories of the town.

I was beginning to understand the language. I thought I was close to understanding it all. There was a wall of foreign sound that was just a word or phrase away from becoming intelligible. Enrique's stories were frequently about the couples who came to him for counsel. Men did not want to be seen with their wives on the street. They especially did not want their wives approaching them when they gathered at the one bar in town. In lovemaking they did not want to see what they were mating their flesh to. They did not want their flesh to be seen. I think Enrique appealed to me as an enlightened man, fresh out of the '60s. What was he to do? The town was so pretty seen from the paths we walked, its walls so white and the geraniums that grew on its balconies so bright, that it was hard for me to imagine these age-old pockets of darkness.

Amparo came there to get out of the city and swim in the summer. Others did, too. In summer the population—never more than five hundred—could double. Spaniards coming back to the *pueblo.* Poisoned cans of mussels could get in, too. I met the young intern who had attended Amparo while she saved her own life. At first occasionally, then almost every night, I sat with him and the schoolteacher around a *mesa camilla* in Enrique's house, with the blanket-thick tablecloth draped over our laps and the coal brazier at our feet, sipping cognac and anise and sampling small sweets in an effort to keep warm. And I straining to break through that wall of foreign sound.

The doctor, the teacher, the priest and the visiting writer. I felt it was a matter of days, at the most a week, before the accents sorted themselves out, the *se-lo-la*'s of my Spanish fell into place. I left that *mesa camilla* and walked home to a dead fire, a cold kitchen and a cold bed. It occurred to me that if I'd had Amparo here with me we could have walked these streets together and set a standard for conjugal happiness that would have rendered Enrique's role as marriage counselor superfluous. And it occurs to me now that my quixotic search for just the right town to shelter us began with my lonely fantasies then. I sought *amparo*, both the sheltering care and the woman, the woman and the word.

.   .   .

SHE'S TIRED NOW, tired of driving and ready to stop. We've followed the river Mino down to its estuary, where the *hostal* we'd expected to find is closed. She'd just as soon stop at the first place we see. We come to a new *hostal*, raw brick fronting the sea, with nothing on either side, and I shrug and say, Go ahead. When she comes back after having seen the room, I tell her I've changed my mind. I won't stay there. With all the places that mean something in this world, in this part of the world, why do we have to stay in a place stripped of meaning, or to which—look at it, for God's sake!—no meaning could ever be attached? She says the room has a stunning view of the ocean. I say the ocean is a great leveler and I'm after something else. We drive on. In the next estuary we begin to see the enormous wooden rafts called *viveros* they use in this part of Galicia to cultivate mussels. They are set out in squadrons against the darkening horizon and remind us of battleships. They stretch on and on.

At the moment we don't know what they are, but the impression they create reinforces the mood that's already settled around us, and we're locked into step the rest of the way.

. . .

BUT, THEN, as a twenty-two-year-old girl, she was waiting for me when the bus pulled in from Sot de Chera on Saturday morning, or was quick to come by my *pensión* if she couldn't meet me at the station. I asked her about her week, the classes she was taking; I told her about the conversations I'd taken part in around the *mesa camilla*. She claimed my Spanish was improving and was very pleased, and it was true, there were moments when it seemed to flow. But mostly it was stacked up in my mouth and felt like a great clogging mess. I'd begun to teach her some English. Her voice in English had a chirping clarity, with the accents all her own. I'd say to her, Come on, to which she'd answer, I'm coming, and even though the words were mine, not hers, she'd give herself over to them with such willing delight that I would shake with happiness.

But while I was basking in it I also thought she was a fool. Why in the world would anyone risk all that she had for me, a '60s reject, a self-reject many times over, if the truth be told, a man who when he turned a pitiless eye on himself could not locate a single truly unselfish deed? But she had. This exotic creature—she didn't know any better. I knew I should tell her how deeply mistaken she was, but then I wondered if what the poets had always said about love wasn't true. That it could redeem. That none of us was so unworthy that love couldn't make us new. And when I saw things in that light I wanted to bow down to her, first to her brother, perhaps, and then to her for finding in me what I feared I had lost for good. I was still alive! Out of the old gnarled heart of me came a fresh sprout, a damp glimmer of green. Thank you, Antonio!

Thank you, Amparo! I was almost prepared to thank Francisco Franco. The old world of Spain was suddenly the most youthful thing on the map. A brand-new peninsula.

The Saturday morning would come, however, when I'd step off the bus and even though she was radiant, open-handed and open-eyed, it would all be a shade off the truth. We'd go through the motions—unbridled motions to the common eye—but by late afternoon, when she'd come back to meet me, I'd know it was about to end. She'd get incredulous and a little defensive when I'd tell her I could see it all on her face. Couldn't she hide anything? she'd wonder, as if she'd been deprived. But she couldn't. Not then. The animation in her face came with an instant's delay, and she was drifting off with that unmoored look in her eyes.

Then she might go to sleep. I'd wait her out, wait until that tear had appeared and slipped down her face. But there came a time when she didn't awake. We were sitting in Valencia's botanical garden, before a cactus garden displaying species from Spain's former colonies. I jostled her shoulder and it did no good. I sat back and stared, not at an orange growing on a tree overhead but at a maguey cactus with its smooth muscular arms tapering to needles. I had to pick her up and carry her through the garden to the gate and set her on another bench while I caught a taxi. We were stared at in another way—as casualties, I supposed, of the unbridled creatures we'd just been. On the long ride out to her parents' apartment, I tried to console her by murmuring Spanish phrases and stroking her cheek. She didn't respond. I had to carry her up two flights of stairs, and for the first time I knew what a weight of life I had on my hands. I could have left then. I could have delivered her into her parents' custody and continued the trip I'd originally planned before Antonio had talked castles out of the air.

For out of my ignorance and love I'd already diagnosed Amparo's condition: She didn't exceed her capacity, we did. We all crowded in with more needy demands than she could possibly satisfy. She'd been raised to be at the center of attention; everybody had a stake in her, certainly her brother and parents, but also people I'd never met. I hadn't even known a man named Flor existed before he told me that all his life he'd been waiting to see that look of love in the *secretarieta*'s eyes.

I, of course, was the biggest drain on her vital energy. If I left her she would come back to life. Wouldn't anybody who loved her do the same?

But I didn't leave her. I knocked on her parents' door, then carried her over the threshold and into living quarters where I'd been forbidden to set foot. Both her father and mother were there, and the three of us gathered around her bed where I laid her, with our differences unvoiced. Although we might not admit it to each other, we knew what we had done to her and it bound us together as nothing else could.

Let her breathe, we were telling ourselves, but what we were really saying was, Let her come back to life.

The Spanish have an expression, *Sana como un pez*. It translates as, Healthy as a fish. And it was true, just as you rarely saw a sickly fish, Amparo looked radiantly healthy. Always. Before she went in for her three operations, nurses would do a double-take and wonder, What is she going in there for? She had such natural color—her forehead glowed with it—and her hair had a surging life of its own. Anybody who knew her would conclude that when she was brought low like this it was because she had been visited by an outside force.

An outsider.

Shouldn't we call a doctor? But I didn't say it.

She opened her eyes and saw the three of us together and indicated that she couldn't speak. Then she closed her eyes, and when she opened them again we weren't there. She searched the room, with alarm but some stubbornness, too. She looked right at me and I was thin air or impenetrable darkness. She closed her eyes. She could speak now. She said, I can't see. Wait. Her mother began to wail inwardly, so that just a high-pitched whimper got through, but her father and I took her at her word.

We waited. She took her time, opened her eyes and smiled. See, she could see. She tried to seize on us and offer reassurance at the same time. That caused a jostling effect in her eyes, and we assured her that we were reassured, we whispered our encouragement to her, take your time, we were in no rush, and she responded with an almost petulant grimace. She pointed at her ear and mouthed the words, Now I can't hear.

Then she cleared her face of all expression, closed her eyes and went perfectly still.

I committed a brazen act, although at the time I didn't realize it. I motioned to her mother and father that we should leave the room. And they obeyed as if they had been waiting for someone—for anyone—to tell them what to do. Señor Ferri's crutch made a lonely plunking sound on the bedroom rug as his weight came down, and on the tile of the hall its rubber tip made a squeak. Señora Ferri muttered a toneless prayer I couldn't understand. We waited, staring at the floor. When our time came Amparo called us all back in and said she was all right now: She smiled, she spoke, she saw, she heard. She had the three of us together, and together we had weathered the storm. We were in the same boat. From that point on I was allowed back in their house and more or less regarded as their daughter's *novio*.

Had she staged it all to bring us together? I've learned not to try to read my wife's mind. The line between her conscious motives and the more ambitious designs of her unconscious, or between the being she commands and that much more variable being she simply bestows, wavers. She claims not to remember any of this scene. Not any? The botanical garden was one of our regular stops. But the cactus garden, the long needled arms of the maguey cactus, the ride she took in my arms, in the taxi, up the stairs, the loss of her senses, the fitful way they reappeared— I think she thinks I'm making it all up. I'm a writer and writers like to find a way to dramatize what might not have been that dramatic at all.

But it was dramatic, and it was no windmill I was mistaking for a great wheeling giant of an opponent.

.   .   .

SHE HAS THE OCEAN NOW, but in a *hostal* overlooking the port of Bayonne, which is an old town (although the *hostal* isn't) with an old granite fort, which is the first thing the crew of the *Pinta* saw when Columbus sent them back to report the discovery of the New World. She has the ocean but not the ocean of crashing waves she had asked for out behind that *hostal* of raw brick, so her mood retains something of that wildness as we walk down these streets. It's as if a high-tide warning were still out, but people are used to high tides in this town, and at the most you might get a little spray in your face. She's giving in, spraying me when I get too settled, but settling in herself to the rhythms she sees around her as the tide recedes. For twenty, maybe thirty minutes, she maintains that skillful balance between the ocean she wanted and the one that's been civilized into the stone of this port. She's a delight. For twenty, maybe thirty minutes, I'm more in love with her than ever.

But it's true what I tell myself. Over the years she's come to want the wildness and the greenness and the space more and more. I, in turn, have turned back to this. The irony is neat and almost charming, but it's not easy to get the whole of us in one place at any one time. Right now that give-me-wildness-and-raw-brick part of her is heading back across the Atlantic, leaving me in an old world with a diminished wife on my hands.

.   .   .

ANTONIO AND I WERE GONE for two weeks. Not castle-hunting (castle-hunting we would never go) but looking for a retirement house on the

costa azul or the *costa del sol* for the couple he'd lived with during his stay
in the United States. We found a house—in an *urbanización* populated by
British, Germans and Scandinavians—but those were two weeks he'd
taken me away from Amparo. Antonio had had the tact and courtesy not
to talk about his sister while we were gone, but I never knew if he knew
that during our absence she was proposed to twice. If he did know, I
don't hold it against him. If his parents had persuaded him to get me out
of town long enough for his sister to consider somebody other than the
outsider he had had the bad sense to bring to her from half a world away,
I could see why he might do just that. I know that he knew at least one
of the men because he was the son of a close friend of the family, and
when he came to call on Amparo he was accompanied by his father, a
wealthy man. The father met with Amparo's parents while the children
were allowed to meet on their own, to sit facing each other over a *mesa
camilla,* I suppose. Later that summer, during fiestas in Sot de Chera, I
saw the man. He may have been my age. He had lank brown hair, he wore
a loose-fitting pale silk shirt, he walked with an insouciant gait. He became
for me the image of privileged wealth, and I thought he looked spineless.

The other suitor, a pharmacist, sent his mother first. These were people from the township where Señor Ferri was now secretary. They knew
what was going on. I have no doubt they had kept us under surveillance
and knew just how many times I had brought Amparo back to her parents' house. The man was not an aspiring pharmacist but the thing itself,
with a pharmacy of his own. He had met Amparo at some town pageant
and had taken her dancing. An older man, eminently respectable, he had
somehow been allowed to escort her unchaperoned. He was a very good
dancer, but he was timid and proud and probably afraid of being rejected, so he sent his mother. Free pills for everybody for life? The Ferris, bless them, said they would not intercede on the pharmacist's behalf,
only allow him to plead his case to their daughter whenever he wished.

He never did.

There were others I would learn about later on. Another would pursue her halfway around the world until, one morning on a town plaza in a neighborhood of Cincinnati, Ohio, he would stand before her and want to know why. An even older man than the pharmacist, he had seen the woman emerge from the child and she had probably come to represent the whole spectrum of womanhood for him. Now that she was a wife and a mother, the spectrum was complete. He had already bought a return ticket to Spain with her name on it, and another for our infant son. At the time we were living on what I made selling encyclopedias in the evening, and the extravagance of the gesture put its gallantry to shame. He showed her the tickets. He would take her back to Spain, where she belonged. He loved her. He worshipped her. He was abject and powerful, and she took our son and ran.

He was an older man. They were all older men. Just as Antonio was an older man. Just as I was.

I asked her to marry me in early May in Sot de Chera, sitting beside the stream. It was still cold in the evening, and I continued to sit around the *mesa camilla* with the priest, the doctor and the teacher, but by then everything was in bloom. *Margaritas* had been out for our first kiss (although she might not remember it), and that had been ages before. Now jasmine climbed trellises and walls. Animal smells combined with the scent of the jasmine to leave a meaty sweetness in the air. She must have been there with her brother, or with Concha. They would have slept in the bedrooms below while I stayed in the one off the kitchen, where I belonged. I could have crept down the stairs at night, forced the issue and perhaps had my way, but I was playing by rules centuries in the making. Not that I understood it at the time. License characterized the world I had left, and I had left it because I couldn't live there; clearly I was seeking some limits. I sat her down on some rocks beside the creek.

She always assumed (feared and perhaps secretly desired) that one day I would begin my trip into Europe. She claimed to feel guilty that I was putting it off on her account. That day I told her that Europe could remain beyond the Pyrenees, I was content to be on the peninsula with her. I remembered the way her eyes had flared and her mouth had dropped when I'd said I loved her. I said it again, with exactly the same words—*Sabes que te quiero mucho*—and then I used the verb again: *Quiero casarme contigo.* I want to marry you, I said. I liked the interchangeable meanings of the word: You want what you love and love what you want.

I honestly believed she'd be thrilled with my proposal. After all, since seeing Jimmy Stewart in those movies in her town's bullring she'd wanted to marry an American. She loved her town and its ceremonial life, but already she'd suffered its smallness and dreamed of space.

But, more scared than thrilled, she said, You should take your trip into Europe first, and if I hadn't been so crazily in love with her I might have given her the powers of prescience she clearly possessed in that moment. She saw what an ordeal we would have to undergo to make it to the altar, she saw looming before us the twin powers of Church and State, perhaps even Franco himself, a bitter old bone of a man. But I, an American, possessed of indomitable willpower and a bulling sense of what I could do with it, brushed her caution aside. I told her we would go together. I told her I had no desire to see Europe unless I had her at my side. My Spanish suddenly flowed and, inspired, I explained how paltry the most majestic cathedral would seem unless she was there to share it with me. She had ruined me for the wonders of the world! I laughed for the joy of the moment and for my own powers of expression and kissed her.

She kissed me back, but in that anxious, half-absent way I had come to interpret as the first sign of her drifting off. Around us were mountains, the muted grays and greens of the rock and the pines, the silvery green of the olive trees terraced up their flanks. The orange orchards were farther down, where the valley widened a bit below the town. The town possessed not a castle but a truncated tower, Moorish in design, where arms might have once been stored. It was terraced on two levels and the creek ran by it. Antonio fantasized about getting himself elected mayor of the town and expropriating the tower for himself. Don José encouraged him in this fantasy. While Amparo and I sat there, Antonio and Don José might have been pacing off the terraces, studying how the tower could be made habitable. El Marqués de Sot de Chera. El Conde de Sot de Chera

A week or ten days later, we were in Valencia in, of all places, a discotheque, with red plush upholstery and strobing red light, where I had taken her dancing. The small dance floor was crowded. She loved to dance and didn't mind banging shoulders with those around her. I was there because it pleased her, not because I shared her enthusiasm. She was tireless. There was no break between songs, but there came a moment when she paused long enough to whisper-shout in my ear, Yes, she'd thought about it and decided the answer was yes, and either because I couldn't entirely hear her or because I was distracted by where we were I came very close to saying, The answer to what? But I stopped myself. I asked her if she'd step outside and tell me that again. But she'd caught the beat of the next song and even though she kept nodding, Yes, yes, and gave me her exuberant open-mouthed smile, she didn't go outside and tell me that she loved me too and would marry me regardless of what it cost until after the song ended. Or maybe the song after that.

But then she did.

. . .

IT ALL MAKES ME FEEL HUMBLE and grateful and, after all the far-ranging and hard times, willing to do anything it takes to please her as we travel her country again. She likes the *rías bajas* of Galicia and the estuaries the rivers form as they widen into the sea, but the water here is as still as the Mediterranean on the calmest of its days and the peninsulas are sedate in their small settlements and unruffled green. Normally this is a rainy, windy region, but since we have been here the weather has been mild. The light is a pale, restful gold. We drive the towns along the coast. A granite cross welcomes us and those little granaries stand up on their stubby legs. Their ventilation slits remind me of gills.

On the map we find the town of Finisterre, the town at the "end of the earth," and drive there.

There's a lighthouse at the point, and finally she has her ocean as far as the eye can see. Three elderly women and one man have found a windproof pocket and sit before the lighthouse in the sun. It's still not her day, I know; the whitecaps are modest and lacy and here are these old folks with time on their hands. We exchange pleasantries. *Que bien que se está aquí!* Perhaps for *los viejos,* they respond, but the young have mostly left. It's true. We have just passed through the town of Palmyra, where a monument has been erected to the one-third of the town that has emigrated to Newark, New Jersey. Nor is fishing what it used to be. European Community quotas are too tight. Costs are too high. The fish have left, too. It is the complaint we have heard all over Spain—and will continue to hear. It doesn't pay to harvest the olives or grapes, we've been told; the work's too hard and the wages too low. The young have gone elsewhere. When the old generation dies out the town will, too. Then, when the young have prospered and return to pay homage to their *pueblo,* they won't find any *pueblo* left.

The time to pay homage is now.

We've violated one of our cardinal rules. We've continued our outing and trusted to our luck instead of finding a place to stay at the start. It's not that the *hostales* and small hotels are full during this off-season;

it's simply that there aren't any in these fishing villages. Not even a *hostal* made of raw red brick facing the sea. We drive into the night. We're down off the main highway onto the narrow roads hugging the coast when our luck holds. A small bay, really no more than a cove, a strip of beach, and set up in the pines a small hotel, all but empty, still open, it's hard to say why.

We take a room looking down through pine boughs to the water. There is even a small restaurant and a menu to order from, but we insist that the owners serve us what they're having, *caldo gallego,* a thick soup of turnip greens, cannellini beans and potatoes, and for the main course *merluza a la gallega,* a fish dish, hake made the way the Galicians like it, with potatoes and onions and a paprika-and-oil sauce. The owners join us for coffee and treat us to a liqueur of blackberries that they make themselves, very *típico.* He is an ex-merchant marine who didn't emigrate, who came home, and she is a woman who was born in a house just above the hotel. The hotel was built on land she inherited when her father died. Her husband had sailed the world, and she had stuck to her patch of land. They had two sons studying *hostelería* so that they would know the correct way to run a hotel.

Galician women have a wistful tone to their voices. That wistfulness can cloy, but it can also run with sweetness down your ear, while the men, used to a life on the ocean, talk less. We like these two very much, Pilar, or Pili, and Rafael. Our son's name is Rafael. We sit there and let Pili melt all over us. She is the cook, and the meal we have been served was superb. Valencia is famous for its rice dishes, just one of which is paella, and Amparo, a fine cook herself, begins to exchange recipes with Pilar for *platos típicos* from the two regions. Galician men are famous for their *añoranza,* a homesickness so severe they might be said to hear their women's voices from across the water, but Rafael is a measured man who has traveled himself out (he talks, unlongingly, of Norfolk, Virginia, and Hoboken, New Jersey) and is content to remain where he is. Neither is political. Many in Galicia are separatists, what they call *nacionalistas* here, like many more in the Basque Country and Catalonia, where we'll be heading. But Pili and Rafa are profoundly Galician. Here is where they belong.

After we leave them and return to our room, my wife and I continue the conversation, this whole matter of what is typical of a region, what it means to live in a place so typically, so integrally, that you can be accounted for down to the finest particular.

Food.

Did I know that in the town where my wife grew up there was a smell on the streets for each day of the week? Start with Monday. The smell of oven rice because everyone wanted to make use of the leftovers from the *cocido,* a meat and vegetable and chickpea dish that was prescribed for Sunday. Tuesday, the smell of roasted red peppers stuffed with rice and tuna, because Tuesday was a market day and red peppers could be bought fresh. Wednesday, a "wet rice," cooked with artichoke leaves and navy beans and, in the fall, mushrooms from the Sierra Mariola. Thursday, the remaining vegetables were baked, and the smell in the streets was of roasted onions, tomatoes and eggplants. Friday, fish, of course; in the winter a hot fish soup. Saturday, an even bigger market day, so fruit and vegetables and chicken baked fresh and especially the intoxicating smells (for a child) of cakes and pastries being baked for Sunday, when people walked through the streets with their sweets and paid their calls.

Sound good? Did I know that there was never a day when my wife was a child that she did not smell these smells? She could walk the streets with her eyes closed and, depending on the season, know the day of the week. When you grow up in one of these regions, one of these towns, you take a variety of wonderful sensations out of your childhood into middle age, but she is telling me the variety is not endless, it's pre-scribed, so in some ways it isn't a variety at all. You lock into place.

Is that really what you want? she asks me, with the ocean stirring be-yond the pines, the thickening smell of the ocean passing through the in-spiriting scent of the pines.

There are days, I tell her, when I would give everything for just that. You lock into place.

It's not as if you walk around dragging your ball and chain.

There are only seven days in the week. There are just so many fiestas and religious holidays.

It's the ocean out there, the wildness beyond the point of Finisterre, that she didn't get her fill of, with the whitecaps no more than little Velazquez-like touches of lace and the old folks taking the sun. Coming back to Spain's small towns, she's experienced both the child's exhilaration and the adult's confinement. She's experienced them again and again.

You can make the argument, I say, that something that has stood the test of time, such as that week's worth of dishes, instead of having a regiment-ing effect frees you for everything else. You could make the argument.

You could.

You know what I mean.

Claro. But tell me anyway.

You grow up with the customs and traditions of that town like a solid base beneath your feet. An American spends most of his life just trying to get his footing. A Spaniard's born with his. You can dedicate your at-tention to other, perhaps more important things.

What more important things?

Things that aren't easy to put into words. The meaning of it all. The meaning of any of it. Or how far you can afford to stray from a good paella before it's all nonsense and you know it.

You used to say my paella was a world unto itself.

It's round, it's sunny. It's got the fish of the sea, the fowl of the air and the beasts of the earth.

El mundo entero, you said.

But that was one of my expressions for her. I'd hold her by the hips, the buttocks, the round of her shoulders, the lovely round of her head, and gaze into eyes that could be bold and demanding and very dark and eyes that could be skittish with insecurity, drained of their color and depth, and tell her she was *el mundo entero,* the whole world, the Old and the New combined, and wonder why I was entitled to have her for my wife and why, of all the Americans wandering loose at that time, I should have been the one elected to help hold the halves—the *many* halves—of her together.

I could make it sound more dramatic than it is. My wife is too many people at once. The artfulness of her self-orchestration is extraordinary. My job is to help hold at bay the discordance that threatens to crash through. Her job is to make me more populous than I am.

It's all words and the pictures they form. But to "know" that on Saturday the smells of baking cakes and pastries will spread through the street and then on Sunday you'll see the cakes and pastries themselves carried as offerings from door to door still strikes me as a godsend. What was a once-a-week occurrence for my wife is a blessing for me. Is it any wonder that I busted my ass to marry the woman back when Franco still ruled this country?

She's quit playing with me and gone to the balcony. The stars are out and the wind is barely blowing. Just enough to bring the smell of sea salt and pine scent her way. She breathes it deeply and shakes a little with the insufficiency of it all. Who's she to accuse me of being a Quixote, of expecting more from the world than on a daily basis it's prepared to give? But she said it herself: Sancho Panza was a bigger dupe than Quixote, following him around knowing what he knew.

I step out and put my arms around her. She leans her head against my shoulder. *Que bonito!* she murmurs as she tightens my arms around her. Hold on to me, she's saying. Hold on. I murmur back, as a teasing sort of promise, that before we are done with this trip I will have found her an ocean that crashes and a *hostal* that does nothing but stand there before it in the rawness of its brick.

TWO

ET ME JUMP BACK. AND THEN BACK A BIT MORE.

We were in Valencia. I had yet to propose to her and she had yet to accept. It was March 19, the day of San José. Two years later our son would be born on this day, and the fact that we named him Rafael and not José struck some as a sacrilege. He was born lean as a skinned rabbit with three or four red hairs and put on display with Spanish infants as chubby and hairy as bear cubs. My in-laws looked at their beautiful daughter and looked at him and wondered what had gone wrong. But we were two years from that date. The day of San José was the last day of Valencia's week-long fiesta called Las Fallas, the day when towering structures made of wood and cloth and other flammable materials and bristling with cartoon figures were set on fire and burned to the ground. These structures were satirical in nature, and the cartoon figures were from the world of business, sports, entertainment and politics. Even Spanish politics. During Las Fallas you could get away with making a fool of Franco's ministers, if not the man himself. At midnight, in every plaza in the city, and to the accompaniment of enormous fireworks displays, the evidence got reduced to ash.

Why this should all happen on the day of San José I don't know. The practice had begun when the carpenters and furniture makers from one *barrio* had decided to use their year's scrap lumber to make fun of their counterparts from the next *barrio* over. *Valencianos* could have a biting sense of humor, and they seemed to have an affinity for noise and fire. They could have a gross streak, too. Many of their curses had to do with where they shat and on whom. A foreigner might not see this at first since the refinement of everything around him was so apparent, but as the *fallas* themselves had become more ambitious and time-consuming to make, you could say the grossness had been refined to an art. A year's worth of effort went into it, and then it was gone. I wanted to be there in a plaza I'd picked out to see it. Such studied and arcane masters of the art of preservation, how could the Spanish suddenly step out of character and see it all burned up? What sort of wildness was this?

Those were the questions I was asking myself when I attended my first bullfight. I was thinking not about the bulls but about the *fallas*. But the bullfights took place all that week of *fiestas,* too. We had come to the last day and I hadn't gone yet and Antonio thought I should. He bought the tickets, but it was Amparo who took me. And since tourists were in town for the *fallas,* we sat in the shade, where tickets were double the price but where we wouldn't be surrounded by people there for the spectacle of the thing who knew and cared nothing about the art.

The art?

Amparo liked the pageantry. She liked the music and the strut and the flourish and some of the preliminary, dance-like movements the bull-fighters and their attendants, the *banderilleros,* made. She liked their costumes, the suit of lights, sequins over satins, although her real preference was for the suits called *goyesco* because they dated from the time of Goya, jet-black embroidery over a background of garnet or gray. She

liked the *mantillas* some of the women wore, and she pointed out to me
when the patterning in the lace was especially fine. It seemed there were
lace patterns handed down in certain families like coats of arms, and she
knew all that. Listening to her I got the impression that within that smell
of quality perfume and cognac and *puros,* plus the scent of horses from
under the stands and perhaps, already, a trace of blood from the bulls,
history was milling around. But listening to her I frequently got that impression and was unprepared for the moment when the first bull burst
into the ring.

I had never seen a more beautiful animal, from the majestic head and
neck to the sleekly tapered trunk to the strutting rump and almost dainty
rear hooves. The bull was black turbulence given a stunning shape, and
I sympathized with it at once—if one can be said to sympathize with an
elemental force. Then a man stepped out to meet it, a man dressed like a
foppish dandy from some century past and wearing what looked like no
more than dancing slippers, and my sympathies shifted. They would
have to. That a man would stand up to that! A man, as Spanish as he
might be and steeped in everything I wasn't, but a man nonetheless. In
the instant when the *torero* stood there with his cape performing his initial passes, the confusion that had characterized my life up to then vanished. What I was watching cut beneath my opposition to my country
and my old way of life and cut beneath the thwarted hopes and baffling
disappointments in trying to get close to a new country and way of life.
It cut beneath my love for a woman. Later I would learn more about the
bullfight, become an *aficionado,* and be able to give names to the passes I
was seeing and shout my *olé*'s when those passes were truly good. But I
was speechless that first time, and I held my breath. The man and the
bull came together; they mated in a graceful swirl of the cape; then they
broke apart. They did this four or five times and life was suddenly elec-
tric to me and very clear.

As clear as a cathedral, the Spanish would say.

Then a whole culture intruded. The *picadores,* mounted on their dray horses, plodded in and made brutal poking jabs into the fatty part of the bull's hump with their lances. The *banderilleros* ducked around and ran across the ring and stuck their tasseled darts into that hump that was already welling with blood from the holes the *picadores* had made. Two other *toreros* waved their capes at the bull. The ring was full of people milling around and performing the jobs tradition demanded of them, and the *torero* I had admired so at the start was seemingly content to let it happen. He stood by the wall talking to some potbellied man while mockery was being made of the bull with which he had done such astonishing things at the start.

At the moment I understood none of this. But I see now that I took it all personally. The man and the bull had had that brief mating, and then a world of outdated ritual had gotten in the way. Amparo was explaining what some of the rituals consisted of and instructing me in certain movements that had an unheralded beauty all their own. The way the *torero* brought the bull to the horse, for instance, or some stylish and provocative step the *banderilleros* made before they began their approach with the darts. She sounded a lot like her brother then, with something appreciative but detached and even didactic in her tone.

Of course, it was what had happened to us. I had met her and wanted to get close, but the world had gotten in the way. That world had a Byzantine beauty of its own, and I wanted it, too.

Which do you love first, the woman or the country?

I wanted the man and the bull.

Then I got them. The *torero* stepped back out into the ring, not with the large yellow-and-purplish cape but with a square of red cloth called a *muleta.* He took his cap off and saluted the president. As an act of dedication, he offered his cap to someone in the crowd. Not a woman. A man, perhaps a mentor. He spoke a few words I couldn't hear even though we were sitting close by. Then he turned to the ring, which had been cleared. Waiting for him more or less in the center, somewhere near that fault line between sun and shade, was the bull. The *torero* approached it with a deliberate and almost feminine step, swiveling one leg in front of the other, until they stood no more than fifteen feet apart. The crowd had grown very quiet. The bull regarded the *torero* as something intimately familiar and utterly alien at the same time. In slow motion the *torero* unfurled the red cloth from the sword he used to extend it. The bull followed the motion of the cloth with its head lowered, tilting its horns back and forth in a quizzical way. The *torero* leaned his weight over his right leg and flicked the cloth once. That put the bull on alert. Before he flicked it a second time the *torero* made a sound, and this time everyone in the hushed plaza heard what he said. He said, *Toro,* but in such a private and passionate tone that I almost ducked with embarrassment. Embarrassment for him, that he would have to put up with our presence in a moment like this. And for us, that we had no bull in our lives that we could talk to like that. Then he flicked the cloth a second time, and this time the bull, clearly provoked but curious, too, and almost trusting in its defiance, came.

Thus began what is known as the *faena,* the heart of the bullfight. After the *picadores* and the *banderilleros* have had their go at the bull, the ring is cleared and the *torero* gets his. He passed the bull with the *muleta* in his right hand, then turned it around, held the sword flat against his leg, and passed the bull with his left. He finished off each series of passes with a backhand pass that had the red cloth fluttering up over the horns. True to its nature, the bull was charging, and true to his, the *torero* was leaning in to work the bull close. At one point he got bull blood smeared on his suit of lights. The *olé*'s were not so much loud as deep and vibrant, with a cavernous sort of echo behind them. Amparo informed me that I was lucky to see a fight like this with my first bull. Not everyone did.

She would not go to many more fights, and there came a point where she would go to none. But perhaps because I was there and it was my first, she was aroused. She kept her *olé*'s to herself, but I could see them trembling in her throat. When she danced flamenco her throat got like that; she'd get a congested expression around her eyes and look as though she were about to commit some shocking act. The *torero* was a Castilian named El Viti, and like most Castilians no showman, rather on the sober and austere side. But I could see his throat trembling, too.

And the bull, of course, was all the turbulence in my life, all the conflicting desires and animal needs, compacted into that elemental shape. The *torero* passed him. But in each pass there came an instant when time and motion ceased, and the man and the bull became one. A man, dressed in his gaudy sequins and smeared with blood, rose out of that muscular black cloud. It got turned around and the bull seemingly circled the man, who stood with a mountainous authority in the center of the ring. Each time they came together the man and the bull accomplished some sort of fusion that I experienced as a swelling surge from the ground up, and that I expressed not with an *olé* but with a groan. The fact was, I didn't know what I was seeing. It was utterly foreign to me. And I remembered that the foreign had played tricks on me before. But in that timeless span that the man and the bull occupied the center of the ring, I felt a wholeness I hadn't felt since I was a child.

Then the man named El Viti finished his passes and stood staring in his pride at the bull, which seemed mastered but in no way diminished. The bull stared back. There was an instant when anything might have happened—they might have fallen on each other in a violent swoon. Instead, El Viti turned his back on the bull he'd come to know so well and walked to the barrier, where he spoke to the potbellied man again and exchanged the sword he had used to extend the *muleta* for another.

A chant rose up around us, something stage-whispered almost reverentially and in no way like acclaim or applause—*To-re-ro . . . to-re-ro . . . to-re-ro*—and whatever it was Amparo said, I didn't hear.

Que dices? I said.

Then I heard. She said it to prepare me and, in the fervor of the expectation rising around us, as a sober reminder to herself.

The kill.

The what?

I had forgotten and I was not prepared. What the bull and the man had accomplished between them was so permanent and strong that I did not see how it could end in death.

The bull had not moved. El Viti returned and performed his only adorned passes of the day, a series that had him turning his back on the bull and wrapping himself in his cloth, *manoletes*, named for the bullfighter who had originated it before he was killed.

With the advent of penicillin and improved surgical facilities not as many *toreros* died anymore. But, except in very rare cases, the bulls did. They died in the sand. Their ears were cut off, and sometimes their tails, and presented as trophies to deserving *toreros* who, in their triumphal tours of the ring might throw them up into the stands, and then they were dragged off by the teams of horses.

The bulls were.

I felt a sadness and a disbelief. It ended in death because there was nothing that didn't, I supposed. There came a point when the *torero*—the bull-man, the man with the bull at the center of his being and his name—became a *matador*, a man who killed. Of course. El Viti was good with the sword. He made one last flick with the *muleta* to lower the bull's head, one last invitation to continue the game, and then came in over the right horn and found the one opening the bull provided and buried his sword up to the hilt. The bull backed off with a confounded expression on its face, some sense of betrayal so deep it could only express itself as amazement; it turned and wobbled back toward the barrier. El Viti followed it at a respectful distance until it fell. Then he made a broad sweeping gesture with his sword, turned an exulting grin up on the crowd, and the crowd roared.

Valencia was generous with its trophies and the president must have awarded the two ears. I don't know about the tail. El Viti fought another bull that day, and there were two other *toreros* who fought theirs, but after all this time what's left is that first one. And in that first one I saw the terms of my own drama with Amparo and her country caught clearly. I might have seen them in any act of sufficient complexity and duration—such is the nature of obsession—but it was in the bullfight that it all came home to me.

In some ways it was an ontological event. It had to do with being. The bull charged into the ring as an avatar of Being itself. It met the bullfighter and in the moment of their meeting their being was enlarged. Then a small fussy hierarchical world got in the way. The bullfighter was kept from his bull until each member of that world had gotten a piece of the bull himself. Eventually the lasting power of the bull and the faith and patience of the bullfighter won out and the ring cleared and they came together again. The large gaudy cape was now a square of red cloth. They came together again and again. If the Spanish would ever let us, if that overstaged world of outdated custom would ever get out of the way, Amparo and I could do that. Love was to feel your being enlarged in a powerful way, and if it took a man and a bull meeting and mating in the center of a ring to make that clear, that was okay. The analogy might be crude, but it was not gross. It simply took everything the Spanish had refined down through the ages and put it to the test. Stand up to *that*, it said. Be *that* in a world wrapped up in history. Again and again, the man invited the bull to pass, and in each of those passes, history, the history of who Amparo had been, of the Iberians, Greeks and Phoenicians and all the rest, took a jolt of fresh life.

Be. Be the bull.

I didn't like the killing. The analogy broke down. I didn't like the exulting gestures the bullfighter performed as the bull went down in the dust. That elegant, elemental being was dragged out of the ring as dead meat. I didn't like the triumphal tour of the ring the *torero* made and some of the silliness the crowd displayed in throwing him their hats and scarves and bags of wine. I liked the moment when it all slowed down to an eternal instant and the bull and the man became one. I liked their ferocity and refinement and saw no reason why Amparo and I couldn't take a lesson from them.

If they'd ever clear the ring.

That night in plazas all around town they burned the *fallas* down. This was 1970. I saw figures from the time, whoever that year had managed to call attention to himself, go up in flames. Caricatures of certain *toreros* went up, too. A lot of slavering after sex and the gorging of gross appetites got ridiculed. And then burned. When the flame got too hot we all had to back up, and then there was a lot of packing of bodies into a confined space—*la bulla,* the Spanish call such a crush—but no one panicked or really even complained and most stood there mesmerized by the flames. When the figures at the top of the structures finally fell, the crowd let out a sound that was part sigh, part groan and part cheer, and turned to start home. Except those who intended to make a party of it. When the *falla* burned, it was not the same as the bull going down, except that after each occasion I had to take Amparo back to her parents' house, where I still wasn't welcome, and deliver her back into that world.

She thought the *fallas* and all the noise around them fun, but the bullfight eventually drove her away. I believe it scared her. I believe it scared most people because they had gotten an intimation of what a man and a bull together could do. But Amparo was not like most people. Most people wanted the bull dead. Even the most squeamish—especially the most squeamish—wanted the bull dead. She wanted the bull alive, and I don't think she really minded the blood. What scared her was that extraordinary sense of growth that seemingly respected no bounds. She felt it, too; I wouldn't have been in love with her if she didn't. But it was all new to her. As I sat by her side I was new to her and frightening in what I could do. And she had yet to know the openness and the wildness and the rampant greenness. So far she'd known only the *pasadobles* and the suits of lights and the especially fine mantillas that some of the older families wore. We both wanted to keep the bull alive, but only I intended to use it to batter down some barriers that had been put up (millennia ago) expressly to thwart me. She wanted to keep the bull alive because, though it scared her, the bull was future growth.

But the Spanish wanted to kill the bull. It was their "moment of truth."

. . .

HOW SERIOUS AM I about finding that perfect *pueblo?* So serious that I can't take time out to visit a city that has been the destination for millions ever since someone discovered that a journey was the perfect emblem for faith and that a place could be equated with its bones?

If they were the right bones.

She wants to follow the pilgrims into Santiago de Compostela. In our wandering around Galicia we've crossed their traditional routes into the city three or four times. It is *un año jacobeo*—a year in which Santiago's day, July 25, falls on a Sunday—and so even in March there are numerous pilgrims on the road. They carry staffs with butternut squashes tied to the crooks. Somewhere on their clothing or backpacks or staffs, a scallop shell will be attached. She wants to follow them into the city. *Un año jacobeo* offers special rewards to those who complete the journey. There are some kids, but most of the pilgrims we've seen have been middle-aged couples caught up in the trend of the thing. History lovers with time on their hands. We recognize each other at once, and in our small rented Nissan we putt along behind them.

I don't want to be here. She pauses before jewelry shops where jewelers put themselves on display working in jet, Santiago's stone. Or shops where women border their cloths with a lace pattern sacred to Santiago. Bakers set out their typical Santiago tarts. An industry is devoted to outfitting pilgrims in the right medieval capes and hats and scallop-shell brooches. Any hole in the wall will have sacred relics for sale.

The walls of the city are granite. The streets are colonnaded in granite. On a good day the stone will hold the hucksterism at bay, and you can walk the streets with a reverence in your step.

Reverence for what?

Santiago, the apostle Saint James and Spain's patron saint, is said to be buried here; they are his bones. At the top of the enormous gold-plated altarpiece in the cathedral, he is depicted cutting down *moros* with his sword. Santiago Matamoros. After each Mass they swing the huge censer back and forth to fumigate a church grown thick with the smell of the pilgrims' exertion. This is what it smells like to cross half of Christendom. And this is what that smell smells like sanctified.

Reverence for the stone.

I stand in front of the cathedral at night, in the enormous plaza of Obredoyo, and the busyness of the cathedral's facade, excessive during the day, is edited down by the light so that only the figures distinct enough to cast a shadow stand out. This is a university town. Students are there, then they are gone, and there might be a few real pilgrims left, and myself. We listen to the cathedral bells toll the hour. The sound is deep, almost too deep for sound; solemn and far-ranging. There comes a point where the bells do pass out of hearing and enter your bones as a mellow glow. Santiago, the Matamoros, in whose name they toll, is always depicted with Moors' severed heads rolling at his horse's hooves, yet his bells make the most forgiving sound I have heard in my life. Certain Catholics learn how to live with these contradictions. What the senses tell us, if caught pure, can instruct us better than legends. There is forgiveness in the air.

Beside me a woman is off in a world of her own, crying. Short hair, grainy chapped cheeks, I would bet she is English or Scotch, or perhaps Dutch, and has made the long trip here, hiking in from medieval France, so that she can cry in this plaza as the bells toll. She could never do that back home. Stand out in your town square crying as your bells toll the hours and they will take you for a slacker, a misfit. So you come here, you spread out and thin out with the sound of the bells until you're gone. Dissolved.

"To cease upon the midnight with no pain."

You couldn't do that at home, where you've got to pull your share of the load.

I don't know if I am serious about this search for a *pueblo*. If I can't find inner peace on my own, what good's a place going to do? There's a plaza where the townspeople gather, an hour when even the most cynical of them will join the promenade. You circle a fountain, a statue, a cross, you greet your neighbors, check on who's growing up and who's pairing off, who's using a cane, who's gone off and come back, who's gone off for good, then you go home to supper, where you sit around a *mesa camilla* with the warmth welling up from under the cloth. There you circle another center with your kith and kin, you sip your brandy or that herbal anise and nibble pastries the nuns in your town have made and tell old stories, until it's time to turn off the light. You do this again and again until you begin to generate a history of your own to add to all the other history you see around you. And history is going to take the place of what? Human history, even in ruins, is a more ennobling force than God on high? Is that what you believe? That that evidence of where another sat or stood on dished-out stone will restore a meaning to your life? Human history is mostly an exercise in viciousness, a succession of rolling heads. You know that.

Quixote.

I was right, the Sancho Panza in me was right. Better to worship the stone. If you're looking for a way to escape the terms of your own trifling existence, better to put yourself in touch with geological history, where you're nothing, an infinitesimal instant in the ageless uplift of mountains and the ageless grinding of them down. Put your hand on a cliff face if you want to get right your place in the chronicle of time. You're an overnight, crevice-growing weed, nothing more. But you have your moment in the crevice. Bolstered, protected, nurtured by stone, you and your fellow weeds can take a certain comfort in that. It's a community of sorts.

Sancho Panza would have said, But Master, my good Don Quixote. Look at that stone and look at us. The stone stands. We're so weak that every few hours we have to lie down. It's as plain as day, *como una catedral de claro.* Why all the fuss?

But my Sancho Panza lies asleep.

. . .

THE OTHER HALF OF THE QUIXOTIC ACT. Let me go back again.

I am astounded now at my own triumphant naïveté. In the discotheque that night Amparo said she would marry me and could we please finish one more dance. We finished the dance and it turned out she had already made plans. We would marry in the Basilica where the Virgin of *los desamparados* was enshrined. We would be transported to and from the church in a horse-drawn carriage. Certainly my family would fly over from the United States so that the two families could get to know each other and unite. Antonio would design her dress. He would design the announcements and the invitations. The wedding supper could be held in Los Viveros, an exclusive dinner and dance club in the center of Valencia's main park. The music would be some pop, but mostly traditional. She would teach me to dance the *pasadoble*. And Antonio, if she knew anything about her brother at all, would make me a present of a Castilian cape, lined with red satin, just like his.

The time had come to try to talk to her parents again. And, once again, she asked me to let Antonio prepare the ground.

I returned to Sot de Chera for a week and resumed work on a book that was going nowhere: that little girl with a terminal illness riding her horse into a lather each day in the woods. I was living my novel, and all I could do with the girl was send her around and around that field until I decided to take her off her horse and let her die. I sat around the *mesa camilla* at night with Enrique and his friends. The nights were warmer now and we didn't have to huddle as much. During our walks along the creek I made Enrique my confidante. He had seen Amparo and me together on her trips there, and now I told him of my intentions. We were sitting beside the remains of an old stone bridge that had once crossed that creek. It wasn't as if I were confessing. I was practicing on him. I was working my Spanish up into a speech. I had to find the right tack to take on this matter of my earlier marriage.

Yes, it was true I had been married before, but it had been brief and childless and had served as a sort of rehearsal for the real marriage to come.

Enrique gave me the word: *ensayo.*

It had been an *ensayo.* I was a better man for it. I wouldn't make the same mistakes. I wasn't exactly asking for a tabula rasa, but it wouldn't be fair to hold that first marriage against me.

I caught something in his eye. He wore thick glasses that made his eyes bold and very round and, when the glasses were clean, very bright. His eyes did a little sidestep, they shifted in a slightly bemused way, as if he wasn't sure he'd heard me right. He then went off on a tack of his own and talked of love as the one emotion that could redeem all past wrongs. But that look in his eyes stayed with me, and that weekend, when Amparo said now I should speak to her parents, the time was right,

I saw the look in her father's eyes, and I realized what was meant by the phrase "to look askance." I told her father my first marriage had been a very instructive rehearsal, *un ensayo,* that I was a stronger and wiser man for it, and her father looked askance at me.

A sacrament was not an *ensayo.* The Church does not sanction *ensayos.*

I understood that. But I had not been married in the Catholic Church.

But in some sort of church.

Yes, you could say that. Some sort of church, not a very significant one.

Ahh . . .

Speaking as a practical matter, I said.

But I got no further. That askance look had turned into a disapproving angle, and he was actually sitting back from me now. I knew him to be a melodramatic man whose nature was to overreact, and I knew his wife to be the master of the frozen, disciplined smile. Both were in character. I also knew that since World War II the Spanish had been brought up on a steady diet of American films, and in not one of those films of the wholesome '50s and early '60s had the hero been a divorced man. The divorced man was someone shifty and urbane who'd had a taste of sin and would sin again. He spoke with a mid-Atlantic accent, or he was a smart-dressing cad from the West. He wore a mustache and there was a glow of rottenness around his mouth and eyes. Was that how the Ferris were seeing me?

Antonio had "prepared the ground." But that was not the same as me sitting before them. I was the man himself, the very one who had indulged himself in an early marriage and had shamelessly declared himself free to do it all again.

With their daughter.

I remembered that divorce had entered on the Christian scene with Henry VIII, who'd deprived his wives of either their heads or their honor—the first of his wives had been Spanish, for Christ's sake!—and told the pope to take a walk.

I was not going to tell the pope or the Ferris that. But I was not going to grovel either. The fact that I'm married now and traveling around Spain with the women who for twenty-eight years has been a steadfast source of fascination in my life I could claim was all due to the fact that Señor Ferri sat back from me when I told him I had learned, I would not make the same mistake, it had been a very useful *ensayo* and an *ensayo* could be a very useful thing, and looked at me askance.

He'd provoked me not into a speechless rage but into good Spanish, and I got a taste then of just how determined and persuasive I could be. I would not be looked at like that, not even by a good-hearted man like Amparo's father! So I reargued my case. I had matured. I was seasoned. A bone breaks and heals and is the stronger for it. Their daughter, in her moments of brittleness and self-doubt, needed someone who had taken his licks and come back. She was a marvelous woman! I truly believed she had the potential to be the most astonishing woman on the face of the earth, but she needed a coach and a cheering section and she needed a fresh perspective on some old problems. I swallowed my hypocrisy, or whatever it was, and told him that what she needed was the American perspective, and I could give it to her. Between the two of us we could bridge old gaps, heal old wounds and usher in a new day.

I went on until my Spanish ran out. It had been Señor Ferri's father who had fought in the Spanish-American War and vowed to stand in any American's path. But his son admired Americans and applauded their generosity in restoring Europe. He regretted what Roosevelt had done in partitioning the continent, but the fault lay in Americans' goodwill and trusting nature, and he excoriated Stalin for his villainy, which, he believed, Americans had been unequipped to deal with. I was an American, and I supposed, similarly unequipped. Without quite realizing it I had struck the right chord. Perhaps in that moment he was looking ahead to his grandchildren. He had wanted to surround a dining-room table with children and had gotten only two. His grandchildren would be numerous and their good-natured American generosity would be tempered by a worldly-wise Spanish streak.

Or perhaps it was my fervor that won him over. Americans had conquered the world with just such a display of can-do willpower, and who was he to hold out? Or he couldn't stand to make his daughter sad, and his daughter would be sad, and mad, if I went away. Or maybe it was just that we liked each other. He was an emotional man who lacked a leg, had a grudge-holding wife and worked for a state that treated its citizens like troublesome children, and perhaps he knew that something had to change. Was I the direction in which things had to go?

But I suspect it was the snails. It is going to sound absurd, but the Spanish do put a great deal of stock in *detalles*, and I knew as soon as it occurred to me that I had hit on a splendid one. It had rained one night that week in Sot de Chera, and the next morning snails had washed out of the roadside grass and bushes and were all over the pavement. I saw them when I went out for my walk before beginning work. Señor Ferri took pride in doing the shopping for the ingredients for some of his wife's more ambitious dishes. I climbed back to my third-floor kitchen and got a plastic bag. There were so many snails on the road that I had to choose among them. I went by the smoothness and the roundness and the sheen of their shells. The sun was out and it gleamed on their slime, and I suppose I went by the quality of the gleam. I had never eaten snails, never been tempted, but more than once I had heard Señor Ferri lament the lack of them in his wife's paellas. He had spoken of them as though they were the finishing touch.

It was still the middle of the week, but I caught the bus to Valencia that very morning. Amparo would be in her classes. I knew when I could catch her between classes, but I resisted that temptation. I could not trust her mother, and Antonio, although I could trust him, would take the whole thing over with his style and the simplicity of the gesture would be lost. I took a second bus and then a taxi and caught Señor Ferri at the city hall in the township where he worked. The office was an institutional gray-green; I heard the desultory clatter of manual typewriters and smelled the standing odor of black cigarette smoke. The only decoration was a photograph of Franco hanging on the wall, but the glass had not been cleaned for some time and Franco's medals were dimmed.

I placed that plastic sack of freshly gathered snails on Señor Ferri's desk, and it was true, they were the most luminous object in the room. He looked up from the letter he was writing, saw who had brought the snails to him, and though it took a moment and was not without a hitch, he ended up beaming at me.

Look what I found, I said.

Hombre . . . pero hombre . . . He searched for words, then found the ones that I was waiting to hear: *Que detalle mas bonito!*

I had gotten the hang of it, gotten into the Spanish swing. That afternoon I took the bus back to Sot de Chera without even informing Amparo and her brother that I had been in town. In Spain, since time immemorial and never more so than under Franco, if a man wanted to marry a woman he went straight to her father to complete the transaction. If he went bearing snails, so be it: He went bearing snails. This was strictly between my future father-in-law and me.

. . .

LEAVING GALICIA, we decide to take one of the pilgrims' routes out. For long stretches, sandy walking paths run alongside the highway, kept level and clear, where the pilgrims stroll and chat among themselves, as though they were on the way to Canterbury and each has a tale to tell. The route is supplied with scallop-shell markers so you can't get lost. When the trail is about to cross the road and veer off across a field, motorists are given ample warning. The government doesn't want them hitting pilgrims.

At Sarria we enter sierra and by the time we get to Pedrafita we are in the mountains and snow. In deciding to follow a Santiago route and not the expressway from Lugo to Orense, I failed to notice the mountains on the map. The Spanish call the passes at their peaks *puertos,* which is the same word they use for ports, and the effect is strange, to reach a *puerto* at an altitude of two thousand meters and to find not a home port at journey's end but a peak that you now have to wind down from in ice and snow, frequently with sheer drops to the side. Amparo won't look; she claims she doesn't know if she can make it; it's her fear of heights, her fear of falling off heights, her claustrophobic fear of never getting out of our small car. When she was a child playing in the *barranco* of Bocariente, climbing in its caves, she knew herself to be fearless and she wonders when all that changed. She means really fearless, as though she'd handed herself over to the elements and knew herself to be as indestructible as they.

At each of these passes or ports there is a café or bar or some sort of rest stop for people who, like her, are suddenly seized by the fear that once they have gotten up here they can't get down. I ask her if she wants to stop and she says no. We continue to see pilgrims, though nowhere near as many. They wear plastic ponchos or other sorts of snow gear, and they trudge uphill with their heads down. In some of the lower reaches, before the really bad stuff begins, carloads of Spaniards have pulled off and built snowmen beside the road and are taking photos of themselves. Pilgrims are posing, too. It is March, off the mountain everything is in leaf and flower, but we have this interlude where we're suddenly back in the world of upstate New York driving through snow, with pilgrims and snow-deprived Spaniards beside the road.

I ask her if she's sure she doesn't want to stop.

She pleads with me to go on. She wants to get off this snowy mountain, back into a Spain she knows.

Suddenly something comes clear to me that I've known all along.

This trip that she's agreed to take with me through the small towns of Spain is a trip she's taking for her own sake, too. She's not just humoring me in my quest for the perfect *pueblo* and supplying a little common-sense ballast to my romantic heavings; she's out to find something for herself. Why, for instance, was she so fearless in that town as a child and why is she such a minefield of fears now? That person she was then—when she had the run of her town, a town that was all history—where is she now? She attended those American movies in the bullring. Thanks to me she's been to California and back and has explored the wild ahistorical reaches, but where is the child, she wants to know, who could dig Roman coins out of rubble and toss them away because they lacked currency in the actual world?

I make a preliminary stab at it: She's out to find the town that can give her back her fearlessness, and then she's out to find a wildness of space she can fearlessly claim as her own.

. . .

MY PARENTS' NAMES are Ruth and Claud, and when Amparo pronounced my father's name she opened the vowels and, unwittingly, gave it a Southern accent, which was charming. Ruth was different. It took her a while to get the "th" sound right, and Mother's name came out "root." I was tempted not to correct her, and didn't for a while.

I taught her to say, Hi, Claud. Hi, Root. I am Amparo. Then we went to the telephone central in downtown Valencia and placed a call to inform them that we were engaged. We were given a booth where we were told to sit and wait, although it would take at least fifteen minutes before the call could be put through. I ran outside to use the bathroom in a bar next door. No more than five minutes later, when I got back, Amparo was fighting to keep her composure. The call had gone through almost at once, and for some time now she had been repeating, Hi, Claud. Hi,

Root. I am Amparo. She has a high voice that sounds flute-high on the phone, and the less composed she got the higher it went until it was the voice of a flustered child.

When I got on the phone and told them the news of our engagement, the first thing Mother said was for incredulous effect: Was *that* her?

Amparo became Empero in her accent. My father, of course, was charmed.

Claud, to my ear, has a gladsome ring to it, a smiling, lighter-than-air sound. Both it and my mother's name are monosyllabic, but while my father seems to rise in my memory (he has been dead now sixteen years), Ruth takes root. Claud and Ruth—in my father's name I hear a not very serious pull to get away and from my mother I hear a tethered tug toward home. Expansion and contraction.

My father was a traveling salesman for most of the years I was growing up, with two and a half states for his territory. On Monday mornings he set out, casting in my child's imagination a large loop over the Midwest (the states were Indiana, Illinois and part of Iowa; later he would take the territory of Kentucky and Tennessee). On Friday evenings he was home. During the weekdays my rooted mother took charge, providing for my needs and depriving me, it seemed, of all childish superfluities. Nothing very serious. Baseball-card bubblegum was bad for my teeth; BBs were bad for the birds I wanted to shoot them into. Dad came home and out of a suitcase smelling of shaving cream and Vicks salve he presented me with small gifts. What wouldn't fit in there he told me to search for in the back seat of the car, which had the toasted and also lighter-than-air aroma of his Lucky Strikes. I found my BB gun that way. On the weekend Dad took charge. Mother devoted her time to her friends or my baby sister, and Dad and I indulged ourselves. We went sledding. He taught me to ride a bike. Together we built my first soapbox racer. Sooner than it should have, though, it quit being fun. On Monday, while Dad was casting one of his salesman's loops in his car,

Mother put herself back in charge. Dad was a good salesman. People bought from him because they liked him as a man, and what they liked about the man was the boy. He kept his boy's sandy hair, dimpled chin and squared-away features right up till the end, when, in a very short span, it all rotted off him. But my weekends with him quit being fun when, even as an eleven- and twelve-year-old, it became clear to me that Saturday meant Monday with a crushing finality.

Real time began on Monday. Why pretend otherwise? Claud was cloudiness and Ruth was rootedness and for a child everything was in a name.

Hi, Cloud. Hi, Root. I am Amparo.

I differed with them on Vietnam, and they probably thought I would head for Canada, where I could heckle them from across the border. Bumming through Europe and staying one step ahead of my responsibilities as a man probably struck them as a likely alternative. But Spain, Spain of the Inquisition, the most Catholic country on the map? My mother had been the daughter of a preacher. Her father had traveled Georgia and Florida organizing First Christian churches and preaching inaugural sermons. He had married a woman half his age whom he'd picked out of one of his congregations. She was fun-loving and a bit of a flirt and gave him four daughters, the oldest of whom, my mother, took it on herself to mother her younger sisters since she considered her own mother too carefree to be bothered.

I don't want to give the wrong impression about my mother. She could have fun. She liked to sing and dance and wasn't above taking a drink. But there was slack everywhere and somebody had to take it up. Have a look around, have a good time, but keep one eye on the morning ahead.

Spain? All those Catholics? How was that having a good time? What kind of morning ahead did I think I was letting myself in for?

Mother didn't actually say that during our phone conversation. She said she was happy that I was happy. She reminded me that she had Catholic friends. And she wasn't all that displeased with Franco. Hadn't President Eisenhower come over to shake his hand and establish relations? *Libertad, si. Libertinaje, no* was one of the government's slogans, and Mother would have gone along with that. And she was looking forward to meeting Amparo, she of the high voice and the chirping lilt. She said she was happy for me. But her tone said, Spain? How backward and foreign could I get? What was I thinking of? Was I about to convert? Should she come over there and straighten things out? And Amparo— Empero. Why couldn't I teach my Spanish girlfriend how to pronounce her name? Ruth. The word meant "mercy, compassion," in case I'd forgotten. I didn't tell her Amparo meant "sheltering care." There was enough competition between them already.

My father didn't say much. His distrust of the foreign was different from Mother's. Mother distrusted the foreign because she didn't like to be confronted with something she had no idea about (that wall of foreign sound would have been anathema to her, and to keep her wits she would have gone after it word by word), whereas my father distrusted the foreign because, as he cast his salesman's loops into the world, he knew that that was where he was heading. He had his territory, but one day he would cast his loop beyond it, and then where would he be? That was what I heard in his voice. Where are you, son? Is it a weekend or weekday? What is the world like out there?

I had a sister, too. She was seven years younger than I, and except for finding her an occasional pest, I really didn't know who she was. By the time she'd reached her teens I was in full rebellion and staying away from my hometown as much as I could. She was kind-natured and I knew she liked animals. She was always hugging a dog. And her kind nature carried over to her friends, who were as loyal to her as dogs were to their masters. Before I left the country I learned of three college boyfriends who had proposed to her, been turned down, yet actually found consolation in the fact that they could count her as their dearest friend after they'd married someone else. It took her three colleges and five years to get through school. I think she managed to graduate without ever declaring a major. Her major was making and maintaining friendships that eventually spread over the map.

We were different although we looked like brother and sister—both fair and blond and blue-eyed and a bit blurred in the modeling of the features. We were both tall with our mother's long legs. And in our long-leggedness neither of us was particularly graceful. We could walk down the street together side by side and no one would have any doubt. But I don't remember walking down any street at her side. That was my fault. She stood by her family with as unquestioning a loyalty as she stood by her friends, but to stand by me she'd have to run me down. Vietnam wasn't just in Southeast Asia, it was in my parents' hometown, especially dense around my parents' front door, and like a lot of others I moved from place to place where Vietnam wasn't. If the transience in the '30s had been caused by the Depression, the transience in the '60s and early '70s was strictly ideological, although "ideology" was a bad word, a life-leaching Establishment word. We moved because we could find few places unpermeated by the values we opposed. My sister didn't do this. She stayed put and let the country's transients come to her.

Her name was Sally. She was exactly Amparo's age. We telephoned her, too. Sah-lee. I loved the way Amparo said her name. Sally was no longer Tom Sawyer's Aunt Sally and, therefore, something like the nation's homespun conscience; rather, she was the salt of the earth—*sal*— taking a leap into the air—*leee*. I wanted to meet this sister Amparo embodied for me in the pronunciation of her name. I taught Amparo the phrase, Come see us soon, please, and then I translated Sally's answer: Only if you'll find me a handsome Spanish man.

We laughed, then Sally added, How about that brother of hers, An-

tonio? and we laughed some more and said we'd arrange it, all she had
to do was come.

Antonio, it seemed, had broken up with Concha. Or they hadn't
"broken up" but had moved their relationship to a higher plane. He was
vague about it, and philosophical, as if he were talking about a character
out of *The Little Prince*. Perhaps he had given her something to write poetry about, and she had given him something to paint. Except that he
didn't paint her. He painted his sister.

I had to remind myself Antonio might be going through something
as intense as I was. He spent his time traveling back and forth between
his apartment in Onteniente and Valencia, just as I spent mine traveling
back and forth between Valencia and Sot de Chera. He'd ride shotgun
for us when we went out at night, be our *carabina,* and then he'd disappear. But he'd continue to talk to me about his sister, her rejected
suitors, those still hanging around. He was warning me not to get com-
placent. His sister needed dedication and the sort of vigilance that only
the most devoted could show.

It was an ongoing pep talk and I was just touchy enough to resent it.
But I needed his coaching, too. There were a thousand ways in which I
needed someone on my side to point out the dos and don'ts of Spanish
society; you could narrow that down to Valencian society, and that down
to the way things worked in the township where the Ferris lived. It was
a wealthy township, thriving on the citrus orchards growing around it,
but there was no real aristocratic heritage in the town and the people preferred to let money talk. They gave money for wedding presents and
then at the wedding dinner announced the amount collected and passed
around a bag in order to match that. They were touchy about people
lording it over them, but really to loosen their purses they needed to
look up to somebody, too. It all depended on how far above them you
stood. It was a delicate matter, which his sister understood. But since in

Spain the man paid for the wedding, I might want to have that bag full the second time around.

I didn't know the groom paid for the wedding. I had to get a job. Antonio set up contacts for me in Madrid and Barcelona. I took a job for the following September, teaching English in an Opus Dei school outside Barcelona that was run by a friend of his. The Opus Dei, a semi-lay Catholic organization, was quickly amassing power in the state. I should not compare it to the Jesuits or other such orders, which had educated almost all Spanish youth. Amparo had spent four years in a *colegio* run by the Teresian nuns. Supposedly the Opus Dei was more enlightened, more liberal than other Catholic orders, and that friend, the director, was a good man.

Though Antonio had had an Opus Dei education himself, he didn't go into it much. Later I would learn that for a time he had taken it very seriously and when he came home for vacations would impose a rigor of religious observance in the house. For one period he walked with pebbles in his shoes and had even taken to mortifying the flesh with a wire brush. I learned later that Opus Dei members carried crucifixes in their pockets that they could finger when they came into contact with a particularly attractive member of the opposite sex. Not the pebbles, not the wire brush, but I could imagine Antonio fingering a crucifix in the depths of his pockets when a beautiful woman approached. This was not the man I imagined at my sister's side.

· · ·

WE ARE IN OLD CASTILE, in the province of Valladolid. It is late March, perhaps early April; Holy Week is less than a week away. The terrain here is a vast plateau, mesa land, in Spanish *la meseta,* mostly planted in wheat. The wheat is green. Poppies have yet to appear in it, although we have seen some along the road. They are a rich clotted red, and when they do grow up in the wheat, and the sun and the wind catch them in just the right sheen, the colors are stunning. The birds here are large black-and-white magpies that really do make a chattering squawk; on top of each bell tower you're likely to see storks nesting, also black-and-white.

But mainly the air is given over to pigeons, *palomas,* and they do their nesting in adobe brick structures, cylindrical in design, called *palomares.* Inside are three and sometimes four concentric walls, and each wall, from bottom to top, is carved out with niches. You add up these niches and you might reach five hundred. These *palomares* are everywhere. We've been told the number was once regulated, and before you were given permission to build one you had to own so many hectares of land, presumably so you could afford to feed the pigeons. They must have become status symbols. I think of those mussel rafts in Galicia, the *viveros.* Could a family of four live off the proceeds of one *palomar?* Amparo remarks that she remembers eating pigeon frequently as a child but that you no longer see them on menus. There's no market left for pigeon eggs or squabs. The *palomares,* a crumbling adobe-red against the land's green, have been abandoned to the pigeons, which nest in them with impunity.

We have been to a town called Tordesillos, located above the river Duero, and are on our way back to Medina de Rio Seca, and we have stopped beside the road. I have just walked around the concentric shells of a half-destroyed *palomar.* I have found no eggs or squabs, but a number of pigeons have been nesting there. Even in the late afternoon it is still warm and Amparo has remained in the car. The wind has died. It could be anywhere on this plateau, but it is here, on my way back to the car, that I stop and take a three-hundred-sixty-degree look at where we have arrived. I can count five small towns. In each town is a church and a cluster of earth-colored buildings. In three of them is what remains of a castle. The church and castle remains are so outsized and distinct against the horizon that they make the houses around them look like rubble that might have tumbled down from the walls. I see no human figures, not even a car entering or leaving the towns. For reasons unknown to me, the earth has erupted in these five spots and created towns, and for someone who has set out to go *pueblo*-hopping I am suddenly faced with a dizzying prospect. *Pueblos* are everywhere. The *palomares* are mostly grouped around them.

When I get back into the car Amparo asks what's wrong. I have taken a deep settling breath. She must assume I've had some sort of experience in the *palomar*. Then she must see something in my eyes, some troubling starry residue, what's left of the vision I've just had looking over the plain. She chuckles, she pats my leg. She's a little sleepy and her voice is not perfectly clear. She suddenly reminds me of the times when our children came to our bed, seeking refuge from their bad dreams. What she told them she now tells me: *Está bien. Está bien.*

Does she go back to sleep? She may. Her eyes are closed. She sleeps quickly and in unlikely places, and ever since those days when I courted her I've never been entirely free of the fear that one day I won't be able to wake her. In truth it's been years since she's fainted. And she doesn't cry much anymore. I don't know the last time I saw those tears slip down her face while she slept, or pool in the corners of her eyes when she's lying flat on her back. She knows herself better now. She gets tired, but who doesn't, and when those debilitating spells come on her she excuses herself and goes off to lie down. If the spells last two or three days, she takes a break and takes them in stride. I may get impatient then, but if I worry it's more out of habit than actual concern. You start off like that, of course, and worrying can become a way of life. My wife wants something—she's convinced me of that—but there's no reason in the world it has to be found here in Castile, among the ruins of castles for small-town noblemen and the ruined mansions for their pigeons.

She sleeps and I drive on.

Then out to the right, past her nodding head, I see a town set perhaps a kilometer back from the road. Rather, I see a large castle, perfectly intact, down to the crenellations and bartizans on its walls, and I see the tower and bulk of a church set at the town's opposite end. Between these two massive silhouettes is the scribble-line of houses and what's left of the town. The castle and the church face each other in such a way that whatever lies between them must live in a state of permanent prostration. I turn in. The dirt road wakes her. The evening has cooled, the light is mild and she can't really believe it either. What was ever there to be towered over, to be *so* towered over?

We don't see anybody. Some of the houses have lace curtains in the windows, so we know they aren't empty. But the doors are shut. It's the hour for the promenade and nobody's out. The houses are mostly made of adobe brick, like the *palomares,* and the walls have been plastered over with mud stuck with straw, which creates the textured effect you see in some fashionable wallpaper. There are a few houses whose ground floors are made of blocks of sandstone, *sillares,* and whose second stories are made of brick. A few of these have escutcheons above the doors, but the stone has eroded and it's no longer possible to read the coats of arms. There is no one at the church, whose bell tower and door are Romanesque and whose buttresses look deeply sunken into the ground. There are two kinds of dogs on the streets: the humped, skeletally thin hounds whose breed might have originally been Ibizan and the small, no-breed dogs you see everywhere in Spain, *chuchos,* as hairy as a woman's muff. They back away from us, with a guilty start, and do not bark.

I have been in ghost towns before in the American West. But this is not a ghost town. People live here under the shadows of this castle and church. They just won't come out.

Walking these streets is a lonely act. We get back in the car and drive to the castle. There is no castle door facing the town; rather, there's a rock wall that someone has plastered smooth, and it is there that two boys are kicking a soccer ball while an old man sits off to the side on a stone bench watching them. There are a couple more benches. It's a little park, built on the lee side of the castle, protected from the north wind.

One of the boys is acting as goalkeeper, so the ball only pounds against the wall when the other boy manages to get one by him. Where did these boys come from? From the way the old man is watching them, it would be safe to assume they are the last boys left in town. Here, beside the castle walls and behind the benches, some flower beds have been laid out and some wiry flowers are growing in them. But they are last year's flowers. We nod to the old man and head off around the walls. Guard towers are located at each corner, and the great square tower of the keep is at the far end; the walls are remarkably well preserved, and standing at their base I find it difficult to imagine how anyone, lacking a helicopter, could have ever gotten over them.

Walking around the castle, we have the impression it is the size of the town itself. Nothing we see on this plateau would even begin to hint that something of this magnitude should be here. Simply as a material object, there is no way to account for it. Where did these huge blocks of sandstone come from? Who quarried them? Where was there an enemy so threatening that something this large had to be raised to stand in its path?

History will give you some of the answers. We can't see the Moorish armies, or the rebellious Castilian armies and the ferocity with which Isabel, the queen of Castile, put them down. We see enormous blocks of stone erected on a plain. We turn a corner, and the evening sun comes across the plain to warm our faces and highlight the red in the stone. The door's back here, a gate of iron bars. We can see inside to the courtyard, which is smaller than I thought it would be, and which allows us to understand just how thick these walls are. The courtyard is overgrown and strewn with rock rubble. The keep angles out to block our vision, but it has been centuries since horses galloped through this gate to pound down the earth inside. Dogs must have gotten in, though, since there's a dug-out, dog-sized space under the bars. And there are crows.

Amparo says she's seen enough.

We circle back around and the old man takes his eyes off the boys to study us. I have noticed that people here in the plain of Castile will stare at you openly but are not at all unfriendly when addressed. Groups of men will turn and stare as sullenly as cattle, then compete with each other in giving you directions.

This old man tells me the castle is owned by a family that lives in Valladolid. They almost never appear. Twice they've allowed movie companies to shoot here—the tower is very well preserved. But they keep it closed.

We ask which movies, but the old man can't remember the titles. I can imagine some enterprising director driving along, as I did, and seeing the castle silhouetted against the sky. I can imagine a traveler from five hundred years back standing where I stand now calling up to someone on the wall.

Cut and print.

It's a shame, I say, that they keep it closed, that they don't open it, at least, to the town.

The old man chuckles and mentions something about the shameless ways of *señoritos*. Then he says the boys have dug out a hole beneath the gate, and even though the owners know what it's used for they don't fill it in. If you want to get in the castle you have to crawl in like a dog, but you get in. Except for the *gordos* of the town; they wouldn't fit. But I would. It's something I should see. Why don't I crawl under the gate?

He can see me doing it. He's grinning and the little tarnished shards of his eyes are suddenly bright. Why don't I crawl in and have a look around?

I give him his grin back. Some other time, I say.

He snorts and turns back to the boys. Each time the one boy kicks the ball past the other he cries, *Gol!* Then the ball pounds against the castle wall.

When you're traveling as much as we are you don't get a shirt and a pair of pants dirty just for the fun of it. Amparo catches me checking to make sure just what shirt and pants I am wearing and says, Go on. I'll wash them out for you—if you don't get stuck.

A generous offer—and a taunt. There's that look she gives our children when their imaginations have run off with them. But as a child she led her own band of followers, and surely she set them some adventurous tasks. Dulcinea was a taskmistress to her Don, or at least that was the role she was called on to play.

Fifty-eight years old and, at her urging, I go under on my back. I've never had much of a gut, but lately, in spite of my exercising and sensible diet, one has begun to grow. I scoop out the loose rock and get my head and shoulders through. My belt buckle hangs up on the bottom bar. I'm looking up through the bars at my wife and beyond her at the craggy underside of the arch. I'm not really stuck—I could always wriggle back out. But I lie there for a moment and shake my head. Twenty-nine years ago I met you and it's come to this. I'm caught sneaking into a castle. What do I do?

During this trip Amparo has been coming out with some apt expressions. On good days she calls herself my little trooper. Other days she says she feels like a wet noodle. Now she tells me to suck it up.

So I do. I suck it up, inch under the bar and stand there on the other side of the gate looking at her. She's out there with late-afternoon cloud shadows passing over the lovely green wheat, and I'm behind bars with a strange sort of emptiness gathering at my back. The boys cry, *Gol!* Their ball thuds impotently against the far wall, and it's as if the sound's coming from another life, a different world.

As I've said, I once did some acting and know what an abandoned movie set looks like. There's no trace of those two movie companies here. Nothing has been touched up. The stone stairs up to the tower door have been worn by seven or eight hundred years of adverse weather, and there's really not a flat place left to get your footing. An actor or his double would have to watch his step. Under my hand the stone of the balustrade is porous and rough. Over the door, which has a plain heavy lintel, an escutcheon has been carved, perhaps at a later date than the construction of the castle itself. The only quarter I can be sure about shows two bears rearing up on their hind legs to eat berries out of an arbutus tree, but that is because I've seen it elsewhere in Castile. There was a time when Spain's plateau was forested and bears roamed it, that vast treeless plain out there.

I step through the door.

I am in a high-ceilinged hall with its beams exposed and an enormous fireplace at the far end. A little light enters on a slant through windows that are narrowed to a slit so that arrows can be shot out but not in. There are few of those. Crumbing niches are carved in the walls, and there are stone protrusions where torches might have been fixed. The air is stale with stone dust and bird droppings and the scent of dried urine. I stand in the fireplace and breathe from the shaft of fresher air entering from above. I no longer hear the boys or my wife. I hear my breath and a voice in my ear that is the wind being piped down from above.

A door is off to the side, with a staircase leading up that is so low and narrow I can't imagine the owner of this castle, or his lady, ever using it. But it's the only way up.

The hall above is identical to the one below, only smaller, with a more intimate feel. It is just as guardedly lit. A fire in this fireplace would roar less. The leftover space has been given to two small rooms, perhaps a kitchen and a bedroom. One is a turret room with a stone bench carved to fit its curving wall. The slit in the window is wider here. You could sit on the bench and study the lay of the land below. If you were a distraught damsel you could pine.

I continue up the dark staircase, hunched and hesitant, like a beggar. On the third floor there's another hall, another fireplace, nowhere near as grand. Coming out of the fireplace is a voice I don't have to strain to hear. It's meant for me. It speaks for me. The light is no longer meager. It's just as dim but within close proximity to a greater light.

I squeeze up along a final flight of stairs. Sunlight and clean air flood over me and, for an instant, I know it's all mine.

I'm on top of the tower, standing to the waist in the battlement's notch. There is old Castile, green and cloud-shadowed, spotted with its small towns and *palomares*. The air below me is swarming with pigeons. So-called noblemen live in those towns and have taken to carving out escutcheons over their doors, but from this angle all houses, even the most *señorial,* are hovels. The plazas the people take their pleasure in are like yards scratched over by chickens and littered with their garbage. There is only one *señor* in his *castillo,* and that *señor* is you.

I see my wife, left stranded outside the gate. I wave. She may wave back—it's hard to be sure. She's much smaller than she was, and like everyone else down there, she's built awfully low to the ground. She may not be my wife at all. There's a good chance I have just waved to one of the subject masses. After all the crazy stuff I went through to reach this point, and with, perhaps, craziness still to come, I now have a chance in my loftiness to put myself out of everybody's reach. This whole Spanish adventure, or misadventure, could be cast in a new light.

Husbands are known to fantasize along these lines.

I take one long breath. I take a lordly look around.

There's a world of squat tubby Sancho Panzas spread out below you, and then there's you.

I remember that this was Antonio's fantasy, to find a castle all his own, and I remember that it was on the strength of that fantasy that I'm standing here now.

Except Antonio wanted to fill the castle with all his art-loving friends. I won't even let his sister, who is also my wife, inside.

Cut and print.

. . .

MY WIFE HAS A THING she does with her tongue. When she's thinking, or distracted, or caught by surprise, she'll flick it back and forth, from one corner of her mouth to the other. I may be thinking of something, too—the two of us may be joined in thought—but I'll see that glistening tip of her tongue go back and forth, and I, for one, will lose my train of thought. She doesn't keep flicking it—no more than three or four times. But that's enough. Her eyes can seem disconnected then, loose in their sockets, as if they were about to roll.

I've been watching my wife do this since I've first known her. I realize that if you discounted her upbringing, her education, all that she's had bred into her by a family and culture so schooled in decorum that it can seem positively baroque, and concentrated instead on that flicking tongue and the eyes about to roll, you might think her mad.

Then the tongue stops flicking and her eyes settle. She takes on the world she was born into and schooled so superbly in. She'll point out to me things I missed, in some cases things I would not have seen in a thousand years. She'll read a face for me and trace a lineage generations back. She'll convince me that the faces you see in Spain can be read in that way. She'll read a human frailty and with quiet compassion instruct me just how to shore it up. When it's a question of the needs of her friends and family, she'll never forget. Spain in its complex calendar of observances teaches you to be like that, and the nuns taught her virtue before they taught her anything else, and her family came along and foisted on her their vision of what a culture could accomplish in one beautiful being. Before they were all done they'd created something truly remarkable and far too good for me. They had created a saint who didn't belong in this world, just as what they had started with, the child with the flicking tongue and eyes about to roll, didn't belong in it, either.

And what was I doing here, caught between these two extremes my wife—my wife-pledged-to-be—was being driven to?

I was talking to her, taking on each of her doubts as they appeared, taxing my Spanish to its limit and coaxing her toward a hypothetical third self but one so possessed of the best of the other two that it would outshine them all—my vision and version of who she should be. I did this in our various haunts around the city, in the citrus orchards and artichoke fields outside the township where her father worked, walking along the creek and climbing into the mountains that overlooked Sot de Chera when she was allowed to visit me there, talking, laboriously placing one block of my Spanish on another, seeking to convince her that when she detected disapproval among her friends, or when her family made their impossible demands on her, or when the world staged yet another of its unspeakable acts, what it meant was that she had to grow as a person and instead of being devastated claim, along with all the other species on the planet, her natural right to survival. And not just to survive, but to flourish.

I had once thought it was the child in the beautiful young woman that I had fallen in love with. Now I knew it was a luminous future self. I was betting everything I had (indeed, the money I'd saved up to see Europe was running low) that my version of the person she could be would outdistance the other two—or three, since clearly Antonio's version could not be equated with his parents'. The day would come, I swore to her, when we would live in a world of our own making, where the warmongers and con artists and bleating huddled sheep that made up this one could not get near us.

I talked myself into such a fervent belief that when my preaching didn't take and she seemed shattered by the day's events, or on the verge of making a tongue-flicking escape into some kind of terminal childish ineptitude, I could despair. In answer to one of my sister's letters I tried to explain it all to her. I thought that with her knack for making and maintaining friends, she could understand. I had met no one with such a capacity to be extraordinary as Amparo, to be the most beautiful being on the face of the earth. My sister, who had always deferred to her older brother, wrote back and said Amparo sounded like the kind of person she would like to know just because she *wasn't* some kind of superwoman. Superwomen, she added, didn't have much fun. I took my sister's point, but Sally didn't know how wracked with doubts and other people's needs Amparo could be when she tried to live a life of the everyday.

So I talked to her. I talked until I couldn't talk anymore, then I took her and held her, and with sudden surges of strength (her *arrebatos*) she held me back. She squeezed and she could take my breath. I loved the feel of the flesh on her back, and the submerged feel of the bones rising beneath it. Her shoulders and arms were round and the crooks of her elbows were always smooth. Her neck was smooth. Where were her tendons? Also submerged. She lived within this envelope of flesh (the cheeks were round and firm, both those of her face and those of her backside), where the muscles and tendons and bones could perform prodigious feats, and within that, where it was all strung together with the nerves, she fell apart.

A child. I couldn't press it. I wouldn't. But with her flesh surging and warm to the touch, I didn't want to go back to talking again, either. I didn't know what to do, but if we were going to marry in the Basilica later that year I had her Church to deal with. This was the Holy Roman Catholic Church about which my mother had such dark suspicions. Amparo and I went together to the archbishop's palace in Valencia to consult the official there in charge of mixed marriages. He was a portly handsome man with an epicurean look who reminded me of an uncle I had, who had been dashingly handsome until he'd made his first million and then had eaten and drunk his way to obesity. Menendez, Father Menendez, was this official's name, but since we saw him only behind his desk it was hard to think of him as a "Father." His professional title was *fiscal*, which in the secular world was also the title district attorneys bore, or sometimes judges. I got the impression that *fiscal* was a catchall term that you might apply to anyone whose profession was the law. That was my father-in-law's profession, just as Menendez's was ecclesiastical law. He explained to us what I would have to swear to before he could sanction the marriage, namely, that I would in no way, directly or indirectly, with overt action or subtle psychological pressure, stand in the way of my wife practicing her religion, and that I would agree from the start that any children born from our union would be christened, confirmed and raised Catholic. I nodded my head and said, *Claro, claro que sí*, no problem.

I was not about to enter into a debate on what I liked and didn't like about the Catholic Church. I was not sure myself. I liked Enrique and the closeness he felt to his parishioners in Sot de Chera; I liked the way he administered the sacraments. When he consecrated the host, there was no liturgical self-importance in his manner or voice. This was a miracle, it was a blessing and it was his job. More than once I sat up close and watched him when he placed the host on a parishioner's tongue, and it was as if he were taking a loving aim.

What I didn't like about the Church was the opulence. Once I got over being dazzled, I didn't like the way it threw its wealth around. Either it hinted at a deep insecurity—doctrinally, I think I'm sound, but just in case I'm not, get a load of this—or it played its believers for simpleminded fools who could be wowed by wealth and never had to be dealt with as discriminating adults. The Virgin under whose gaze we would be married, the *virgen de los desamparados,* was covered in those jewels she'd inherited from the wealthy widows of the city. The Church kept piling it on. There was a third interpretation, of course. And that was that there was no outfit or altarpiece or chalice or vestment too sumptuous when it came to portraying the riches of the divine. Our worldly attempts always fell short. Instead of being offended by such excessive shows of wealth, we should be heartened by their very inadequacy. The best was yet to come. In the meantime, learn to live at ease with the things of the world. Cover yourself in them if you get the chance. It's all an emblem. Don't be such a Kentucky kid with a hang-up about all that glitters.

Sure, okay, I said, Catholic kids from the cradle to the grave.

Father Menendez asked if there were any impediments. A formality, but was I single? No impediments that I knew of. I had been married briefly before, a youthful indiscretion, but I was as single as single could be.

Single in the eyes of my church and state?

I was tempted to argue the point. They weren't *my* church and *my* state. I'd been baptized as a Presbyterian and divorced in the state of Ohio and had left all that behind. But it's not a point you argue with a Spaniard, whose ties to Church and State are indissoluble. Much less with an ecclesiastical *fiscal.*

I said that I was.

Menendez smiled. I believe it was his first smile of the day. He'd worn an expression of beatific (and well-fed) pleasantness until then. He was glad that impediment was out of the way. It would help him if I could get a letter from my church and another from my state stating that I was single and free to marry.

I said that I was sure I could.

Menendez nodded. He never stood—he was too comfortably ensconced behind his desk. We never shook hands. But he made a good-bye wave with his right hand that I thought had vaguely something to do with a benediction, and then we stepped out of his office and onto the street, where the life of Spain swarmed up to meet us.

Franco's Spain.

Franco would take care of his business and I'd take care of mine.

I wrote the office of civil records in the Cincinnati courthouse and asked what it would take to get a copy of the divorce papers sent to Spain. I wrote to my parents—I addressed it to both of them, but I was under no illusions about whom I was really writing—asking if they could get the current pastor of the Presbyterian church there to draw up a document stating that in his eyes I was single and free to marry. A formality—they were not to think I was already caught in the coils of the Catholic Church. We had time. It was only June and we were not planning to marry until after Christmas. I wrote to my sister, whom I had last seen the preceding summer, when we had watched the Apollo landing on the moon together. I again extended an invitation for her to come visit.

Then I pep-talked Amparo and kissed her good-bye. She and her family would be coming to Sot de Chera at the end of the month, and the next time I saw her would be there.

On the twenty-fifth of the month I turned thirty. Don José had his wife and daughter and two other women from the town come in and clean the house from top to bottom in anticipation of the Ferris' arrival. I swam in the creek that curved around the town, then lay out on the warm rock. The vegetation in the creekbed was lush—oleanders and plume-topped bamboo grew out of the rock, fig trees along the low walls. Four teenaged girls from the town were swimming in the creek with me. I had noticed them on the streets the last few months, and although they were among those who laughed when the diminutive Enrique and I made our rounds, I thought them friendly and fresh and I enjoyed their smiles. From the start we'd exchanged greetings and lately had begun to chat about the weather and events in the town. This was the first time I had seen them in bathing suits. It was my thirtieth birthday, traditionally a day to take stock, but not for me. I watched the girls climbing out of the creek. There wasn't a skinny one in the bunch; if anything they were plump, but not with that frothy fat that teenaged girls back home put on sprawled on a couch, munching something out of a bag. This was solid flesh, lightly toasted and glistening with creek water. These girls would lead uncomplicated lives. Compared to Amparo's, their lives would be blessedly simple. It occurred to me that I could fall in love with one of them—even at my advanced age. But a lot occurred to me in those days, and I felt ageless lying out on that warm rock. It occurred to me that my country was still at war and that I couldn't hide out for the rest of my life in a remote valley such as this. And it occurred to me that when my country began to behave in a way that I could stand, I might go back. Meanwhile, I had these girls to entertain me, whom, I was quite aware, I was seeing through a prism of Amparo's flesh. They were beautiful. Tomorrow they wouldn't be, but today on my birthday they were.

. . .

WE HAVE BEEN IN SEVILLE during *semana santa,* Holy Week, on three occasions and have always talked about being in Valladolid when they carry the statues of the grieving Virgin and the suffering Christ through the streets to see if what they say is true. They say that compared to *semana santa* in the north, Seville's is orgiastic; they say that if we are judging by the south, we will find *semana santa* in Valladolid forbiddingly austere. In Seville the Virgins are carried by as many as twenty men on large, ornate structures called *pasos.* The canopies that shelter the Virgins are of gold and silver thread and are lit by tiers of candelabra. The gowns and jewels the Virgins are dressed in flicker in the candlelight, which, when viewed from afar, can make them seem more like sumptuous pagan deities than a mother who has just seen her only son crucified. When they pass you can't be sure whether it is grief or rapture you see in their faces. All are beautiful. They are serenaded by men and women stationed overhead on balconies, *saetas,* these songs are called, and you can't tell whether the singers' voices are grieving or enraptured either. With great conviction, but sounding a lot like cheerleaders, too, worshippers standing rows deep along the street chant, *Guapa, guapa, guapa!* when the Virgins pass, and *guapa* is the word the Spanish use for good-looking, sexy and all the rest. It takes forever—those *pasos* are very heavy and have to be carried from the home church to the cathedral and back. Meanwhile, bars and *cafeterías* along the route serve enormous quantities of cool sherry and *tapas.*

In Valladolid, the processions are said to be solemn, the members of the individual *cofradías*—something of a cross between neighborhood associations and spiritual guilds—marching behind the Virgin masked and the whole thing stone-quiet. If you eat or drink, it is with an almost consecrated air. The statues of Christ and his persecutors are reputed to be of great artistic value, worth dwelling on and taking to heart. Castilians—Castilians from the North, the old Castilians—are not like Andalucians. Andalucians live to get out on the streets; Castilians get out there, too, but at the crucial moment they take it all home.

Amparo has always wanted to go.

We talk about it. We're in the town of Medina de Rio Seco, twenty-five kilometers away. We have friends in Valladolid, Tomás and Marta, who would go with us. He's a town secretary, something like Amparo's father, except that he travels from town to town, and she is a pediatrician. But we discover from what we hear on the street that a number of people in Valladolid are coming to Medina de Rio Seco to witness the processions here. Tomás and Marta, when we talk to them on the phone, hint that they would like to come to Medina, too. The implication is that *semana santa* in the city, as impressive as it may be, has become unrecognizable. To get the real thing you have to go back to the towns.

I sometimes think that is the one abiding truth in Spain. It is the very truth that we have taken to heart as we travel the country. Do not cut your ties! Do not! Practice your professions, make your fortunes, live your sophisticated urban lives—but come back! And if you don't have a *pueblo* to come back to, pick one off the map and make it yours.

Buy in. To call it "gentrification" is badly to misunderstand the Spanish soul. Like the bullfight, *pueblo*-hopping can be an ontological event. Where is Being most being, most real, ore-rich with the potential for its own transcendence? Travel the country until you find it. Home in there.

It is *viernes santo,* Good Friday, when Tomás and Marta drive over. Two professional people, they have postponed having children until their careers are well under way, and now they have just had two in a rush. Marta is still nursing the most recent, and there is a flushed and milky softness about her skin. She is very happy. Tomás takes an opinionated leap into almost every subject, but has learned the trick of retreating behind his wife's almost universal appeal before he becomes truly objectionable. She scolds him and he's back on track. The truth is, Tomás has some interesting things to say; Marta might have heard them all before, but we haven't. They aren't old friends and we don't see them that often.

I congratulate them on the birth of the baby. I have just read an article in the country's best newspaper, *El País,* claiming that the birthrate in Catholic Spain is the lowest of any nation in the industrialized world. That same article went on to wonder what would happen to the metaphorical concept of brotherhood (as in "the brotherhood of nations") if brotherhood as a physical fact failed to survive. A generation ago my father-in-law had wanted to surround a long dining-room table with children so that his wife could cook for them all. But Franco died and Spanish women saw their chance. They were now doctors and judges and mayors of some of the larger cities. Many were not mothers.

I congratulate Tomás and Marta for bucking the trend.

Do I know what worries Tomás the most? He doesn't see how he can be a good father and keep from passing his whole system of beliefs, and all the defenses he's developed over the years, and all the complex compensations for things he hasn't gotten—in short, the maze of a man he admits to being—down to his children. The newborn is a daughter. If he keeps his distance and doesn't feed her and change her diapers as often as he should, it is because he can look into those clear trusting eyes and feel the whole of him passing into her. Why should he be inflicted on her? Many days he wouldn't inflict himself on himself. So he backs off.

Tomás's hair is receding. He has a high domed forehead and eyes that go hard and round behind his glasses. He walks with a sort of disarming shuffle, and when he is coming toward you, you'd think him harmless, a bit goofy. You smile. You giggle. You're his baby daughter and he's your daddy, the clown. Then those eyes bore into you and you're in trauma land before you know it.

I tell him I sympathize with him. That is one of the risks of waiting so late to have children. It's only when you get to Tomás's age that you begin to think such things. Younger, you plunge in and do the damage and wonder later how your kids got so screwed up.

Amparo takes offense. Our children are not screwed up. Our son has a wonderful talent and a clear head, and our daughter has managed to combine the discipline she learned as a dancer with a very sociable nature, and both have enviable futures ahead.

True, it's all true. But Amparo doesn't know our children as I do. I know the parts of me that went into them, and I know that none of those parts was entirely at peace with itself, resolved.

Tomás is serious, grinning and half hidden behind his wife, who, as a mother and pediatrician, knows that close affectionate contact more than offsets the hang-ups you may pass down to your children. Plus the fact, there are those dirty diapers to change and pablums to coax down unwilling throats.

She tsks her husband. I have the impression that this is a topic they've been discussing on the way over to Medina de Rio Seco, and Tomás, true to his brooding theatrical nature, doesn't know when to let it alone.

We're about ready to set out into the town to watch those *cofradías* parade their crucified Christs and his virgin mother through the streets, but this conversation about fathers and children comes back to me later, when a number of statues of Christ and the Virgin have already passed. Medina de Rio Seco is known for its main street, its *calle mayor*, which is colonnaded with stout columns of wood that have aged and weathered and now have a glassy petrified look. I am standing beside one of those columns, my hand on wood that was there, in that precise spot, serving that same function, eight hundred years before. Before us a *cofradía* is stopped so that the statue bearers can take a rest. The *cofradías* are made up of men and women of all ages, including children, and on *viernes santo*, all are dressed in black. The men wear penitents' robes with the hoods down and the women wear satin dresses with their hair caught up in buns and long mantillas hanging from combs. The women are dressed like widows. Some of the girls are very little, with round eyes and chubby cheeks, and their hair is pulled back and tightened in buns. They, too, are dressed in black—identical to their mothers and grandmothers and older sisters. They are very well behaved, and the two or three mothers there to herd them along really aren't needed. They are the littlest of the widows and know their parts. From their wrists rosaries dangle, and I wait to see if one will begin to twirl it and treat it as a toy.

But none does.

Something in me objects to this dressing up of small children in black. Then a moment occurs.

That *cofradía* has stopped. The little girls are directly in front of me, and just behind them comes a line of those hooded men. There's a pause in the music, and those heavy platforms the Virgins and Christs are borne on have been lowered off shoulders and allowed to rest on staffs that serve as props. Before me stand these tiny widows and hooded and penitent men. Then one of the little girls crosses the street and approaches one of the men. Amparo and Marta are talking about the beauty of the children and how faithfully gotten up as grieving adults they are. Tomás is flexing up and down on the balls of his feet, as if the moment is preliminary to something else and he's impatiently waiting it out. And, really, it's no moment at all, just one of many pauses in the procession. But that little girl crosses to the other side of the street, goes up to one of the hooded men, and he bends down to her. They talk. I can't see his face, of course, but hers is attentive. Then she smiles up into that black mask. Because of my angle and the fact that his robe and hood hang to reduce my vision further, I can't be sure, but he may reach out and touch the side of her face. She turns and, her rosary dangling, her mantilla floating almost to her knees, returns to her place. That is all. Soon the bearers will pick up their loads again and the musicians will set them a pace. This *cofradía* will pass and another will come along behind it.

But the child is so convincing as a small grieving adult and the man so hooded in his own sinful self that the fact that they could step out of their roles in that way almost seems shocking. It sets me up straight. I realize that this is the sort of coexistence I've been looking for all my life, a life balanced between the part you play in a mystery that transcends you and the part you play here on earth, where no disguise is so daunting that it can keep your hand away from the side of your daughter's face.

That night I tell my wife about the man and his daughter, but I see her tongue flick between the corners of her mouth and I know her mind is somewhere else. The next morning as we stroll through the streets she tells me she's come to a realization. Perhaps she'd been expecting too

much from *semana santa* in the north. It wasn't austere, it wasn't rever-
ent, it wasn't for her even a particularly spiritual experience. She's prepared to say that Seville, with its sensuous overload, is truer to the spirit
of what it means to grieve a death and rejoice in a resurrection. She's re-
membering moments in her town of Bocairente when she was a child.
The crucified Christ passed, the grieving Virgin, and no one made a
sound, not even the children. Some men and women wept openly. She
knows she's impressionable, too sensitive, unfit, as I've reminded her, to
suffer the assaults on our moral nature that the televised world inflicts,
but she still doesn't see how when a statue of a man agonizing on a cross
passes, people can go on scratching themselves or gossiping with their
friends or eating *tapas* or drinking wine. She doesn't mean a statue of
Christ; she means a statue of a man in mortal pain.

I am aware that this realization of my wife's constitutes a key moment in her search for some living connection to her past. And I'm more
than aware that I'm the one who dragged her out on this quest. But, as
petty as it may sound, it's my moment against hers, and I tell her that at
bottom I disagree. If these rituals have evolved from religious to cultural
and even social occasions, that is not necessarily a bad thing. Maybe a
less pure thing, but surely it keeps more people in touch, if only glanc-
ingly. And it keeps the pope and the whole stifling bureaucracy of the
Catholic Church a little at bay. If an atheist or agnostic wanted to parade
with the devout, he should be allowed to. At any given moment a small
grieving facsimile of a big grieving adult should be allowed to step out
of line and go up to her father, who should be allowed to touch her face.

My wife gives me a long, puzzled look. This is not the sort of assess-
ment she's used to coming out of my mouth. It's shot through with com-
promise. It seems I've settled for some feel-good Hollywood solution to
an age-old dilemma. Jimmy Stewart is up in the saddle, Don Quixote
down on the ground.

Go to whose house? Pepita's? I hear my black-robed father saying. Maybe after the siesta. Oh, there goes that statue of Christ again, bleeding on his cross. Why don't you run back in line and we'll catch up.

The next Monday Tomás drives by and takes us to three towns. He has to put in an hour in each, taking care of legal matters for the week. The first two are towns on the verge of extinction, but somebody has to be there to represent the law, other than the occasional pair of *guardia civil*. The third is called Uruena, in the province of Valladolid, built on a bluff overlooking Tierra Campo, the breadbasket of Spain. Most of the town's streets are rectilinear, which leads Tomás to believe they were laid out by the Romans. Its houses are sandstone in the first story, brick with diagonal wooden beams in the second. For effect, I believe, some walls are spread with that subtly textured mud, which is reminiscent of Japanese rice paper. Most doors are framed in stone, either squared or arched with stone wedges. The town is walled. You can walk along the parapets and look out over the plain. The least suggestion of a hill will have another town on top of it, but none is as strategically located and *señorial* in its bearing as Uruena.

We could get in on the ground floor, Tomás claims. Strange to talk about a ground floor in a place that the Romans laid out, but if we acted quickly we could buy here cheaply. A new expressway passes close by, but so far only an English couple has discovered the town, and Tomás points out their house to us, stone and brick fitted with new, dark-varnished windows built up against the town wall. We thank him for the tip, but the fact is we haven't told Tomás we're looking to buy, not even that we're looking for a town. Perhaps it's something we give off.

· · ·

THAT SUMMER the town was Sot de Chera, for with the Ferris come to spend the months of July and August I did not have to travel back to Valencia on the weekends. I kept my room off the kitchen, two floors away from where Amparo slept. For a few days I tried to keep writing with my portable Olympia on the kitchen table, but soon gave that up. Amparo and I swam, took hikes up the creek and into the mountains. We hiked all the way up to the top of the cliff looking down on the town. Behind us was open sierra where herders grazed their sheep. There were sheep-herders' huts made of stone where they slept when they chose not to come down to the town. We stooped to enter one. There were some dishes, some rags, scraps of yellowed newspaper. After the civil war, die-hard guerrillas, who called themselves *maquis,* hid out in these hills for years and slept in these huts. It was impossible to tell who had occupied it last. There was a human reek that went deep, well beneath the occupations of either shepherd or guerrilla.

Antonio was there on occasion that summer, and when he took walks with us he spent a good part of his time sorting out the herbs and flowers he found and explaining to me the part they'd played in his and his sister's childhood. *Romero,* rosemary, the Spanish used to season any number of dishes and they used it to freshen their houses. We never came back from the sierra without a sprig of it stuck in our breast pockets. Its scent cleared your head and kept your thoughts pure. Did I know what else it was used for? It was once customary for the bridegroom to bathe in a solution of *romero* before presenting himself to his bride on the wedding night. Customs such as these should not be allowed to die out. There was folk wisdom in them, and there was almost always beauty. Antonio held a sprig of *romero* beneath my nose. I was to imagine my whole body enveloped in its scent, a world of rosemary kept alive on the skin.

Could I? I could. I could imagine an envelope of freshness so fresh it felt brash.

On the weekends Señor Ferri joined the family in Sot de Chera, and I met him at the bus. He wouldn't let me help him down, but I was allowed to carry his bag and walk him home. Since I had taken those snails to his office he had unofficially given up his opposition to me and at times, and very unofficially, treated me like a son. He showed me how to eat a snail, how to hook it in the foot and coax it out without squirting myself in the process; how to de-bone a *lenguado,* the Mediterranean sole; how to extract the ink of the squid, which his wife used in one of his favorite rices, *arroz negro.* He was a big-handed man but extremely dexterous with a knife, and I let him teach me the correct way to peel all sorts of fruit, beginning with a grape. When I finally managed to peel a peach in one paper-thin spiral he practically cheered.

He brought me a book, stories and poems by Gustavo Bequer, a real romantic, something like Spain's Edgar Allan Poe.

My future mother-in-law dressed meticulously each morning and Amparo spent a good hour working on her hair. She was an intriguing woman whom I might have taken a more positive interest in had she not been out to thwart me at every turn. She got herself up elegantly, then spent most of the day in the kitchen. She could laugh a lot, to the point that tears rolled from her eyes, but she was simultaneously aloof and judgmental and you never doubted that at any moment she had made a reckoning and knew just how things stood.

In her small, hemp-woven chair she set up an observation post in front of the house, and while the rest of the town was engaged in the *paseo,* she sat and greeted townspeople as they passed by. But her mind never wandered—I'd bet on that. The dreamer in the family was her husband, and he'd passed that fatal tendency on to his son and daughter. The town was small, and if you didn't go out on the highway, the streets for the *paseo* were limited, and it was just possible that a woman as keensighted as Señora Ferri might be able to tell you where anybody who'd stepped outside was at any given moment. If she had to locate you, she could. If she had to locate Amparo and me, she could; yet, since we weren't going off into the night where we might imagine we could hide from the eye of God, she let us go for hours at the time, up into the hills or far down the creek. The weather turned dry. There was always danger of brush and forest fires—they had become a real menace in Spain—and with our passion running high it was just conceivable we might start one of those.

If we made it through the day we had the terrace in back to cool off on and a sky of stars overhead framed by the encircling hills. The air was very clean, and we watched meteors streak across the sky and listened to the creek rush by and smelled everything the heat held down during the day, but especially small bushes of flowers called Don Pedros that were as sweet as the jasmine but lay less heavy on the air and opened only at night.

The night did not tempt us into sin but relieved us of the heat of the day. We entered a state of truce.

Don José might come by to sit with us; Enrique the priest would, too. For three weeks a woman in her midthirties from Bocairente came to visit and to help in the kitchen and house. Her name was Maruja. Her family had been in the Ferris' employ since Señor Ferri had been *el secretario* in that town. She had babysat for Amparo and would later become Amparo's closest confidante and one of our dearest friends. Yet another wealthy friend of the family showed up to spend a long weekend in the town, and during that time he spoke to both of the Ferris. It didn't surprise me that he, too, had a son. I overheard what he said. Perhaps he thought I couldn't understand Spanish or shouldn't be credited with the ability even if I could. He put it clearly and cast it in the broadest possible terms. I think he had something to do with Franco's government, and even if he didn't, with his well-fleshed face and the burr-trim to his mustache and his expensive cologne, he became Franco's representative to me.

Spaniards live by exaggeration, but I really think he meant it when he said that Amparo was not just a lovely young lady, whom he would be deeply pleased to have as a daughter-in-law if the occasion ever arose, but also a national treasure who should not be taken out of the country. Especially by the Americans, who in defeating Spain in 1898 had stripped her of the last of her empire. Now they wanted our greatest works of art. They already had *Guernica,* which they could keep, but they must not be allowed to abscond with the most beautiful expression of the Spanish soul it had been this gentleman's good fortune to ever behold. Give them *Las Meninas,* if need be. But—*por favor!*—not their daughter.

To their everlasting credit the Ferris told their visitor that I had already entered into relations with their daughter and they had given their consent. They must honor their word.

They had not consented—to the extent that they had spoken a word to be honored—but they did that night. Señor Ferri did the talking, but his wife was there and in her submissive silence she backed him up.

We had a last visitor that summer. With almost no advance notice my sister came, and I realized very quickly that my mother had sent her to scout things out and see what I had gotten myself into. Go over there and see how backward and benighted those people really are, she must have told her daughter, without it occurring to her that her daughter might be seduced by the country, too.

Sally was tall and very fair, and watching her walk around town I got a sense of how out of place I must look there, too. She had gotten the upbringing I had. We were taught to be mindful of others' rights and above all to respect their privacy, which included the privacy of their property. But it was the first time Sally had been out of the United States. She was not as self-conscious as I, and in Amparo's company could easily be persuaded to stick her head into someone's door, because it happened to be half open, and then into someone's patio since, clearly, it had been planted with all those flowers and made shiny with all those ceramic tiles to be put on display. She was not at all reticent about trying out a few Spanish expressions, which she mangled. *Tengo sueño* (I am sleepy) became *Tango sweeny* in her careless, fun-loving phrasing. She did not understand that Americans should not breeze in and plunk their bottle of ketchup down on the dining-room table; rather, they should emulate the European ways and accept without argument the fact that they were in the presence of their cultural superiors.

Sally didn't argue, but she didn't ape the Spanish ways, either, and when she was invited to suck on the shrimp heads, practically slurp the mussels right out of the shell, detach the mackerel's tail from its mouth and eat it down to the bone and then eat the bones, she resisted with an incredulous laugh. Cultural superiors? How do you say "you've got to be kidding" in Spanish? With his napkin tucked into his collar, Señor Ferri took great pains to show her what he'd shown me, and Sally regarded it all as a theatrical event, staged expressly to amuse her. She *was* amused, she was having the time of her life, and with a glance in my direction that said, Who knows, I may get to like all this, she took a stab at everything.

Whereas I ducked and winced a lot. It was like looking at myself with the accent differently placed—Sally was easygoing and I was intense, but we were both oversized and underbred and capable of making enormous fools of ourselves simply by being the people we were. There was a moment when I realized the whole enterprise was doomed from the start. You don't marry an American such as my sister and me into a family like this. Big and blond and unschooled, we had no business sitting at the same table with the smaller and finer-featured Ferris. There was something surreal about it. Salvador Dalí might have painted us sitting there like that, but for Dalí, whose whole stock in trade was the incongruous, the perverse, it would have been the most natural thing in the world.

I got depressed and this world of high gray rock and creekbed fecundity went stale for me. Then I got over it. Clearly Sally had delighted the Ferris, and since I had barely known her as an adult and tried to keep her away when she was a pestering child, thanks to the Ferris I began to discover what a delightful sister I had. When I began to see her and not a version of myself, I liked what I saw. Americans can have a warmth of spirit and an easy educable nature, if I could judge by my sister. The Ferris, when they judged by her, reasoned that my mother and father could not be as bad as they might have feared. Sally took one look at Amparo and hugged her and hugged her, as if she were all her favorite pets and girlfriends rolled into one.

Señora Ferri, true to her nature, was the last to come around. She had a horror of broken mirrors, perhaps because she spent so much time sitting before one. Midmorning, as Sally and I were finishing breakfast on the terrace, someone in the house knocked a mirror off a shelf and it broke. Señora Ferri screamed—with a mixture of horror, foot-stamping anger and resignation before the fatedness of it all. Not knowing what had happened, Sally and I rushed inside. Once there, my sister was quick to size it up. She collected the broken pieces of the mirror in a dustpan. She held the dustpan out to each of us and, in the way that Spaniards display their best dishes before serving them on plates, invited us to look. She had placed each of the pieces reflecting side down. Then she asked for a cloth sack and with Amparo holding it open dumped the pieces inside. I was to translate. I told Señora Ferri that if she took the broken mirror down to the creek in the evening and dumped it in, no harm would come.

That evening Sally took the sack of mirror shards down to the creek herself. She wouldn't hear of a symbolic dumping so we worked downstream to a spot where no one was likely to wade in. There she shook the shards into the creek.

Señora Ferri was won. It had been *un detalle* of the first order.

Antonio no longer had to serve as chaperone. As long as my sister was with us, we might go where we pleased.

We went to Cuenca, we went to Toledo. We went to Madrid. Then a number of Amparo's classmates decided to go to Ibiza, and as long as

Sally was there as her traveling companion, Amparo was allowed to go with them. We got on a boat and went to the Balearic Islands. Ibiza had recently been discovered by the roving hippie community, and it would take the minister of tourism a year before he realized the hippies were tourists who added nothing to the nation's economy, at which point they would be rounded up and summarily dumped beyond the Spanish borders. But there were also some well-heeled tourists from the continent and Sally went off with one of them. A Dutchman, with a puffy dissipated look around the eyes, yet my little sister saw something in him, or fell for some line of cultivated European bullshit, and gave it a shot. I thought of Antonio. Shouldn't I be vetting her suitors? Shouldn't I be looking after my little sister? We were with Amparo's friends, playing the guitar and doing a lot of syncopated clapping, and then we were off by ourselves. Ibiza is a small island with two small cities on opposing shores. Powered on by some crazed desire, it's possible to race back and forth between them and live the illusion of having exhausted an island. We got on another boat and went to a smaller island, Formentera, and exhausted it in one day. We came back in time to collect my sister. She'd gotten rid of the Dutchman. He'd invited her to come to Holland with him and she'd turned him down in favor of her brother and future sister-in-law.

Southerners have an expression: "Hug my neck." Sally hugged Amparo's neck. Amparo was short (but not squat) and Sally had to bend over to do it. We took Sally to Onteniente and introduced her to Antonio, who was just as short, and she had to bend over and hug his.

Meanwhile, my mother had persuaded her current minister at the Presbyterian church to write a letter insisting on how single I was and what a fine person he knew me to be (even though we had never met). The Cincinnati courthouse had sent a copy of my divorce papers, and the photocopying of the day was so erratic that some paragraphs were barely legible. It made it seem as though I had been married in another age. We had to have both of these documents translated, and those letters typed on manual typewriters, notarized and then signed with the flourish the Spanish use instead of a signature, which made it all seem older yet. Positively archaic. I felt I was slowly, and at no little expense, being written in. When we presented these documents to Father Menendez, he glanced at them and smiled, then waved them all away, as one would a formality, or as a priest, at ease behind his desk, might wave his blessing. He said he would look at them more carefully, but that all was in order. He would be in touch. We were to go in peace.

Sally was pleased, Antonio was pleased and, I thought, relieved. He began to talk of the wedding, which Sally, unfortunately, would be unable to attend. So, for her benefit, he talked it up in greater detail. Amparo's dress would be made of velvet, perhaps trimmed with some sort of fur since the wedding would be in the winter, and for himself he'd design a velvet suit of his own with an Edwardian cut. For the invitations he'd settled on an image he'd discovered on a medieval tapestry. It showed a knight and a *dama* playing chess in a forest. They were surrounded by animals, some their possessions or pets, others belonging to the forest, but all made to seem lovingly attendant on the knight and his lady. They were playing for the lady's consent, of course. Depending on the outcome of the game, the knight might have to go off to the crusades before he got it (taking with him his hounds, his ferret, his falcon and his horse), and the crusades might be long, but the outcome was foregone. If he survived they would marry, and all those animals would lovingly assemble again.

Sally was happy for the animals, but I have often wondered what Antonio meant by the comment about the crusades. Franco often referred to his fight against the godless Republic as a crusade. How much of an ordeal for us had Antonio foreseen?

The invitations were ordered. We were to marry in the Basilica, under the gaze of the Virgin of *los desamparados* and the orphaned cherubs gathered beneath her skirts. We would arrive and depart in a horse-drawn carriage. The date was December 26.

Sally and Antonio claimed to have understood each other. From the day they met until Sally got on the plane, the standing joke was that Antonio could redesign the invitation to make it a chess game for four and the wedding could be double. He charmed Sally. He put on his elevator shoes and gave her a small cultural tour. He took her to art museums and sorted out the various styles and periods of Spanish painting for her; he walked her through the religious life of the country, from hermitages to cathedrals to monasteries to convents. He took her dancing. He talked with her for hours, and his accent was charming. He told her about the many people he'd met in the United States who, though suspicious at first, had all come to love him, as he'd loved them from the start. Sally saw through him, but she also knew she had no idea what was on the other side, and in that sense she didn't "see through" Antonio at all. He was more of the same for as long as you cared to look.

She sat through a showing of his paintings, which she thought were lovely. And she was right. No one painted women misting up out of rock the way Antonio did. If she thought these women resembled Amparo she didn't say so. She said Antonio was "some character," but every time they got together she suffered a sort of disorienting assault that had her surrendering to him again and again. And I thought: So that's what it looks like. You're big and you're blond and you watch him perform and he's a trim little Latin who makes gestures that are like wand-waving arabesques, and the best you can manage as your wits desert you, is, "What a character, what a clown."

Amparo, Antonio and I took Sally to the airport. She kissed us all. When she got on the plane, I discovered I wanted her back. This was a sister I'd just met, and now she was going off. Then I discovered I wanted it *all* back—the little girl she'd been, the boy I'd been, the fields and creeks where we'd lived, my weekday mother, my weekend dad and my Aunt Marie sending news of all my far-flung cousins and pasting bunnies and chicks in the margins of her letters, as if that was what the country was as Herrins spread over it, a pasture of hopping bunnies and chirping chicks and not a predator in sight.

That weekend I got in a small Seat I had bought and drove to a town outside Barcelona, San Cugat de Vallés. On the way I was stopped by the *guardia civil*. I did not know that the *guardia civil* served as traffic cops, but a pair of them sped up behind me on their motorcycles and pulled me over, for no reason I could understand. I began to protest—compared to the tailgating Spanish who swerved in front of you and forced you to slam on your brakes, I was a model driver from whom they all should take lessons. I began to tell them so. Then I stopped. These really were the *guardia civil*. They had helmets rather than their mouse-eared hats on, but their jackboots and wide leather belts and their shirts a shade darker and more menacing than army green all hearkened back to their fascist past, which, I had to remember, was also their fascist present. I couldn't read their faces. Their features were not unfamiliar, but their flesh seemed molded out of hard rubber and their eyes set like stone. As they examined the ownership papers for my car and then my American driver's license, it dawned on me that they could do to me what they wanted. They asked for my passport. A number out of place, an illegible stamp, and they could put me in jail. *Incomunicado*—the word alone was enough to flood my stomach with a stinging cold, something like the touch of dry ice. Señor Ferri administered one kind of law; this was another.

What they did was let me go, brusquely, with a short slashing gesture up the road, as if I had only seconds to get out of their sight. They must have wanted to scare me. There goes a gringo who thinks he can barge in here and walk away with the crown jewel of Spanish womanhood. Let's bring him down.

That Monday I was on the job trying to teach an elemental English to Spanish kids uniformed in little blue blazers. I am. I was. I will be.

.   .   .

WE TURN NORTH. The Asturias are out there, the *picos de europa* covered in snow. It is mid-April. The winter has been severe, and the snow in the mountains has worked its way to the plain and brought the wheat up out of the ground. Towns go by with their outlying *palomares,* any one of which could be a diamond in the rough beneath the rubble. We don't stop where we might have before. Our disagreement over what *semana santa* could and should be has not gone away; rather it's left a quietly widening gulf between us. We're here because the old ways, in their purity, have been compromised to the point that they can accommodate me. I could live here. And we could not live here if those ways have been compromised to the point that they make mockery of the Spain my wife knew as a child.

We are driving into the north, the province of Palencia, site of some of the best Romanesque architecture in Spain, and another stretch in the pilgrims' route. We take a room in a *hostal* in the town of Carrión de los Condes, and as chance would have it, our window looks directly onto the main door of the church of Santa Maria. We are not in Spain to visit churches or cathedrals. We have done that—the cathedrals in Seville, Granada, Toledo and especially the shimmering, light-charged cathedral in León. Our intention is to stay in the streets and plazas and get a feel for the way the people live in their towns, and for the way the towns grow out of the land. But we get up in the morning, look out the window and see this door. Maybe it's the morning hour and the surprise. Maybe it's this disagreement we've had. I call her to the window. Gently, I insist it will be worth it to get up before the light changes and come see what we have here. She grumbles, but she knows I'm not bossing her. And she comes.

Our window frames the porch, which rises on ocher stone columns to frame the door to the church. The morning sun lights the porch floor to within a step of the threshold. The door is concentrically arched in a *medio punto,* and there are four low columns on each side with capitals of human figures and vegetation designs. Around the next to the last of the arches, small human figures with large heads are fitted in side by side, so simple they might have been carved by a child. Over the door is a frieze carved in higher relief, where the figures are larger and include at least three mounted on horses; a crowned figure sits in the center. There's a story being told here; everywhere you look in this Romanesque world a story's being told in stone, paint or tapestry for an almost entirely illiterate populace, but the porch roof casts the church door in such shadow that from my vantage point it's impossible to read it. And it doesn't matter anyway. I didn't call my wife out of bed to decipher a church legend. I called her because the morning light lit the way, and because there was such a simple, elegant dignity about the door that anybody could enter. The wooden door itself stands open, but I don't want to go in. I want to stay up in my window and let the bright light and the warm glowing shadow do the rest. But what I want my wife to feel is that for once in my life I'm present before a truly catholic door, and that that is what the word means.

A door cut to a human scale that anybody can enter.

She understands me. That doesn't mean our differences are over, but it does mean we have a door in common anytime we want to go in.

She kisses me and gets back into bed. I would like to make love to her before a door like that. I am suddenly sure that is one of the things such a door is meant for. Come into the cool close warmth that a door like that promises and take your solace. We are directly on the route to Santiago, and that is what the pilgrims must have done.

I am still sitting there musing when I hear the first bells summoning the faithful to Mass. I don't hear my wife rise out of bed and get dressed, but as people begin to arrive at the church, she presents herself before me and says that she is going, too. I have gone to many a Mass with her, but somehow she knows I'm not going to this one. After twenty-eight years she knows my moods, and the mood in which I'm sitting there before the window would not survive the priest in his robes, the altar boys, the censer, the chalice and host and all the rest. While she's making her way down the stairs, I watch mostly the old hobbling in through that door; a few kids, slicked down, are dragged along, too. And more of those little girls. Then she comes up behind them. She's got a sweater on and some dark slacks, nothing exceptional, what she had at hand when she got out of bed. Recently she's cut her hair short, which gives a lovely roundness to her head. The back of her neck is bare. There's a mole, which in the past I've lifted her hair to expose, and from that window and in that light I'm able to see that mole now. She knows I'm watching her. She waves a mock-annoyed hand over her shoulder, brushing me off. Then, before she steps into the church, she turns and smiles, and the shadowed warmth coming off that glowing red stone is all over her face. I smile back and curse under my breath. That a goddamned priest gets her for the next hour and I don't! It isn't fair! I didn't marry her for this! I should go down there and pull her out, like the barbarian from the West her family, Church and State had me pegged as from the start.

That afternoon we are out on the pilgrims' route again, midway between Carrión and the next town east, Fromista. To the south lies the flat, barely undulating farmland of *tierra campo*, and to the north, at the arable limit of it all, mountains surge out of the land and we're looking at the *picos de europa* under snow. Eliminate the cars, and a pilgrim would have seen the same thing five hundred years ago. In the midst of this vastness I have a sure sense of something having been paced off to the finest unit of measurement, and that, I think, is the way history mates with the land. Human history, as it's chronicled most, is all about strife, but I feel none of that here. I can imagine armies, yes, galloping across the plain, threshing the wheat and pulping the grapes, but I'm not in the mood for armies now. Quixote was embattled but Quixote had a philosophical side, too, and if Sancho was listening to his master when the philosophical mood was on him, Sancho learned a lot. What did Quixote imagine fabulous foes to fight against for? For this, for the land and its towns set out in well-behaved lots, crossed on a daily basis by the pilgrim's steady tread.

As we stand there, pilgrims pass. It looks to me like a family, the father and mother our age, a son and either his wife or sister. They all have staffs and the mother a scalloped medallion around her throat; no butternut squash that I can see. They carry raingear in their backpacks and wear boots and different-styled hats, the father's pulled down like an inverted bowl around his ears. The father's face is splotched red; it's the sun he'd hiding from. When I mention the snow waiting for them in Galicia, the father explains that this time they're only going as far as León. Sometime later, when the weather's a sure thing, they'll take it up from there. They've learned that to get their passbook stamped all the way through to Santiago they don't have to make the whole trip at once.

It is said that pilgrimages to Santiago dropped off after the discovery of the New World. The world no longer ended at Finisterre. Pilgrims wanted to go all the way. Now the way is so crowded with jets that you can be in a holding pattern over Kennedy for hours, describing great multinational circles up in the sky. Pilgrims have come back down to earth again, if only to walk as far as León.

In the church of St. Martín's in Fromista, Amparo calls me to the base of one of the columns in the nave and instructs me to look up. At first I'm not sure what I see. As with most of the columns, human figures are carved around the capital, and two of those figures are pilgrims—that much is clear from the staffs they carry. But others are there with their arms entwined, a group of three and a couple, and they're all gazing off at something with those lidless stone eyes. The threesome seems to be composed of a woman standing between two men; the men have their hands clasped over the woman's breasts, and she, in turn, is holding their clasped hands. The couple is holding on to each other more tightly, and the man, it seems, is attempting to shield the woman's eyes. Their heads are all disproportionately large, with long rounded jaws and chins.

I think of that family we just met on the trail to Santiago, and something tells me that is the comparison Amparo is inviting me to make. These people on the capital walked to the west with the sun of their belief blazing in their eyes, until their sight was burned clean and there was nothing left to see. The family we greeted on the trail was on a weekend outing, and there is no comparison to be made. And no dispute. During *semana santa*, a little girl should be allowed to step out of line and go up to her father, who should be allowed to touch the side of his daughter's face—I still insist on that. But my willingness to accommodate old rites to modern times will extend just so far. I tell my wife, instead, that it's touching, it's fine, the way those people above us huddle together and take strength from each other, while the pilgrims stand like sentinels at the corners of the capital. Then I put an arm around her shoulder and nudge her around to face the apse, where a crucified Christ hangs on wires suspended from the ceiling. There is no altar, no gaudy *retablo*. The windows are narrow, and the alabaster they're paned with takes the harshness out of the light. St. Martin's is a very intimate space at that moment. The Christ on his cross is part of that intimacy, and not a man in mortal pain. We stand there like that until my wife, shorter than I, and with the surer plant, simply slips out from under my arm and leaves me listing to the side. My staff, my Sancho, who, as she herself said back at the start of all this, can out-Quixote his boss at times.

I am not her boss. We are a team.

We drive on, farther north, to Aguilar de Campó. A river, the Pesquegra, runs through the town. Spring has come to its banks and the poplars that line it. As in town after town in the province of Palencia, the sycamores that grow in the plazas have been pruned with selected branches left to entwine, and now those stumpy sycamores are in leaf and a canopy is beginning to form. We walk the plazas. We pass through the gated walls. A footbridge built by the Romans crosses a branch of the river and we sit on stone benches carved into its walls. The town is not too small; there are signs of prosperity. In the colonnaded *plaza mayor* there are almost always people, and at the hour of the evening *paseo* there is an easygoing, very fluid throng. We walk there. Another long strolling avenue has been built along the river and we walk there, too. The kids seem to prefer the river. They sit on the benches, three on the seat, three more up on the backs, and eat sunflower seeds, spewing out the husks as they chatter. Pigeons wheel in. We watch another kid, a loner, pull a small but handsome trout out of the river. To the south of Aguilar the land is still relatively flat, but to the north the hills begin to swell, and I feel as though I were about to be borne up on the crest of a wave. In addition to the flowers and baking bread and the scent of olive oil that you get in almost all Spanish towns, there's another smell in this one, sweet and very mild; it's everywhere, and it too seems capable of bearing you up. We are told that Fontaneda makes cookies and crackers here, cookies we've had with *café con leche* for breakfast for years, and that every morning they turn on the ovens, pour in the honey and cook them up.

We meet a couple at the *hostal* where we are staying. They are retired, English, very pleasant and polite, but I get the sense they are saving themselves for something, measuring themselves out. They have driven down from Oxfordshire, on, for them, the wrong side of the road, and will spend the next ten days going from town to hamlet to see if they can make a discovery. They are on the trail of the Romanesque. They tell us about English friends who do the same thing, and about acquaintances from the continent, too, who come to the province of Palencia and get back on the dirt roads and find maybe three or four churches in one day. Untouched. The towns and hamlets are all but deserted. There'll be an old woman left who has the key. Depending on the weather and the mood she is in, she may or may not let you in. Inside, there's no telling what you might find. It is a glorious moment. They were such simple, devout, humble and strong-willed people, the Spanish back then. They were not out to outdo their neighbors. They had one belief and it went into the stone.

Then this English couple gives us a tip in case we want to get out on the trail ourselves. Matalbaniega. The road is bad, with deep ruts. It needs more traffic. But if we make it, the woman's name is Pina, and the day the English couple went there the weather was fine and her mood was good. They wish us luck and urge us not to lose heart. There's a church out there in this part of Spain for everyone with the steadfastness to find it. And once we find it, what then? Are we to "go native"? He has a hound's hanging chops and she a wren's twitching face, and more English they could not get. But we take their tip.

The road is worse than bad; in our lightly built Nissan I judge it to be impassable, but Amparo urges me on. Once I learn the trick of straddling the ruts our chances improve, and by the time we make Matalbaniega I am ready to make a day of it. Matalbaniega dribbles down off a hill. Old stone, covered with lichen, has settled into the ground and whatever headroom these houses once had has been lost. The last thing you expect to see is fresh brick and mortar; and the next-to-last thing men working on a car. Two men are working on a car before a freshly built house. They direct us to one of the two other habitable houses in town. The old man we find there is named Manuel. He stands with his feet flat on the ground, his arms hanging straight at his sides. It's hard to imagine him taking a step. Pina is his sister, and she has the key. For some reason he asks us to go up to the church and wait for her there. Perhaps he doesn't want us to see him move, as if there is some old family secret as to how he does it.

We walk up to the church, which stands on the brow of the hill, its stone whitened in the years of unobstructed sun. With so few windows and those so narrow, a Romanesque church approached in this way might resemble a bastion more than a site of holy worship, and this one at Matalbaniega presents a broad, nearly bare wall. There is no bell tower or bell gable. There is a single, semicircular apse, and at the other end the closed-off ruins of another structure, a small monastery, Amparo suspects. A cow trail and narrow dirt road dip down off the hill to our left. Falling off the hill just to the right of the church are a few moss-blackened stones of the cemetery. The brother of the woman we came to find is coming up the road, but the woman is leading the way.

I wonder if she's angry. Her face is red and she is walking with a churning little step. She steps in a cow pie that her brother manages to avoid. But she's got on ageless brogans of some sort and the cow pie is mostly dry. Her mouth is open and her teeth are nearly gone; I think she's about to shout at us when I realize she's smiling and she's out of breath and she's hurrying because she's afraid we won't think much of her church and will pick up and leave.

Her name is Pina, which is short for Agripina, a Roman name, she tells us at the start, as if establishing her credentials to be our guide. And her guide's fee will be adjusted accordingly. Her brother doesn't say a word. He's taken another of those wizened, rooted stances and creates something of a mystery just by his presence there. His sister has the key. Actually two keys, one to a conventional lock and the other perhaps the original key to the door, a good eight inches long with a single notch.

The brother is there because they are a team and for time immemorial his sister has done the talking.

Who are we? Where do we come from? Where else have we been? Where do we intend to go? She assumes we are on the trail, for that is the only reason anyone would brave the roads we have and end up here. We name St. Martín's and a couple of other churches we've seen. We mention the frescoes we've been told are painted on the church walls here at Matalbaniega, scenes of the Last Judgment, heaven and hell, and she shakes her head and the gray curls that frame it make a stormy little shudder. We've got our churches wrong. Not Matabaniega but Matamorisca. The woman with the key there is Ángela. But the paintings are not all they're made out to be, and Ángela's church is second-rate compared to hers. With a commanding gesture Pina motions us to follow her around behind the apse.

I've already noticed the rows of stone figures carved under the eaves, *canecillas,* they're called. She points up to them on the far side of the church. She has us count down until we get to one that is clearly is the shape of the upper half of a woman's body, although the weathering has badly blurred the lines. Do we know what that woman is doing? She gives us a moment to figure it out. There are two rope-like protrusions seeming to frame the woman's body, but other than helping to support the eave we haven't a clue what she might be doing.

Pina chuckles knowingly. She glances at her brother, who may allow the creases at the corners of his mouth a slight movement upward. Pina tells us that that is the only *canecilla* of its kind in all of Spain. That woman is giving suck to two serpents, one at each breast. Do we see it now?

If those rope-like protrusions are serpents they do seem to end at the level of her breasts.

There is nothing lewd about Pina's laughter now. It is pure civic pride. Ángela, she claims, can't show us anything that good. But we should go to Matamorisca and see for ourselves.

Then she uses the two keys to open the church door, although I suspect the old iron key is pure theater now. Inside, we might as well be in a cave. Until our eyesight adjusts from the sunlight to the near darkness there is nothing to see. The smells are not of incense, not of hymnals or missals, not of the wood of the benches serving as pews, but of cold earth and stone. And for the moment we stand there, I fill up on that smell and let it go to my head as I would a drug. The smell is pure, so pure it's rank. We're standing on ancient paving stones, hollowed where feet have most often fallen, and Pina doesn't have to tell me they're the slabs covering tombs, although she does. The church fathers—*this* church's fathers—and the most illustrious of the monks are buried there.

Amparo is impressed by the church, which predates her childhood, with its incorruptible memories, by plenty. But she is also ready to leave. I haven't forgotten I've promised her a *hostal* of raw brick, and the ocean is nearby.

Outside, Pina situates us on the best vantage the hill offers and points us any number of ways. Cantabria is to the north, Asturias to the northwest—the *picos de europa* span the two regions. The valley before us is spotted with towns, all huddled up to their churches, which she names and relates a detail or two about, and by the time she's directed us to the town farthest out we are already in the province of Santander. The Basque Country is close by. She allows a dreaming glint into her eye and a husky fondness into her voice. I can imagine her standing here every so often, letting her gaze roam free. Plodding up the cow path, then plodding back down. But I know I've got it wrong. There is not the first hint of sentimentality about this woman. She's one with the dying town, her taciturn brother and the stone-cold church. She sells what she's got to those who manage to make it up her rutted road. She doesn't charge a peseta, will not accept anything like a tip. Yesterday she had the English here. Today an American, married to a Spaniard, who's looking for a town so durable and uncompromised at the core that it can hold its own in a wildness of space. As long as Pina has possession of the keys, the world comes to her, which makes the road to Matalbaniega another pilgrims' route. I like her. I think her church is the real thing, as pure as it gets. And I share her doubt that Ángela will show us anything better, although I jot the directions in my breast-pocket notebook, and she sends us there.

THREE

IF SANCHO WAS LISTENING TO HIS MASTER, WHAT DID he learn?

He learned this:

God knows whether there is any Dulcinea or not in the world, or whether she is imaginary or not imaginary. These are things the proof of which must not be pushed to extreme lengths. I have not begotten nor given birth to my lady, though I behold her as she must necessarily be, a lady who contains in herself all the qualities to make her famous throughout the world.

And this:

Recollect, my friend, that all knights cannot be courtiers, nor can all courtiers be knights-errant, nor need they be. There must be all sorts in the world, and though we may be all knights, there is a great difference between one and another. For the courtiers, without leaving their rooms, or the threshold of the court, range the world over by looking at a map, without its costing them a farthing and without suffering heat or cold, hunger or thirst. But we, the true knights-errant, measure the whole earth with our feet.

Quixote did not create his Dulcinea, although he beheld her as she "necessarily" must be. If he was going to adore her, there were certain qualities she had to possess, otherwise he would not adore her. And, clearly, he did adore her. Therefore . . . Sancho could have finished the rest. Dulcinea was real, real enough to drive her devoted servant out into the world of heat and cold, hunger and thirst. One reality ensured the other. Dulcinea was real and so were these bruises and bumps and scars, which Sancho could reach out and touch.

Touch them, Sancho, and read in them the wondrous qualities my lady must necessarily possess. We shall push on.

Here is the true Quixote for me. His need is such that there must be a lady whom he can serve. But she is not his phantom. If anything, her reality exceeds his. In her service, then, he quests after a superior reality, which on other occasions he might have called his soul's redemption, but which he knows is his body's business now. Courtiers in their easy imaginings may have their pallid souls redeemed. Quixote measures the earth.

Did Sancho know what he was signing on for? Another of the Spaniards' ontological dramas? An embattled old cuss, Don Quixote liked to thump a goatherd's skull for what it told him of his lady Dulcinea's inestimable beauty.

The quixotic quest: outward in space, backward in time. We push on.

We have left the plains of Castile, with its castles and *palomares* and Romanesque churches, and entered the mountains of the Asturias. We are not really following any plan or itinerary now. *Sobre la marcha*, the

Spaniards say, play it as it goes. The *picos de europa* have been out on our horizon for days now, and we simply allow ourselves to be drawn in their direction. Briefly, we're in the region of Cantabria, then back in the Asturias. The valleys have grown lush, cut by rushing streams, which, with their white-flecked riffles, look marbled. The valleys are terraced but not so much for crops now as pastures. The terrace walls are earth-rounded, not rocked. Black-and-white cattle graze on these terraces, which as they broaden might be called upland pastures, a phrase I've always liked. Sheep graze there, too. Higher, though, the terraces give out, and we're into the craggy grays and greens of the ridge peaks where Spain is still muted, inhospitable and very austere.

. . .

BARCELONA IS FOR LATER. I love Barcelona, it may be my favorite city in the world. I love its wide boulevards and its narrow twisting streets. I love its grid of nineteenth-century mansions and I love its Gaudi. Past the politics of the day, its people are honorable and hard-working and at ease with their leisure time, not as striking in appearance as the Andalucians or the Valencians, but handsome enough, and I love them. I think of Barcelona and the word is "established"—as though by natural right. A city belongs here—this city. Before its port, within its cradling hills. No one in Spain inhabits his city with more unostentatious pride than a Catalan. I lived here for three years. Our son was born here. Toward the end of the second book, Quixote made his last foray here and came away impressed. But Barcelona is for later, after all that I'm about to recount is done.

During that time I lived downtown, caught a train over the hills and taught in the town of San Cugat de Vallés, and on Friday afternoon got in my Seat and drove five hours along the coast to Valencia. There's a stretch between Tarragona and Viñaroz where the wind can be so strong, if your car is as small as mine was, that you're forced to pull off. I pulled off more than once, had a coffee and waited it out. Other times I rode it out. But, to one degree or another, there was always this great howling gust to get through before I got to the woman I loved, who, of course, after a week's separation, had grown to striking proportions, deserving of such a powerful wind.

She claimed that over the week she'd forgotten what I looked like. She tried to call me up before her mind's eye and failed, she said. I laughed at her—such an eager and anxious and impressionable child. I have a face of unexceptional features, clear eyes and a dimpled chin. Fair-complexioned. Forgettable enough, I suppose. But that wasn't what she meant. She meant in her love for me she reached out and I simply wasn't there. So she stood for an instant in the door, sizing me up, assuring herself that I wasn't an imposter, before she stretched up to hug me around the neck.

I laughed. She, in turn, has large prominent features, and I never told her that I had a problem similar to hers. I never doubted she was who she was, but between her eyes, nose, mouth, forehead and chin there was always one feature that stood out, upsetting the balance and jarring the rest, so that the first look I took at her after that drive down the coast was an adventure. Beauty, real beauty, is always in danger of becoming grotesque. At any moment—after a week of not seeing her at all—I might open the door on a strange and unsettling sight. She would wait to see if I was who I said I was, and I would wait to see if her features would settle into a facsimile of the person I knew.

Not the same problem at all. Not even similar.

This went on for about six weeks. Then the *fiscal*, Father Menendez, called us in for a Friday-afternoon appointment, and I had to ask to be released from the Friday classes I taught.

He was back behind his desk with our papers before him. I know I saw him on his feet because he was a shorter and less imposing man than his full breadth and girth behind his desk made him seem, but I can't remember when. When Amparo and I walked in, he was making a perfunctory show of going through our papers. He welcomed us and motioned us to our seats. Actually, when I was seated before him, I saw that he was thumbing through our papers as though making sure he hadn't overlooked one he'd missed before. Then he laid his glasses aside and, in a tone of patient forbearance, as though we'd misunderstood him from the start, he said, Your first marriage is still valid. You'll have to take care of that.

The word he used was *solucionar,* which is normally translated "solve" and carried the implication that some things couldn't be. But that was not his tone. His tone was that we had one more bureaucratic hurdle to clear. So, clear it up, take care of that.

Then he met my eye. It was a look I've seen only on a priest's face. Not on a Protestant preacher's face, but on a priest's—a composed and irreproachable mask, as if Menendez had turned his attention to eternal matters and absolved himself of any earthly mistakes. If I could achieve that state of mind I might absolve myself of my mistakes, too.

I said I didn't understand. There were the papers showing I was single in the eyes of the church into which I'd been baptized and the state where I'd last lived. For an instant I wondered if the translator had done me an evil deed. But I'd read the translations. *Soltero,* they said.

Amparo remained silent. But I glanced over at her and her expression came out of the same world as Menendez's: a look of resignation before forces that she'd been warned might one day oppose her and been raised not to resist. She didn't move—her face might have been hung with tiny, perfectly positioned weights. Menendez wore his mask and Amparo wore hers, a face that the tide of history had washed clean of all distinguishing features and made into an emblem. Of what? What martyred saint? What incorruptible virgin?

All that meant that Menendez and Amparo could talk to each other without exchanging a word. Thinking about it now, I realize that was the moment when I dug in my heels and said to myself, I'll be goddamned!

To Menendez I said, I got the papers you said I needed. I did exactly what you said.

He acknowledged no mistake. He thumbed through again and came to the name of the church where my first wife and I had been married. The chapel in the College of the Bible in Lexington, Kentucky. As provincial as it sounded, it was a sect whose sacraments the Holy Roman Catholic Church recognized as binding. I made a chuckling groan. Menendez may have heard it as a growl. But it was a groan.

Something had occurred to me that Menendez knew nothing about. My first wife and I had married in that college chapel because my preacher and church organizer of a grandfather had gone to school there and excelled to the extent that they'd put up a plaque in his honor. We'd married in the chapel of his alma mater to please my mother and . . . well, because, one place was as good as another. But what I suddenly saw was my grandfather standing at the pulpit of a church where he was preaching the inaugural sermon, eyeing an out-of-town visitor in the congregation, my grandmother, and then standing at the church door, where he shook her hand and told her, loud enough for her girlfriend to hear, too, Young lady, I'm going to marry you.

And he got his way.

And I wouldn't get mine? I'd be goddamned! Because of a hypocrite like Menendez and my grandfather with his roving eye?

But I was stunned, sobered, and my mouth was dry. What was I supposed to do now?

Behind his pleasant, self-absolving smile Menendez said that was up to us. Then with no change of expression he informed us that, while the Catholic church does not recognize divorce, it does recognize annulments, and it might be worth inquiring whether there were any grounds for annulling that first marriage of mine.

Worth inquiring? Whom was I supposed to ask? We stepped outside the archbishop's palace and I never felt more in a foreign world. Amparo belonged to that world.

They won't let us, she said to me in a voice that was the equivalent of that expression I'd seen on her face, even-toned, impersonal, foregone. Then she added in a meek and peeved aside, which, nonetheless, was a voice I recognized, a voice I knew, It isn't fair.

Civil marriages were performed then in Spain, but unless they were accompanied by marriages in the Church they were considered excommunicable affairs. During the brief second Republic, in certain sections of Spain Church marriages had not even been allowed. Valencia had been one of those sections. Couples married during the Republic had to remarry in the Church once Franco came to power.

We were sitting at a table on the *plaza de la virgen,* facing the Basilica where the Virgin of *los desamparados* was enshrined, when Amparo told me that that was what had happened to her parents, that they had been caught between the godless civility of the Republic and the triumphant reestablishment of the Church during the Franco regime and had had to remarry. It turned out that Amparo's grandfather—not the one who'd fought in the Spanish-American War but her mother's father—was a renegade of sorts who had resisted the Church at every turn, to the point of naming his daughter Delia, simply because no Delia appeared in the saints' calendar. A civil wedding for his daughter suited him fine. Then the war came. His house was near the medieval city gates, *los torres de Quarte.* Between his house and the gates stood the church and convent of Saint Ursula. During the civil war the *cheka* had used the church as a tribunal to try unregenerate priests and nuns. Amparo's grandfather claimed to have heard their screams. After the war was over, during a heavy rain, blood suddenly appeared among the flowers in the convent garden, and those missing priests and nuns were dug up. It was regarded as a miracle—that blood of martyrs blossoming with the flowers of spring. Citizens were allowed to file through as witnesses. Amparo's grandfather was not one of them. But when his daughter's name was changed to Maria Delia in the city registry and his daughter took her wedding vows again before a priest, he did not say no. It would have been pointless. He became a man like so many other Spaniards of the time, caught between competing atrocities and somehow canceled out.

So when Amparo said, They won't let us, she had family history to back her up. And her family history, in that respect at least, was the nation's in miniature.

Whereas I, after my initial outrage, kept returning to Menendez the man. Why would he have wanted to put us through our paces if he'd known it was impossible from the start? Was the war still on and was the Church still taking its revenge on godless civilians? I didn't think so. For all his self-satisfaction, Menendez, I suspected, had made an honest mistake. If I were single in the eyes of my church and state, why, he'd reasoned, wouldn't I be free to marry? He was prepared to approve a marriage after getting the non-Catholic party—me—to agree to do everything his way. Then someone tougher and less comfortably ensconced behind his desk had straightened Menendez out. The Church does not make allowances, Father Menendez. The Church punishes home along well-established paths. Menendez, partly ashamed of his mistake, partly sympathetic to our plight and partly relieved at being overruled by someone on high, had put a pleasant face on it. But he'd been trying to tell us something: Get that first marriage annulled and come back. And he'd been hinting: Make the right inquiries and getting a marriage annulled was a piece of cake.

I talked myself into believing that after all was said and done, Menendez might just be our ally.

It was the first time Amparo referred to me by the name of her nation's Don. *Que quixote eres,* she said. You just don't know.

But I told her I had a hunch. In retrospect I even thought I had seen

Menendez wink. I would make my inquiries. We would get this straight-ened out. We have a saying in English, Where there's a will . . . but I stopped. If I was reduced to mouthing clichés, all was lost. I kissed her and brought that leap of trust back into her eyes. I told her she could count on being married on December 26.

.   .   .

I HAD A FRIEND I taught with who moonlighted in the evenings in a lan-guage academy in Barcelona, where he taught professional people Eng-lish. One of his students was a lawyer. We met for coffee before his class. The lawyer was a Catalan—factual, friendly and entrenched in his op-position to the Castilian police state. Three million pesetas, he said, and an annulment of my first marriage could be had within a month. It didn't matter whether my first marriage was an abomination in the eyes of God and man, three million was the standard price. Three million pesetas at the time was forty-five thousand dollars. My friend and I were poor lan-guage teachers and the lawyer was learning English and just starting out. We laughed. The rich man's divorce. The very rich man's divorce. But the lawyer was stating what was common knowledge. There was plenty of uncommon knowledge out there, too, and cases in which annulments had been granted on very peculiar grounds. There were edicts and dis-pensations and sanctified loopholes that any good ecclesiastical lawyer would be able to tell me about. The three million was for no questions asked. Otherwise they would ask a few.

This really isn't about my first wife, but the fact is, we were curiously alike. We had almost identical needs. We'd belonged to a fairly con-tented crowd until a day came when we'd suddenly been struck by the insufficiency of it all. From that day forth, we'd done one of two things: Either we'd kept in a kind of thrill-seeking motion in the hope of hold-ing that insufficiency at bay, or we'd talked ourselves into believing that with a crazed commitment of some sort we'd find a way to make that insufficiency good. Obviously, there was room for only one of us in any given marriage, so we'd divorced and wished each other well.

This is about my second wife, Amparo, and the country that bodied her forth. Of my various fears for her, one has always been that the day would come when the country that gave her to me would take her back. We will all lie with the Phoenicians, the Greeks and the Romans—that is not what I mean. I mean that the day would come when her experiment with the life she'd fashioned for herself as my wife in the United States would end and the country that accounted for her in all the particulars would want her back. She would disappear from my side, and when I came to look for her all I would find would be castles, pilgrims' trails, terrace walls, orange and olive trees, bulls and goats, virgins and churches and stone Christs. And the sea. The sea as it glittered a three-toned blue, and the sea as it broke, a battleship gray, against some isolated point.

Finisterre. End of the earth.

We have reached the sea at the Asturian town of Ribadesella and she has taken the umbrella and left. This is not a *hostal* of raw brick but a turn-of-the-century home converted into a hotel. There is plenty of wood—the floors are wood and the frames for the windows and doors—and there are easy chairs and old rugs. I have a bottle of Ribera de Duero wine that I have brought up from Castile and a window looking past a balcony onto the drizzling sea. I have been reading. But I have given up. This is a rainy area and workers are working in the rain, laying a new sea walk, a *paseo maritimo*, down to my right. Two sounds alternate: a jackhammer pounding into the old concrete and the revving roar of a bulldozer as it moves the earth around. My wife would have walked away from that, following the bay's crescent out to its western point, where, when I get up to study the scene, I can make out a few figures—fishermen, I suppose—standing before the surf. The ocean, the Cantabrian Sea, is not storm-tossed. This is no storm. It's a dampness, whether misted up from the sea or dropped from the sky, it's hard to say.

A woman has come into the room, the daughter of the owner of the house. We talk for a while. The bottle of wine stands unopened on the table because I have forgotten to bring a corkscrew, and she offers to bring one from the kitchen. I tell her to bring a glass for herself if she'd like some, too. The Duero is the river that cuts through Castile, and the wine from that region is strong and full-bodied. I never learn this woman's name. She takes a sip of the wine and puts it aside. She has thick features and slumberous expressions and gestures. She wants to talk, but her speech begins to labor, and finally she seems to lack the energy to force it out of her mouth. For a moment, she's steeped in a sort of inertia, during which time she simply looks at me and smiles. I assume she's slow-witted, but the smile is peaceful. Her eyes are slightly bulbous and a cloudy hazel, and they, too, are peaceful. The woman works. She's in this room dusting, and I've already seen her spading around the bushes in the garden, but it's the way she comes to a halt that takes my attention. It's if she were a piece of the furniture, or a bush outside, and the smile on her face and the quiet in her large opaque eyes hint at an intelligence I know nothing about.

She starts talking again, with a churning effect, and tells me she's a *maruja*. On nice afternoons, she says, she and the other *marujas* in the town get together and walk before the sea. But the repairs to the sea walk and the drizzling rain have kept her in today.

Maruja is the nickname for a spinster in small Spanish towns.

In times past, Spaniards castigated *marujas* with a vehemence reserved for sexual deviants in other cultures, but the look on this woman's face says, Here, it's who I am, I'm in hiding, I'm in public view, take your pick. I'll listen to what everybody has to say.

Eventually she dusts her way out of the room, and I am left with the wine, the book, the sea and the noise of bulldozers grunting into earth and jackhammers pounding rock. When the workers are quiet, I can hear the sea, and it gives off a restless, tight-compassed sound, like a body shifting in a narrow space in search of that one comfortable spot.

I'm bored. Vaguely depressed and feeling all of fifty-eight.

When Amparo returns the rain is running off her face. That beautiful broad forehead is lacquered with it and it's sparkling in her long lashes. Her eyes are bold and concentrated and as buckeye-bright as when I first met her. Her hair is plastered wet and her mouth is open on the teeth and tongue. I notice that her umbrella is strapped closed. It's impossible to believe that gray drizzle wetted her like that, and for an instant I believe she has jumped into the ocean and come to stand before me with an expression that says, Here, you want a jolt, you want to get in tune with the elemental flow of things, take a look at this.

So, as with the woman who's just been here dusting, I take a closer look. Amparo is charged up, all right, but at the moment none of it's for me. *Que tiempo más malo!* (What miserable weather!) *Que maravilla!* (How wonderful it is!)

That evening when we go out for supper she has *fabada asturiana,* and pauses in her eating just long enough to say, I am in bean wonderland! *Que lástima* (what a shame) that you can't be, too.

I don't digest beans well, and the trip through the mountains has left my stomach queasy. I applaud her for her good fortune, but she's not in need of applause. She's gotten out in front, out of ear-range. Sancho's had his outing and is warning his master he'd better catch up. The next morning we're on the road and up the coast, ticking off towns until she directs us inland. She's actually taken an interest in the map. Towns she likes the sound of—Comillas and Cabezon de la Sal—and towns she'd been told way back in her childhood not to miss—Columbres, Santillana and Covadonga, where the Virgin appeared to her beleaguered Asturian countrymen and led them in hurling rocks and spears down on the Muslim hordes. The reconquest started there in Covadonga. We visit the Virgin's cave—*la cueva santa*—for a moment's worship, and then drive on.

.   .   .

MY EMOTIONS WERE RUNNING HIGH. Lacking forty-five thousand dollars to buy an annulment, all I had were the strength of my emotions and my determination to keep them running full throttle. My problem, I see now, was that to sustain the driving force of my desire I had to call on what was most American about me—the willingness to pound and pound until I was admitted or had knocked down the door—while simultaneously trying to persuade myself and everyone else involved that that was a way of being I was through with. I didn't phrase it like that. I was aware that I was calling on something in myself that, if considered apart, would disqualify me from being considered the person I aspired to be. I got up in the morning with my stomach tensed—a linesman poised on the line of scrimmage, ready to plunge ahead—pep-talking myself. I'd be goddamned! I'd be good and goddamned! Who the hell did they think I was? It wasn't long before I began to wince. Whom was I imitating? Football stalwarts such as Woody Hayes or Bear Bryant? Or LBJ and Richard Nixon as they pleaded for peace and understanding with their bombs? Not that I actually named those fellow Americans. It was a state of being, a state of being so powerful that it overwhelmed the mind. There were no words. I got up full of myself—the pressure was actually physical— and I got up unwilling to spend another day inside my own skin.

Country or woman, it didn't matter. I was going to be married on December 26.

The school I worked in got some of my excess energy. Schools such as mine were training future leaders, and we were instructed to treat the students, to the degree possible, as responsible young adults. Somehow, I convinced myself that the more exposed these students were to people like me, with plights like mine and with needs equivalent in their pent-up, bursting force to some of our great natural phenomena—a Niagara, an Old Faithful, a Grand Canyon of a need—the better for all of us. I allowed my students to organize debates, and since I knew they wouldn't get excited if I assigned a topic, I encouraged them to choose their own. They chose three: birth control, the independence movement among the Basques and, as the subject of our first debate, divorce.

I had not breathed a word about my civil status. Perhaps it was something I was giving off. Here stands a man begging to be debated.

The week of the debate the students' enthusiasm grew. I could see it in their eyes. If I taught them a new rhetorical construction they were already casting ahead to see how they might use it to strengthen their position. By debate day they were primed. I was met at the class door by the leader of the sixth form, Jorge Otero, a pale, wispy-haired man but, as I recall him now, with a fascist's lantern jaw. What was I intending to cover in these upcoming weeks? I told him where we were in the textbook. And nothing else? I said we were about to have debates, and with a gentle, forgiving and very charitable forbearance he explained to me that only topics with two sides can be debated, and the topics I had chosen, unfortunately, did not qualify. Against birth control and divorce the Vatican had spoken, and Basque independence had been ruled out by the state. I had not mentioned these topics to him. He had gotten his information elsewhere. I corrected him. I had not chosen the topics, the students had; they were excited, their English was about to blossom. Otero, schooled to be a patient man, continued to shake his head. He laid a hand on my shoulder and smiled. *Trabajo en equipo*, teamwork, was the school's motto, and we stood there as a team, committed to defending the one and only side of these, by definition, undebatable topics.

When I informed the students they groaned, but a few of them snickered knowingly, and after class they explained to me that there were two Opus Dei spies in the class—two so that they could keep an eye on each other—and were about to give me the spies' names when I stopped them. I taught them the expression "Shut the fuck up!" A handy word to know, "fuck," if you saved it for the right occasion. As in "I do not fucking want to know."

When I described this scene to Antonio he told me he'd known many a man like Otero in the Opus Dei, with the same sort of mild-mannered and servile fanaticism. He insisted, though, that the school's director and his friend, Pablo Pujol, was not that sort. I could rely on him, confide in him; for the next fifteen minutes Antonio sang me Pujol's praises.

For a week I dutifully taught my classes and observed the Opus Dei members as they patrolled the halls and manned their offices. When they went to their pockets I couldn't decide if they were fingering their crucifixes, scratching their balls or counting their money. They were certainly wealthy, sanctimonious and uptight enough to be doing all three.

But I'd come too far not to trust Antonio now. I went to Pujol for advice. And since what I wanted from him was the name of an ecclesiastical lawyer I could consult, I ended up telling him where I stood.

Pujol looked like a Spanish actor I'd come to like, José Luis López Vázquez, who specialized in sad-sack roles. López Vázquez's eyes hung mournfully, and while other characters would die or disappear during the course of the movie, López Vázquez was always there at the end, as a mute witness to whatever chicanery or abuse the movie had depicted. The censors left him alone, and it was easy to think of José Luis López Vázquez as the conscience of the country.

Pujol heard me out with similarly heavy eyes. Every so often he murmured some comment under his breath that I couldn't understand. At some point it occurred to me that I was not the sort of man he'd want teaching his young boys. But it also occurred to me that I was not the sort of man who should care what two-bit directors like Pujol and the state he worked for and sought to furnish with properly indoctrinated young men thought. Time to get up and leave and keep going? Time to tell Amparo and Antonio, in all their Old World ways, good-bye? By the time I'd finished my explanation to Pujol, I realized I'd just confessed.

I'd always been fascinated by acts of confession. Someone kneeling at a confession box in a dark corner of a church with her heels splayed out reciting her sins in a desultory whisper could incite in me a high degree of wonder. Would it be stretching the point to say that during the act of confession this woman's life had come to this? Once she'd risen to her feet absolved of her sins, would it be wrong to think that a new life had begun? The next breath she drew would be sinless and, if she could keep her mind blank, the one after that. It all depended on whether the black-clad priest huddled inside his box uttered the words *Yo te absuelvo*.

So I sat there in front of Pujol's desk, my life come to this. Strange to think that a boy growing up in the hard-drinking, golf-playing Protestant reaches of Kentucky would come to a dead stop in a small town outside Barcelona, Spain, called San Cugat de Vallés, but there I sat, prisoner of love, sinner supreme, waiting to hear whether I'd been absolved.

And Pujol sat behind his desk shaking his head and uttering in a low, pained voice, It shouldn't be, it shouldn't be.

I warned myself to be careful. Menendez at the start had been a sweetheart, too.

Pujol asked what he could do to help. I told him I'd been told I needed an ecclesiastical lawyer; a lawyer, I hastened to add, who knew what the Church offered as an instance of its grace, not how the Church could be gotten around. A lawyer, it went without saying, in keeping with my modest salary. What did he think?

Instead, without answering my question, Pujol asked me how Antonio was. Antonio was our link, and whatever service Pujol provided me, it was understood, would be in honor of his friend. I had learned that it was customary to mention that linking friend at this moment. (The word the Spanish use is *enchufe*, which means "connection," as in the connection you make when you plug a light into a socket.) The detour into the friend's life should be brief and laudatory. But that heavy-hanging look in Pujol's eyes, as though the whole human comedy had passed his way, and that sympathetic tone to his voice made it hard for me to say that Antonio was fine, painting a lot, he sends his regards, and leave it at that.

I said I'd be honest. I was nowhere near understanding my future brother-in-law. Yes, he was painting, but it was as though he were marking time until he was visited by his next enthusiasm. I mentioned the castle-buying scheme that had brought us together. And I alluded to the great stake he had in his sister's life. Not how, in his enthusiasm, he'd groomed me to stand at his sister's side. But Pujol would have deduced that.

He said he remembered Antonio's "enthusiasms." The Opus Dei had been one of them. For a while Antonio had inspired them all with his zealous high spirits. Then he'd cooled off. With Antonio it came down to tying these enthusiasms together so that he didn't suffer too much of a lull. He was glad that I'd come along to befriend his friend.

He wrote the name and address not of a lawyer but of a well-situated priest in Barcelona whom I should go see.

I felt myself being handed on. The priest's name was Puig, very Catalan. He had studied the Church carefully and had a doctorate in theology—certainly the reason Pujol had thought of him on my behalf.

He spoke some English. He clearly relished the opportunity to speak with somebody outside the confines of his parish and gave me all the time I wanted. How did I find Spain? Ah, yes, the Valencian women—although I wanted to add that Amparo in no way resembled the typical Valencian woman, who could be as highly wrought and devious in her beauty as the Church. Whereas Amparo . . . Amparo in her purity . . . I said Valencia had given me the love of my life and left it at that. Father Puig sympathized. His smile was a fine, knowing crease, and the smiling crease at the corner of his eye came close to a wink. I liked him. It was impossible not to. Somehow the talk strayed to bullfighting—probably because Amparo had taken me to my first fight—and did I know on what this winning iconoclast of a priest had written his doctoral dissertation? The bullfight as a Christian allegory. Christ as the sacrificial bull? Or Christ as the bullfighter, transfigured in his suit of lights? We spent a long hour. Then, as the bull is handed on from the *torero* to the *picadores* to the *banderilleros* and back to the *torero,* who stands with his sword transformed into a *matador* now, Father Puig gave me the name of a friend of his who, better than being a lawyer, taught ecclesiastical law in a university and could advise me better than anybody he knew.

The university was the University of Navarra, in Pamplona, and maybe it was the running of the bulls there that had brought that particular friend to mind. I combined two days off with a weekend and drove there. Did I know Navarra was known for its fierce devotion to the Holy Roman Catholic Church and had furnished the cause with a disproportionately high percentage of soldiers during Franco's uprising? I did not. Past the bull running and the trout streams that must have been nearby, I knew nothing about Pamplona or Navarra. Not that the University of Navarra was a Catholic university, also Opus Dei-run? I did not.

Pamplona was built on a hill, inside a loop of a river. I walked the city. I wrote Amparo from there. You felt defended here, borne up, within the river's freshening embrace. You could look off across the plain and see mountains rising in the north. We would live here someday! We must! Standing out on the city's ramparts I felt an instant's loneliness unlike any I'd ever felt before: a sense of utter incompletion, an insupportable lack. The distance separating Pamplona from Valencia took on a metaphysical dimension. I thought of Zeno's parable of Achilles and the tortoise. Halve the distance separating you from the woman you love; then halve that. You might think one day you'll arrive, but you never will.

The University of Navarra lay outside town. Professor Alvarez gave me half an hour. He was the first Spaniard who asked me if I knew the difference between liberty and libertinism. I supposed I did. Are we at liberty to commit acts of libertinism? I supposed we weren't. So liberty, by definition, carries a sense of its own restraints. It would seem so. I wanted to remind Professor Alvarez that he was not a priest but a scholar with a fund of knowledge that might be helpful to me, and that if he planned to lead me in Socratic loops for the next half hour I didn't have the time. But I didn't have anywhere else to go. We are at liberty to marry but not to commit acts of libertinism within the marriage bounds. Did I know what the ultimate act of libertinism was? No, I didn't. I was to think. I was afraid Professor Alvarez was confusing me with one of his students whom he could send away with a problem to solve. Self-dissolution was the quintessential libertine act. Are we at liberty to destroy the very grounds on which our liberty is based? Only if we are incorrigible libertines, I ventured to answer. A marriage that contemplates the act of self-destruction from the start would therefore be a contradiction in terms, would it not? I nodded and slumped. We are not free to destroy the grounds for our freedom, if that's what you mean, I said. We'd be left hanging in air. Slumping, I might have seemed to be hanging there before Professor Alvarez. Then he snapped me up. If within the bounds of your marriage, which you freely entered into, you and your wife made a pact to commit the ultimate act of libertinism, your marriage would be null and void, having contradicted itself from the start. Would it not?

He gave me a triumphant little laugh. Then he did tell me to go off and think about it and come back and tell him what the solution to my dilemma should be. I let my nerves unravel then. I groaned. My Spanish stacked up in my mouth. I couldn't come back. I lived many kilometers away. I worked. My fiancée, *mi novia,* was a delicate creature. She'd been raised to submit to the powers that be. She had a rebellious nature but without the nerves to back it up. When brought to her knees she had this look, this submissive, schooled expression, that Spanish girls like her must have worn since the beginning of time, or since Isabel, the Catholic queen, had cleansed the peninsula of all extraneous races and creeds. I didn't know how many disappointments she could take.

I tried to tell Professor Alvarez I urgently needed to bring it all down from the realm of rarefied speculation to the world of nuts and bolts, but my Spanish got nowhere near that. Nuts and bolts. I made a pantomiming attempt to describe the objects in question, how they screwed together to achieve a fit, and he surely misinterpreted that.

Libertinism.

I asked him for a name.

He gave me the name of a lawyer in Madrid, the biggest libertine in the profession, I supposed.

I drove to Madrid, up on its arid plateau.

This lawyer had a narrow office looking out on Madrid's broad Avenida de Castellana. Alvarez had been his teacher. The narrowness of the office looking out on that broad busyness below made me think of the arrow slits in castle gates and walls. The lawyer's name was Juan Solares. He looked like a harried but still irrepressible boy, with lively squirrel eyes and a turned-up nose. He spoke in breathless salvos. Professor Alvarez seemed to inspire a great deal of merriment in him, and he recollected a moment when as a student he had gotten a similar tongue-in-cheek Socratic treatment. I had not been aware that it had been tongue-in-cheek. Oh, yes, but with the best intentions. Liberty and libertinism, eh? Juan Solares would do what he could to help me in honor of his old professor, whom, in his eminence, he clearly revered.

I had to tell him the story of how I'd met Amparo, though, which meant the *Cristoforo Colombo*, Antonio, the high seas. I tried to describe Amparo to him, the wealth of things that went on in her eyes, her large and mobile mouth. The fountain effect of her laughter. Time was, a man knew how to speak in praise of the lady he loved. But I was in a foreign land, limited to a language not yet my own, and, as with Father Puig and

Professor Alvarez, I reached a point where words—anybody's words—mocked what they sought to celebrate. I fell back on Amparo's incomparableness, insisting that no one in my country even came close. Solares nodded wholeheartedly. It turned out that although he'd gone to Narrava to college and lived in Madrid, his mother's family came from Valencia, and during summers there on the beach he had gotten a wild adolescent's impression of what female beauty was all about. I had to listen to the tale of a teenaged romance. The traffic roared by below in regulated surges, spiked by the drilling din of motorbikes without mufflers. And somewhere in that street noise and that noisy, rollicking story of his, Solares was telling me what Alvarez had meant. You are at liberty to get married, but if you tell yourselves in advance, If this doesn't work we'll get a divorce, you are inviting in the ultimate act of libertinism. And since liberty and libertinism don't mix, just as creation and destruction don't, you are involved in a nonsensical act, which could be grounds for annulment. I protested that no one married in the United States without knowing that divorce was a possible outcome. And Solares said, Not good enough. You and your first wife . . . and he waited for me to give her name—after all, hadn't he already told me of a youthful indiscretion of his?—but I kept her name to myself. You and she, he went on, sat down together somewhere—out beside a swimming pool, he supposed, or on the edge of a bed—and spoke the words, which could be recalled to the comma, translated, sworn to, notarized, stamped and sealed. I promise to marry you and to divorce you if I don't like the way things work out. That's how seriously I take my marriage vows. Do you promise me the same thing? Get her to say that she did, and we'll draw it all up and submit it to the Tribunal de la Rota and see where we get.

Tribunal de la Rota?

The Roman court that makes these decisions in two or three years' time.

I wasn't being gallant. The reason I hadn't given my first wife's name was that I didn't want to mix our life together with this one. I had an intimation of what it would be like to dump those cloudy turbulent times on this time-sealed scene that was Franco's Spain, and I quailed.

Wasn't there a special favor I qualified for? Some obscure dispensation?

I asked for a name.

Midway down La Mancha in the city of Albacete, Solares had a friend I might find it interesting to talk to.

I drove to Albacete. It was a nondescript city set out on a plain. A depot. The friend, Ramón García, lived in a nondescript neighborhood of high-rises containing small apartments, each with a balcony crammed with plants and hanging wash and orange canisters of butane gas. The apartments smelled of gas and the olive oil used for cooking, even with the balcony door open. The background sound was always the radio from someone else's apartment. One of the songs of the day was *"Espera un poco, un poquito mas,"* which translated, "Wait just a little, just a little more," and which Amparo, before Menendez's reversal, had adopted as our song and sung to me promisingly, as if a final countdown to our wait had truly begun. I'd now begun to interpret it as a song of eternal postponement, bringing to mind the lovers forever out of reach on Keats's Grecian urn. I heard that song again and again. Ramón wanted to know how Juan was, and we went through Juan Solares and his office above the bustle of Madrid. His irrepressible good humor. His *simpatía*. Ramón and Juan had been companions in the *colegio*. Sooner or later every boy in that *colegio* had undergone a crisis, a dark night of the soul, if you will, and Juan had been there to help pull them through. I didn't interrupt. Ramón began to tell a story of some *genialidad* of Juan's and I began to tell mine, so that the two stories ran parallel for a while. I was on my way to completing a circuit of the eastern half of Spain, surely there was someone . . . Then it occurred to me that I really didn't know *why* Juan Solares had sent me to Ramón García, only that I would find him interesting to talk to.

A woman entered with a tray full of bottles, soft drinks, beer and tonic water, and another with small pieces of bread, cheese, *serrano* ham, almonds and olives. I stopped my story, Ramón García stopped his, and we thanked her and served ourselves. She was a woman perhaps nearing forty. I don't want to say nondescript (I realized, even then, that in seeing every woman in light of Amparo I was seeing no woman as she truly was, a blinding side effect of consuming love). Thin shoulders, thin-faced, a pleasing demeanor, distrustful eyes. Ramón, at her side, was more bearish. No evidence of children. When we paused in our eating, Ramón began to counsel me. Either he had been listening to my story all along, or Juan Solares had called ahead to fill him in. As Professor Alvarez might have called ahead to Juan, and as Father Puig might have contacted the professor after Pablo Pujol had contacted him once Antonio had made it clear to Pujol that I was to be regarded as his newest enthusiasm.

There were good men in the Catholic Church, and the Church, even as an institution, was not bad. To deal with the Church requires patience and a historical long view. The Church took its sacraments seriously— really, would we have it any other way? Ramón went on. The Church loomed large in Ramón's life. It was the rock you clung to, even though it might have been the rock that had sunk your ship. When, finally, you swam away from it, it was still the rock of reference in your life. Ramón talked like a preacher, in parables, in metaphors extended to the horizon. There was a reason: He had been a priest. Shipwrecked, he had eventually let go of his rock and swum off. He had married this woman who had served us. He had made dry land and this apartment looking onto hundreds more like it. His story bore on mine in that patience, faith and steadfastness (on that rock) had seen him through, and now he was an unembittered man who was reaping his reward. I could be, too.

Espera un poco, un poquito mas.

I had learned my lesson. I thanked Ramón and his bride (with the distrustful eyes) and did not ask for a name.

I drove through the towns of La Mancha at night. They were closed, a glimmering bone-white in the moonlight. When the Spanish slept they battened down the hatches and slept. All I could do was keep an eye out for the *guardia civil* and drive through. Perhaps the desire to drive the *pueblos* of Spain with my wife at my side came from that night when, with almost no traffic, the towns handed me on. I don't want him, you take him in. Sorry, not me. I went through a self-pitying stage of the night, then I got angry and clear-headed and with my little Seat took a kind of aim. I was through begging. I'd give them a chance. But if the Spanish continued playing hard to get, I would just take Amparo away from them. They had until December 26. This stage took me out of La Mancha and into the mountains rimming Valencia. Onteniente was just beyond those mountains, and Antonio never went to bed before four A.M.

Full circle? Not quite. I caught Antonio with a brush in his hand. He would pour a watery acrylic mixture over a canvas, dab at it with rags and rollers and sponges until he had created a texture that was both craggy and fine, then study it until from out of those creases and crags and patches of deepening color he saw one of his women emerging. Then he would paint her before she could disappear.

I sat there until he caught her. He got her form, the windswept line of her gown and hair. The face was for later. Anyway, the face was always the same. I told him where Pablo Pujol had sent me and that Pablo Pujol had sent him, Antonio, his warmest regards. I recounted the circuit I'd been on. Amparo, it turned out, had been trying to reach me. Tomorrow, which was a Monday, I was expected in Valencia. Antonio would call ahead and explain my absence at school. Everything was about to be resolved.

Antonio tried to keep a secret. But his imagination fed on itself and improved endlessly on what it saw. After all, witches didn't mist up out of that rock. Ladies did, worth waiting for, fighting for. We lay side by side in his twin beds, and before I'd gone to sleep he told me what I had in store. The archbishop of Valencia. Antonio and his father, plugging one *enchufe* into another, had gotten Amparo and me an audience with the archbishop himself.

Amparo was waiting at a café outside the archbishop's palace. After having been disappointed at stop after stop around the eastern half of Spain, I couldn't make myself believe the archbishop was going to right all wrongs in a single stroke. I arrived in a frazzled, jumped-up state and tried not to let my disappointment show. Amparo, I could see, was of two minds. She wanted to believe what Antonio had led her to believe, that *enchufes* counted for something and that when archbishops granted audiences it was because they had favors to bestow; a girlish, dream-chasing expression flitted around on the surface of what was solemn and stricken and without a recourse to her name. That second Amparo didn't have a name. I wanted to shake her. Tracing my route from Barcelona to Pamplona to Madrid to Albacete to Onteniente to Valencia and arch-bishopland, I looked for some way to make her laugh.

We saw the archbishop the hour before lunch, one-thirty in the after-noon. He was a small man dressed in gold-embroidered vestments and seated in a large, high-backed chair upholstered in velvet. His beanie was knocked askew. We pleaded our case to him but we had no new ar-guments to make. We were open and innocent and trusting and had been misinformed. We were in love. We were looking to the Church to give us a new life. I tried to do something with Valencia's *patrona,* the Virgin of the Uncared-For, setting myself up as one of them, one of those or-phaned infants peeking out from under the Virgin's skirts in the Basilica, only in my case I had come to Amparo for my *amparo.* I got tangled up. There was no telling what came through, other than my earnest and boyish desire. But it didn't matter anyway. I was convinced that the archbishop, looking undersized in his vestments and high-backed chair, had gone to sleep. The priest there to take care of him seemed to think so, too. Like a referee about to signal the end of a match, he was on the point of waving us silent. But Amparo knew better. Priests never slept.

And archbishops never, never slept. Or, you could say, when they slept the whole history of Roman Catholic Christendom awoke and spoke through them, so they continued to function anyway.

With his eyes still closed, the archbishop drew a rattling breath and told us he would pray for us. He said he would pray for us as if we could expect concrete results. We were still God's children. He'd pray for us and get back to us tomorrow. He'd pray for us and, meanwhile, we could start folding those invitations into their envelopes. The priest at his side gave us an open-eyed smile, astonished at this unprecedented act of generosity on the archbishop's part. They were a team, a sleepy get-lost and a wide-awake what-more-could-you-ask.

I kissed Amparo good-bye right out in front of his palace. I kissed her with an urgency and a smack meant to be a cannon shot across the arch-bishop's bow, and across the bow of each of his little minions I had met on this trip. But my knees were weak. I had barely slept for the last four days. I had disillusioned students to teach. To buck me up Amparo said, He said he'd pray for us, didn't he? and I'm afraid I laughed in her face.

. . .

THROUGH CANTABRIA and into the Basque Country. Getxo, Barakaldo, Galdakao—names that are hard to pronounce. We stop in Durango, probably because we can say it on first try.

It is not a town where she'll have any desire to stay. There's a small river running through it; there are bridges and a few older men fishing from the banks. There's greenery—patches of grass and spring flowers. At the town center the stone buildings are nice. We stand in front of the *ayuntamiento*, the town hall, which, in whatever town we visit, she never fails to locate, in honor of her father, who worked in one all his life— where, as a girl, she went to bring him home for lunch. Basque *ayun-tamientos*, as a rule, look like little fortresses to me, and the one in Durango is no exception. But a cold wind is blowing down out of the mountains, which are visible off to the north, lush pastureland halfway up the slope, then forests. The mountains are beautiful, the blocks of apartment buildings thrown up before them are not. I suggest an early supper, but Amparo skips it and goes to bed. She's been riding a high since the Cantabrian sea charged her up; today it's run out on her and stranded her here.

And the town of Durango makes her nervous. If truth be told, the Basque Country makes her nervous—not because she fears being the unlucky victim of a terrorist's bomb, but because something in the Basque dilemma speaks to her about the terms of her own love-hate affair with her country, its richness, its geographical and demographic diversity and its oppressive hegemonic weight. And I suspect it's not just my wife. Most Spaniards sensitive to these matters need a figure in whom they can embody their contradictions. Someone who can lash out for them and someone who can love the land as blindly and trustingly as a child. There must be Spaniards out there for whom entering the Basque Country is like entering a land of dreams. The same dream, in the course of a night, can arouse and deplete you many times over. Tonight my wife is not up to that.

This is not the place to recount the history of the Basque struggle. Most Spaniards would say, How wrongheaded and, at least as long as Franco ruled, how gutsy and how romantic. Basque resistance to Franco was the resistance that Catalans and Valencians and even Galicians might have mounted and didn't. Under the current constitution, however, the Basques enjoy more governmental autonomy than they've ever had a historical claim to, and the separatist element among them, given to acts of outrage, has lost the sympathy of nearly all Spaniards. On a number of occasions the separatists have seemed ready to give up. Then there is a resumption of the shootings and bombings and the nightmare continues, or the sleeper becomes aware that he has never fully woken up.

That separatist element is known as ETA—Euskadi Ta Askatasuna,

Basque Fatherland and Liberty—and its signs, slapped on the walls of buildings, on monuments and bridges, in dripping black paint, are all over town. I pass bars that display the ETA flag in their windows and photographs of ETA heroes imprisoned or killed. There may be a block of these bars, something like a martyrs' row, right in the center of any Basque town. There is one in Durango. Teenaged kids are hanging out in front of its doors. But, then, there are teenaged kids hanging out all over town, on the plazas, under the arcades, beside the river. When Amparo passes these kids she stiffens, and I think I know why. There's not one of them who doesn't have a decision to make. Kids that age elsewhere might turn to shoplifting to express their defiance, or some effrontery they can commit with their cars, but each of these Basque kids has to decide whether to be a terrorist.

Not everyone will put it to himself like that. ETA has managed to alienate even a majority of Basques. Its killings have come to seem like senseless slaughter, and its so-called "revolutionary tax" has been thought to have ruined a once solid economic base and to have driven off foreign investment. But kids know better than adults—it's just that what kids know is not always available to them as knowledge. It's more like a climate, information they absorb. ETA is there for them. Their measure of their courage is ETA. The alternative to their free time, to their aimless, jobless milling around, is ETA. The name of what they know least and fear most about themselves is ETA. The decision will have to be made.

It seems heartlessly unfair to me that a boy—and not just a boy—born in this country should be confronted, inescapably, with that dilemma, should have to go from his mother's womb to the enwombing world of these aggrieved and unavenged towns. Amparo, mother of two, of a son who expressed his defiance through a skateboard and some unruly taunting of police, stiffens with the thought that if her son had been born here he would have been driven to those dream extremes. And whichever extreme he embodied he would have somehow been expressing her. The violent son, the sacrificial son. The mother enraged, the mother in mourning.

A contemporary *pieta*.

. . .

ONCE, when I was a boy of ten, my friends and I were playing King of the Hill and a fight broke out. I charged up the hill, which was a terrace in a neighbor's yard, and an older, bigger boy knocked me back down. He was using his fists. My mother was standing behind the neighbor's picture window observing it all. The neighbor had her nose pressed incredulously against the glass, but my mother stood back with a coffee cup in her hand and let it go on. This was a weekday. My father, who spoiled me, was gone. If I took my licks and didn't give up, Mother reasoned, I'd thank her later on.

She was right. I hadn't given up, and I thanked her then. Pablo Pujol, to his credit, tried again. This time he inquired around and gave me the name of the best ecclesiastical lawyer on the scene. Except that he wasn't on the scene. He was in Rome. I wrote him. I told him I'd heard rumors of certain dispensations—Saint Peter's or Saint Paul's—that would wipe my slate of sins clean in exchange for a conversion. If I became a Catholic my Protestant past would not be held against me. That, it stood to reason, would include my ill-begotten marriage. I was prepared to come to Rome and fall on my knees before whatever representative the pope named, if that was what it took. If the Church could sell an annulment for forty-five thousand dollars, I could fall on my knees with my fingers crossed and make the appropriate sounds. Or if the Church would settle for a pilgrimage of some sort, I could perform one. Two Irishmen taught with me at the school, and one of them claimed that a thoroughly documented pilgrimage to Santiago entitled me to another sort of dispensation, although he wasn't sure what. My mother might pull her hair and count me as lost, but I'd play their game. I'd worship their relics. In the cathedral at Valencia the desiccated arm of Valencia's patron saint, San Vicente, was on display. It looked exactly like a carob pod—that flat and bumpy and that shade of brown—enlarged to perhaps three times the size. If not San Vicente's arm, was there some other saint's body part before which I could perform an obeisance? Flagellation? In Mexico I'd seen the *penitentes* whipping themselves out of the desert and on into church. I could do that. Amparo herself had seen women climbing the zigzagging ascent of the rock-sharp *via crucis* on their knees after one of their prayers had been answered, and that was okay. I could take punishment. I had knees begging to be bloodied.

Some other body part of mine? Let's talk about it.

My *enchufes* were holding up. Within two weeks I had an answer from the lawyer in Rome. The Spanish are florid letter writers. It was never "Dear Sir." It was "My most beloved and estimable sir." The lawyer, a Spaniard working out of Rome by the name of Francisco Morales Cabanes, was deeply grateful to have the opportunity to serve me—*muy agradecido*. Unfortunately, the various dispensations I had asked about—and most specifically Saint Peter's—did not apply in my case. Yes, it was true, Saint Peter's dispensation would, in a manner of speaking, absolve me of the sins I'd committed before converting to Catholicism, but my first marriage could not be considered one of them since it was a sacramental bond that the Church recognized as valid. In other words, I might have sinned myself silly in that benighted youth of mine, but in the Church's eyes the one thing I'd done worth preserving was marrying my first wife. Sorry, it was the sole bright spot on an otherwise blemished record—if I cared to view it in that light. That is, Saint Peter could absolve me of drunken fornication, outraged protesting, destruction of government property, tax evasion and, yes, whatever innocent shoplifting, joyriding or vandalizing I'd committed. But not that marriage.

My grandfather had made enough of a name for himself in the First

Christian Church to get a plaque put up in his alma mater, wooed his wife out of a Saturday-night congregation with his flashing black eyes, fathered a first daughter who became my mother and who revered her father to the extent that even though she opposed my marriage she insisted the wedding be held in a place where she could look up and see her father's name and reputation upheld even as I stepped off, she was sure, into hell.

And for that I was unentitled to any blessings the Catholic Church could dish out? Because of my mother and grandfather and a two-year farce of a marriage I was to be denied the love of my life?

In his last page Francisco Morales went into a lengthy peroration. Floridity aside, there was something going on with his prose. I was to think back. I was to wrack my brains. I was to retrace my memories into the dimmest reaches. I was to make the superhuman effort it took to do all this. Was I back there yet? Was I at least getting close? Could I, in what Morales knew must seem like the dark ages to me now, or even further back at the dawn of time, recall with enough conviction that I could write it down on paper and take it to a translator and take the translation to a notary public so that it could made official and sent under the right stamped seal to him, there, in the holy city, Rome . . . could I recall if I had ever . . . and delicacy aside now, the law demanded clarity on these issues . . . consummated that first marriage of mine? Because if I hadn't, my marriage would be invalid from the start, or would still be hanging fire (he used a more discreet term, *pendiente*). A word from me to him to that effect, properly presented, would set the whole process in motion. That my first wife might remember it differently would have to be considered, but so too would the fact that from what Morales had heard of the '60s in my country something of a sexual free-for-all had taken place and proving who had done what in that regard would be all but impossible.

No offense intended. (*Sin la menor intención de ofender su altísimo honor o el de su ilustrísima patria.*)

No offense taken.

I read the letter through again. It took a second reading for me to realize that I was being coached, in time-honored Spanish style, to plead impotence on my wedding night. And on all subsequent wedding nights. Morales could not advise me to lie, he could only insinuate that it might be possible, at such a distant time (little over three years had passed since our wedding date), to misremember. Americans, in addition to being sexually promiscuous, had no sense of history. Everybody knew that.

No offense.

If I was willing to make pilgrimages, worship relics, bloody my knees ascending the stations of the cross, couldn't I admit to a sexual malfunction at the crucial moment?

I thought I could. I actually drafted most of a document that I would get translated and notarized stating that I had failed my wife miserably in my matrimonial duties. I went on to excoriate myself for being an imposter in the taking of my vows and to excoriate the times in that licentious country of mine for making me cower when I should have crowed lustily . . . but I couldn't finish. Who would want to marry such a man? If I got my rhetoric going I might make the Church believe I had failed my first wife, but in the process I could portray myself only as a dishonorable weakling. I might get one marriage annulled but not the second one approved.

But that was not the real reason. The real reason I didn't finish was because, as the saying had it, there was some shit I would not eat.

I wrote Señor Morales that consummation had occurred. What I was willing to swear to was that my first wife and I had openly discussed the possibility of divorce before we'd married. I'd go on the record as having done that. Morales wrote back asking for the name and address of my first wife. I hesitated, but friends of a sort we had been at the end, so I gave him her name and the last address I had. The diocese corresponding to that address would have to investigate. I experienced a kind of visceral shudder. Morales hinted—very lightly—that this can of worms could be left unopened if I'd get over my macho sexual pride. I wrote him back, in an equally roundabout way, that he'd have to open that can.

Then I forgot about it because shortly after I sent that last letter off to Morales, Father Menendez back in Valencia had a change of heart. Amparo was excited. Could I come at once?

I got the Irishmen to cover my classes and drove through that howling wind between Tarragona and Viñaroz to be at her side.

Simply put, Menendez told us, as we sat before him in his *fiscal's* office, we had been too honest. By now my Spanish was quite good. *Demasiado honestos* can mean only one thing. But I cocked my head as if to give him my good ear and wondered if he would mind repeating. I was curious if a priest could say that twice: "too honest"? He could: *Sí, demasiado honestos.* Then he looked down. I shot a glance at Amparo, who managed to glance back, but mainly her eyes were trained on Menendez. We had come because Menendez had called to say he was willing to reconsider, but this phrasing of his had put her on alert. She knew what she knew about the Church and its history and some of its bizarre ways. In her convent school every morning while she and her classmates ate breakfast the nuns would read to them from the lives of the saints, and she knew you could eat bread and marmalade and listen to the gruesome details of a saint's martyrdom at the same time. That was the kind of balancing act she'd been brought up to perform.

But "too honest"? Virtue on a sliding scale?

My first thought was that the lawyer Morales had contacted Menendez and Menendez was chiming in. You did but you didn't. On this matter of consummation, I'll blink if you will.

But that wasn't what he meant. He meant he was sorry for us, and it suddenly occurred to me that when Menendez had dashed our hopes that first time he had not been a happy man. Amparo had insisted I just didn't know, but perhaps I did. Perhaps being a Catholic priest in Franco's Spain did not mean you had nothing in common with a kid from Kentucky with its stripped-down, straight-talking Protestant ways. Could I have been right? Had Menendez been caught, as we had, and was he now sorry as hell?

Poor young people, too honest for their own good. It's time they were rewarded.

But Menendez could not pretend we had not told him what we had. What he could do was not stand in our way if we went to some other diocese in Spain and told a different story. And then, if permission to marry were granted in that diocese, he would not stand in our way if we applied to have the license transferred to Valencia. That was, he implied, a bureaucratic matter. He approved transfers of that sort every day. He would be offending his fellow *fiscales* elsewhere in Spain if he failed to. The marriage could take place right here, if we moved fast (he did not put it in quite those words), on December 26, in the Basilica, under the figure of a Virgin sheltering the homeless and loaded with jewels from the wealthy widows of the city.

I flashed on the sleepy figure of the archbishop with his beanie knocked awry. It wasn't just Menendez who'd have to look the other way. I almost asked what it would take to get the archbishop on board, too, but Amparo was squeezing my wrist now with a fierce sort of joy, and although her eyes were still fixed on Menendez they were brimming with tears.

We thanked him. We tried not to gush and Amparo tried to keep her tears from falling on his desk. Bygones would be bygones. Poor man, what he had gone through on our behalf. While I had been racing around Spain Menendez had been going through a dark night of his own. I wanted to go up and cuff him on the shoulder. Those shadows under his eyes, that sag to his face—he would eat and rest better now.

We drove straight to Amparo's house and told her parents. Her father immediately called his son. Two hours later a friend dropped Antonio at his parents' door. To get permission to marry in another diocese Amparo would have to establish a residence there. An employer would have to front for her; so would a landlord. Witnesses would have to be lined up. Señor Ferri knew both what it would take in City Hall and what sort of network of friends. Once again we were in Antonio's hands.

. . .

THE TIME I'VE SPENT watching her sleep, waiting for her to awake, so that I can bend over and kiss her on the forehead and receive her first smile of the day, knowing her smiles, their entire range, from the one that puts a brave face on another day of pain, malaise, ailments that no doctor has diagnosed to our satisfaction, to the smile so utterly unburdened and free for the day that I can only compare it to the rising of the sun—for me and on me alone. She sleeps and sleeps, then she awakes smiling. I kiss her.

And why shouldn't there be a town that would, in exchange for the limits it imposes on our range of activities, relieve her of her pain? We'll live with this if you allow us to live without that. On her good days she's such a delight to be with, what town wouldn't want to make her that deal?

Spain. Imagine it, Sancho. Rid it of all that would do my lady harm and what a paradise it would be!

We leave the Basque Country. The towns are lovely in their close green hills. I think she thinks they're diseased.

We enter Navarra. The valleys broaden, scoop out deep broad hollows where wheat and grapes grow. Towns are situated on the slopes, the warm ocher of their stone giving off tints of red in the afternoon sun. Pamplona lies ahead, and although we said no cities I'm curious to see how the city might have changed since I came here looking for help, and Amparo doesn't object. I was a lonely man then, being kept from the woman I loved. I have to remind myself that I won.

But I get lost driving in. We can't find the *plaza mayor*. When we find it, it turns out to be an industrial gray, more shabby than austere. We circle out from it, and a policeman points out to us the route the bulls run during the fiesta of San Fermín. The bull route is commonplace, the bullring more of that industrial cement, and the statue of Hemingway erected before it is a melodramatic affront to what was clear and direct and best about the man's prose. I recognize none of it, nothing. Not until we position ourselves on the old city walls do the remains of the outer defenses seem familiar to me, but the river does not trace a loop partially to enclose the town. It flows by and is gone. I remember writing Amparo from this town, telling her that here, one day, was a place we would have to live. It was borne up, I said. I see now that I made it up. I saw what I needed to see, what my longing made sure was there. It occurs to me that I could present this to her as the ultimate tribute, a city made over on her behalf, but I find it too depressing. I have never been in this city before. I have been in a fantasy Pamplona. Years ago, driving around Spain attempting to clear away all obstacles to our marriage, I was in a Spain of the mind.

We eat a late lunch there. We were right. No cities. Towns.

She will have recognized a certain drivenness to my driving. I turn us south. I don't quite know what I'm doing. We pass by towns that normally we would stop in and explore. She catches sight of one, Ciranqui, still in Navarra, in her side mirror and insists we go back. Perfect. Perfectly preserved. The steep streets, the stone, the plaza and the church. A *casa señorial* with its carved escutcheon at every turn. Unspoiled. Untouched. No empty houses. No stores. Where do the people shop? Where are the people? We're fifteen minutes walking the streets before we meet a woman who tells us this is the way they like it, not a single sign or trace of glitter to catch the eye. Many of the home owners, it seems, are city dwellers who come to enjoy the town on weekends as it exclusively once was, and remains. It is clean, the streets swept. Under its arches and in its brief tunnels the dankness is so pure it might have been distilled. The woman speaks to us in an appealing voice, a lulling lisp, a background of pollinating bees, no sting. Honeyed. When Amparo and I get back into the car she gives me a look that says, We asked for it, here it is, a town with no smoke or motors or screaming come-ons, minus almost everything but that soothing voice. Who's conjuring whom? What is going on?

We pass through Estella, and she looks at me again. This is a town full of life, with its old *barrio,* its river, its commerce mindfully situated around its *plaza mayor,* which is ample and colonnaded and filling with promenaders. Just driving through, we can tell it's a town where a balance has been struck. We can see it in the way the people pace and hear it in the modulated ease of their voices. It is time to start looking for a *hostal,* but I don't stop. Amparo chooses not to say anything. We enter the region of Rioja.

Known for its wines, of course. More wheat and vineyards, then it's all vineyards, and the stocks have just begun to leaf. This is one of the moments to marvel at them; the other is when they're heavy with fruit. But now the tender green leaves issuing from those shaggy gnarled stocks, stocks that will yield for decades before they need to be replaced, speaks of rejuvenescence in the simplest sense. We're at the end of April, and it's everywhere. On the plains of Castile, towns were located three or four kilometers apart, with those crumbling *palomares* clustered around them, but here in this wide upland basin of Rioja it's all vineyards, the stubby, tough, all-but-petrified stocks coming back to life, sending out their shoots of green over just-turned earth.

I won't say I'm bored. Quixote would have found nothing to engage him here, and neither do I.

We cross the river Ebro. We come to the city of Logrones, and skirt it.

We enter another expanse of vineyards, highlighted by the setting sun. There are birds, swallows, not many; most of them will be flying over the wheat. Amparo sees a magpie, big, black-and-white. Scouting. The magpies will be there later to eat the grapes. A scarecrow would not be beside the point. A gangly, whirling dervish of a bird-grappling scarecrow. With his boulder-sized sidekick.

Save the grapes!

Suddenly we're in the sierra. It will have a name. Sierra de la Demanda—Amparo looks it up—which is a little too contrived for my taste. I laugh and question her eyesight (she's just begun to need reading glasses but has left them behind in one of the hotels), or I question her motives. What "demands" will she make of me?

Stop and find us a place to spend the night, she says.

I can do that, I say.

But I can't. The valley we are driving up has narrowed precipitously and the towns we pass in the widenings look half deserted and stripped of their accommodations. They are returning to the rock out of which they're built, towns that are losing their right-angled edges to the years and are coming to resemble the excrescences of the hillsides, excrescences wonderfully shaped to resemble towns.

Natural marvels.

I tell my wife I'm looking, as she can see.

But for whatever reason—that pall hanging over the boys of the Basque Country, the boy I'd been when I'd spread my lovesickness over Pamplona and never seen a thing—I'm driving like an American now in a particular American mood. There is a mood you can enter in that country of ours when you feel that, as vast as it is, it is still possible to outdrive it and get the best of it once and for all. Under the influence of that mood, boys point their cars toward California and let rip. I'm feeling some of that now, here in the Sierra of the Demand.

And Amparo knows me well enough to know it. She says, There may be places to stay, *casas rurales* [a kind of bed and breakfast] if not hotels.

I tell her we can look. But in the next town we come to I pause only to glance up and down a couple of intersecting streets before blasting on through.

This is not doing any good, she says. Tell me what's the matter.

Tell me what's the matter with you.

With me? It's been a long day. I'm tired. I want to rest.

It hasn't been that long. You couldn't get out of bed until almost noon. Put the seat back and lie down if you're sleepy, I say, my eyes fixed on the road.

She doesn't answer, but the seat stays up.

I really don't expect her to say another word until, perhaps, we go to bed. Then it will be *buenas noches,* but so clipped and cool it will be like the barrier she's erected between us.

She surprises me. She says, I agreed to come with you. We've been doing this for almost two months now. Name me one town that comes anywhere close to meeting your standards.

I pause for a moment, eyes straight ahead as I run out the gears and we get through another town. Then I name three towns. One in Extremadura, Zafra; one in Castile, Aguilar de Campó; and the last town we passed in Navarra, Estella.

She says, If I took you seriously enough to come out on this . . . this what?

Quest, I say.

This quest, then you can take me seriously enough to answer my question. We did not stop in Estella. We could have.

I liked the feel of it, I say.

Stop it. And her cool composure almost cracks.

Scratch Estella. Substitute Finisterre in Galicia, then.

You did not like that town, she insists. You just liked the name.

Down at the bottom of this narrow twisting valley we're driving along, it's nearly dark. We're ascending. I look up and most of the light left in the sky seems to be falling on a mountain peak still under snow off to the west. She won't say it again—find us a town with a hotel. But the clock is ticking, and for every minute I subject her to my maniacal driving she'll make me pay.

I don't really believe that. It's just that that feeling of being handed on has come over me again—town to town, authority to authority, what difference does it make?

We drive for another ten minutes without passing through a town. Her voice sounds apropos of nothing now, except the silence she's sculpted around her.

Some mornings I'm so tired I have to lie there and recuperate. I'm not making this up.

I pause. A long beat. Then, Be honest, I say, but not without gentleness. Most mornings.

Most mornings.

I can almost always tell by the day before, I say. You get too excited or you get upset and the next morning you pay the price. This argument today will keep you in bed the good part of tomorrow. But you know that.

She doesn't answer.

It's amazing, I continue. We make love and blow the roof off the house and you couldn't be happier, and I'm thinking why should that lay you low? Why shouldn't those nerves of yours be singing? Why shouldn't our lovemaking pick you up and let you fly?

I *do* fly, she says.

In your dreams.

It's lovely, she says. Sometimes I fly all night. You don't, do you?

A little. Along the ground.

Lástima, she says. It's a pity. She means it. She'd share it with me if she could.

Goddamn it, Amparo! I plead.

When a sign directs me off the highway three kilometers in to a town called Villoslada de Cameros, I follow it, although the sign has mentioned nothing about accommodations. I don't expect to find any. I expect to have to knock on doors to see if anyone in town will let my wife get the rest she needs, that someone like me, with his own heavy crowding needs, has driven her to.

But there is a *hostal*. It's there just before we cross a bridge into town. The bridge is stone, and it's barely wide enough for one car. At present, cows occupy it. Most are plodding up into the town, but two are bucking the traffic and coming down to drink from the stream. Their bells clang dully in counterpoint to the rushing water. No one is herding these cows. There *is* a man in charge of the *hostal*—I'm almost surprised. We take a room without asking to see it. We are told it looks out onto the town, over the bridge.

The next morning I'm up early, writing in my notebook certain ideas I've had. Then the present intrudes and I set my work aside and slip back into bed. She's waiting for me, I know. She went to sleep in an unreceptive mood; nonetheless, she doesn't want me to go off and leave her in Villoslada de Cameros. I lay a hand on her hip. There's a moment's pause, then she turns to me, and, as gingerly as if we were nursing a tiny flame along, we begin to make love. The flame begins to crackle and she's fully awake. I hear the cows outside again on the bridge, this time going out of town and up to their pastures; I know because I can hear them pass below our window. The clanging of their bells is the farthest thing from the rhythm of our lovemaking, but lovemaking, as inspired as it is, can adapt to almost any rhythm. We make love to the sound of cows plodding by. Before it's over we're half laughing, half sobbing our vows again. Then she's asleep and I'm dozing in her warmth.

· · ·

AMONG HIS FRIENDS Antonio numbered a certain actor and actress in Madrid. She was Julia and he Gregorio; they both worked steadily, and Julia, especially, had enjoyed considerable success. She had a wider range than her husband, who, an Argentine, was pretty much restricted to the role of a *galán*. Julia could be a breezy-minded redhead, in the style of Lucille Ball; then she could do roles when she seemed washed pale and plain and hardly had to exert herself to express the resentment of the unchosen, the barely seen. There'd been something about their marriage, some hitch, some hurdle that had made Antonio think they would be sympathetic to our predicament. Plus the fact, they were always acting. They acted on the stage twice a night, a before-supper performance and another at eleven o'clock. All Spanish actors did. You were that person you were paid to be double-time. It stood to reason you would leap at the chance to be somebody else.

Antonio called Julia and explained our case. Then he put me on the phone. Julia had a theatrical voice. It was like a spray of sultry perfume. An angel, if she was disposed in your favor, might breathe over you like that. She would do it. Like Pablo Pujol, she wanted to express to me how ashamed and sorry she was that her country had put me through so much grief.

I said that Spain had given me Amparo and how could I possibly complain?

I was not there when Amparo auditioned for her role as aspiring actress/live-in maid. I was down to my last peseta at the conclusion of each week and had to tear up the coast to teach my classes. I taught them breathlessly, I am sure, which must have made the students wonder what all the excitement was about. Did all Americans pant when they conjugated the verbs swim, swam, swum; lie, lay, lain? Antonio operated on as many fronts as it took and informed Pablo Pujol that I might be shaving some of my class times close, but he would have me there. Antonio had solicited the help of other friends in Madrid to serve as witnesses. These were two older women—one of whom was the owner of a gallery that had given Antonio his first show—who loved Antonio and would gladly perjure themselves when it came time to swear that they knew of no earlier marriage that might disqualify me for this one.

A new round of handing me on had begun.

When I was summoned—no more than three weeks had passed—I

begged a single midweek day off, which Pablo Pujol, in the name of his dear friend Antonio Ferri, gave me, and I drove again to Madrid.

Julia I liked. She stuck by her tack of grieving for me, and when we talked she looked deep into my eyes. Her eyes were lively, then suddenly stricken by what I must have been going through, and how was I not going to like her, suffering as she did for what her country and church were doing to me? Her husband barely got out of his satin bathrobe before going to the theater for the afternoon's performance. He was observant—he observed Amparo assiduously—but gave off an air of professional restraint, as if he'd not yet been handed his script. Unscripted, he had no comment to make. I didn't dislike him, but I saw the limits to his range.

The hour came when Antonio had us all on stage. Menendez's counterpart in Madrid was nothing like Menendez. The office where we filled out our application and signed our oaths had nothing in common with the archbishop's palace in Valencia. It was a large office with a counter, beyond which were situated a number of desks. In the immediate vicinity I saw no priests, although one passed through in back. Franco's photograph hung on the wall. The man who attended us—a functionary with a harried look who kept uttering *bueno* under his breath—didn't really see us until he recognized Julia and Gregorio, and then he swallowed a *bueno* or two. But the stir the two actors caused quickly died down. This was Madrid. This was the bureaucracy of Church and State grinding on.

We'd been too honest, we'd been told.

Antonio said when I came to the question about a possible impediment, including an earlier marriage, I was to write no. I wrote no. I'd be a liar if I said I didn't flash on my first wife in that moment, whose characteristic expression, when she wasn't mad as hell, was an affectionate needling grin. Julia and Gregorio swore that Amparo had been their employee residing at their house for the last six months. We met the two other witnesses to our trustworthiness and good faith and they also signed. Amparo's paperwork somehow got left for last, and although Antonio had dressed his sister in a drab green suit, befitting a maid, she was something of a showstopper as she filled out her page and signed and looked tremulously up at me. Julia managed a wet eye, which she dabbed at with a handkerchief. Gregorio still hadn't warmed to his part, and although he wished us well there was a judgmental set to his jaw. Or perhaps that was how Antonio had directed him. Antonio was no fool. A hint of disapproval from one of us might throw any suspicious functionary off the scent. Gregorio was to stand back, and nod, and all but shake his head at what this gringo was getting away with.

I had to remember that we were not married and I might not kiss the bride. We applied to have the wedding transferred to Valencia for December 26, still more than six weeks away. Amparo and I walked for an hour in Retiro Park, by ourselves. We didn't talk much. We were trying to establish a rhythm that would take us through the weeks ahead. To the innocent eye we might have been pacing like man and wife. Then I got back in my car and drove to Barcelona to teach, and Amparo, because she'd told herself she would and because a small superstitious voice told her there was always a price to pay, went off to clean Julia and Gregorio's house for them while they spent the afternoon on the stage.

Back in Barcelona I took a deep breath, and no telegram or phone call came to tell me I might not take another one. In a town next to the town where I taught I rented, for not much money, a large furnished stucco house within a grove of pines. It had high windows and cool tiles on the floor, but the day had been warm when I'd seen it and I rented it for the entire year. The couple in Barcelona who owned it were too old to use it even as a summer residence anymore. The four-poster bed was theirs. The mattress had lumps and swales that might have gone a century back, and there was one pillow of double length, a his-and-hers joined.

This would be our first house. I tried to picture Amparo in it, which brought its largeness, its draftiness, and its mustiness to the fore. In the kitchen there wasn't an inch of luster left, and I wondered if there wasn't some act of propitiation I needed to perform, some invocation of the lares and penates to get them on our side. I sat in a wicker armchair on the sunporch and waited for Amparo to walk around the corner. When she didn't, I asked myself just how I'd jinxed our cause now.

Nevertheless, I moved in. The weather turned cool and I turned on the two butane gas heaters, and lit a fire in the tiny ornamental fireplace, and more or less ran from one pocket of warmth to another. I walked down the railroad tracks to my teaching duties; I kept in shape. I made my phone calls from the *central* just off the town square. A family ran it—husband, wife and a daughter in her twenties. Occasionally a young man helped out, the son or son-in-law. It all had to be done manually, sticking those pegs in their corresponding holes, and the connections they gave you couldn't be counted on to last long. I called my parents from there, my sister. I tried to get things said quickly before the line went dead. I gave my parents the date. Families married families in Spain—it would mean everything if they could come. No time for my mother to inquire, Are you sure, really sure? How well have you thought this through? Or to insinuate: Get yourself caught in the coils of the Catholic Church and they'll bury you over there. Talk to you soon, I shouted down the line.

I waited out the weeks. A letter came from that Roman lawyer I'd forgotten about. He'd received a letter from my ex-wife. The lawyer wondered if she was sufficiently aware of the gravity of the situation, for, to judge by the letter's tone, she was too amused by the whole thing to do us much good. She'd said she would cooperate, but the lawyer's question to me was whether my ex-wife was capable of swearing with a straight face that before we even married we had agreed to divorce, if it came to that? He quoted her. What did it mean, he wanted to know: "We had to warm up in the bullpen before we could get in the real game"? A pen full of *toros*—just what was the lawyer being asked to imagine? A colorful lady, but the Tribunal de la Rota didn't respond to color, just sworn facts.

I was to pass along his warmest regards to a certain Sergio Masmitja, who would ask me to pass his along to his friend, Pablo Pujol.

I wrote the lawyer back and told him that, sadly, plans had changed. Days had darkened (I would follow his example and pile up the figures), a hard cold winter was about to set in. He should forget my petition. And anyway, my ex-wife was incorrigibly the way she was.

He wrote back commiserating with me. If bullpen was like bull market, then, he understood, good times were ahead. I was to take heart. He would keep my wife's letter on file.

Sergio Masmitja. Pablo Pujol.

I passed along the latest regards and stopped it there.

Every chance I got I drove back to Valencia, but I had missed so many teaching days that I couldn't take much time off. Father Menendez had been good to his word; the transfer for a marriage on the second day of Christmas in the Basilica had been approved. If we were going to ride to and from the church in a horse-drawn carriage we had better reserve it. We went to the jewelers to choose the wedding rings and have our initials engraved. The invitations with Antonio's drawing of the knight and the lady playing chess in the forest went out. Mostly they went to people I didn't know, residents of the town of Albal, where Señor Ferri was town secretary, who could be expected to provide handsome gifts of cash. The wedding dinner and dance would be held in that nightclub, Los Viveros, in the center of Valencia's largest park. Amparo and I went dancing there to get a taste. We'd been dancing in a strobe-lit discotheque when she had told me, yes, she would marry me, and this was a sophisticated step up from that. A small orchestra was playing now. We danced—I tried—*pasadobles,* rumbas, fox-trots and waltzes.

I had a moment sitting there between dances when I was struck by the utter unreality of it all. Not even a year had passed. I hadn't ventured

out on an existential quest but had crawled under an old historical blanket and tried to hide. Not even my historical blanket. What possible rel-
evance could the Bourbons' struggle with the Hapsburgs for possession
of the Spanish crown have to my life? The Republic versus the monarchy?
Franco's time-tested dictatorship faced with the anarchists, communists,
freemasons, socialists, and all the rest? Just who were the Falangists?
The Carlists? My country's history that year had resulted in the bombing of Cambodia and the killings at Kent State. I was barely aware. You
can step out of your history and take refuge in another's easily enough,
precisely because that other's history is unburdened by your own pride,
grief, guilt and joy. As theater it will almost always be good. But the day
comes when the backdrop lifts and you see the theater's pipes and bare
patched walls. Then you look at the woman at your side. Who is also a
child. Who is a beautiful wise woman, whose intuitions have the wealth
of the ages behind them, but whose emotions of the day are as quick and
unmediated as a child's. She's worth it, you think. Worth what? you wonder. Step out of your own history and the "it" and the "what" have no
antecedent you can name.

I stopped that Sunday on the way home and stood before the Mediterranean. *Mare nostrum*—a lovely phrase, especially lovely in Latin but
nice in English, too. Our sea. A Spaniard, Frenchman, Italian or Greek
gazes toward the sea and it's as intimate as a backyard pond. Ours.
Theirs. On a clear day a North African will be looking back over that
table of blue. A sea of history, violence, war, all of that, barbarities as
deep as the human imagination can plumb, but each morning it's born
blue again, and calm. A cradling sea, as if everyone who stepped up to its
shores were a babe. Every one of *them*.

The next week Amparo visited with Antonio to see the house. They
immediately began to consult on how they could redecorate, but eventually Antonio went off to see Pablo Pujol and his many other friends in
Barcelona and left Amparo to me. Now I had a chance to observe her in

the house—in the living room, in the kitchen, on the stairs—and as I'd suspected I saw the house's bigness and draftiness and ill-suitedness with her standing in it. Any jewel needs a setting and I admitted that this was not hers. I showed her the bedroom and the bed. She tested the mattress and I lay down at her side. There were pine boughs outside, heavy with cones. The panes of the window were dirty. The sunlight that fell on her as she lay on the bed was hazy and mottled with cone-clustered shadows moving over her cheek, neck and shoulder. The woman I kissed then was a woman with bright and dark patches under a film of haze. I kissed her hard and she kissed back. I lay on top of her and pressed until she opened her legs. I could have taken her virginity away from her; I ground into her and could have ground her down. Between the two of us we could have rendered her family, Church and State null and void. We could have howled our defiance and our relief out that dirty window and past those prickly cones. Why didn't we? Because we wanted to belong. That's all I can answer. As tough as they were making it, there was a stratum of desire beneath the flesh's desire that was as solid as bedrock, and with the strength of that desire we wanted to belong to them.

We rolled out of bed and stood glaring at each other. We'd taken a shaking and were not very attractive to each other then. We had too many masters and were being pulled out of shape. I hated myself for wanting to violate a shrine, and I hated myself for not blowing all shrines to smithereens.

My history was the '60s. Whose history was this?

FOUR

THE MOMENT IS CLEAR TO ME. ONE OF THE IRISHMEN at our school had left, and until a replacement could be found the rest of us were picking up his classes. For the first time I was teaching children, ages eight and nine. In the corner of the classroom, two burro's ears growing out of a cap were suspended from the ceiling, and I'd been told to use the punishment sparingly. But to use it when I had to. As mischievous as they could be, especially around a foreigner, none of the children wanted to be forced to sit in the corner beneath the burro ears and be designated the "burro for the day." I couldn't quite see why. The burros I had seen in Spain's towns had meek manners and affectionate faces. But, for a Spaniard, they carried shameful associations. They meant you were stupid and slow and could never catch up. Sancho Panza, they all knew, had been mounted on one.

I had just placed one of their number under the burro ears and was trying to quiet the rest down when the form leader appeared at the classroom door. I assumed the noise had attracted him, and it was true, when the children saw him standing there they drew a collective breath and held it. He was the kind of man any cause wants on its side—cleanly groomed, properly behaved, stern and square-faced and eminently fair. He wore the blue blazer the children wore, a V-neck sweater, a white shirt and a maroon-and-blue-striped tie. His black shoes had a settled luster.

He called me out. I had a phone call. A phone call that wouldn't wait till the end of class. He would keep the children under control until I returned.

I immediately thought of my parents and the blood dropped out of my face. The form leader, whose name won't come back to me and whose face is little more than that generic cut, placed his hand on my shoulder, and it is the weight and pressure of that hand I still remember. Firm and steady, as though to bring me down from my excessive height to his more stable size. Teamwork. *Trabajo en equipo.*

Tranquilo, he must have said. They all did.

Mis padres, I must have murmured. For I'd checked my watch and if nothing had gone wrong my parents would have been in the air at that moment, coming to Spain to attend their son's wedding. And if something had gone wrong, I would, of course, be called.

When I picked up the receiver my mouth was dry. But it was not my parents or some representative of the airlines calling to tell me what had happened to them, but Amparo. Her voice in its high tunefulness was still high, but the tunefulness was gone. The *fiscal,* Father Menendez, had just called to report a change of heart, she informed me. A change of heart? A seizure of conscience was what she meant. Menendez couldn't ignore what he knew and already he knew too much. Therefore, he would not allow the marriage to go on.

I said, I remember, Too late now. My parents are already in the air.

For a moment Amparo was silent and I could hear only her puzzling breath. Too late now? My parents were in the air and that meant the marriage had to go on? For an instant I must have believed my reasoning myself, and for half an instant she deferred to me and the something I knew that she didn't. Then she got over it. *She* knew what *I* didn't, and for the second half of that instant I might have been that slow-witted child wearing the burro's ears.

Goddamn! I cursed impotently. Goddamn that Menendez to hell!

Amparo told me her father and brother were scheduled to see the *fiscal* that afternoon to make an appeal. Within three hours I would be driving to the airport in Barcelona to pick up my parents, at which time my mother, as a force, would make her presence felt.

It occurred to me that Amparo and I could go back to Madrid and she could go back to being a live-in maid and we could marry there. But Menendez's seizure of conscience had come accompanied by a confession: He'd told his counterpart in Madrid what he'd done. Madrid was out of the question. Julia's and Gregorio's parts were over.

Goddamn . . .

And he said, Amparo reported, if we tried this anywhere else in Spain we'd better not let him hear about it.

"Tried this"? He's the one who told us what "this" was! When you've been "too honest" let me explain to you the only recourse you have left.

Amparo's voice began to fade. I breathed deeply and planted myself. I'd seen *toreros* plant themselves before their bulls, but I wasn't thinking about *toros* or *toreros* or other things Spanish with their macho bluff. I was thinking, I'll be goddamned! I'll be good and goddamned! As a kid, I'd charged up that hill and that playmate had knocked me back down, and with her coffee cup balanced in her hand, my mother had said to herself, Let's see how long he can keep it up.

I told Amparo I'd call her back once I'd met my parents. I cheered her up and got a bit of that tunefulness back in her voice, if only wanly.

Driving to the Barcelona airport, I thought more about Menendez. For Menendez to have set us up from the start so that he could do this to us at the finish was more than I was prepared to believe. From the start he'd been uninformed or misinformed; either way he'd not been up to the job and should have known better. One mistake had led him to another. He was a man who had put off making tough decisions about himself until now, when we, unwittingly, had put him to the test.

I entered Barcelona, took Muntaner down to the Diagonal, which would take me to the Plaza de España, the Gran Via and out of town on the airport highway. At, perhaps, the very moment I'd been driving over the hills that cradled the city, Antonio and his father had met with Menendez, and my future father-in-law had accused the *fiscal* of everything from simony (the selling of annulments) to sadism (playing with our feelings for his own perverted pleasure), and the truth was that Menendez hadn't flinched. Menendez had made Señor Ferri, a devout Catholic all his life, ashamed of his Church. And what was more (and perhaps for him more important), his future in-laws were already in the air, and was this any way for a Spaniard to treat his guests? Unruffled, Menendez admitted to no mistakes; he said only that he was sorry, there was nothing he could do except be more vigilant the next time anyone tried to brush the sacred bonds of matrimony aside. That, according to Antonio, was when his father stood, and, with one hand supporting himself on the desk, brandished his crutch over the *fiscal*'s head. Menendez stood. Antonio was worried about his father, whose blood pressure was high, but he saw then that Menendez was a short man—short-legged, maybe even squat—who needed a broad desk to sit behind, and that the rich color had fallen out of his face. For that moment he was speechless and Antonio got his father away. If there had been any doubt before, there was none now. We had an enemy who wouldn't stop short.

When I explained all this to my mother, her first comment was: I'm not sure I understand. The same man who told you to go ahead now tells you to stop? The same man?

I nodded. I could have made an observation about one man's complexity and the convoluted ways of the Church, but didn't.

I'm not surprised, she said, but there was a light shudder in her voice. Not surprised that her worst fears had been borne out? Are you, Claud?

My father said, If she's worth it, sounds like you're going to have to put up a fight.

She's worth it, I vowed.

Sally sure thought so.

My mother, who couldn't stand being disconcerted for long, said, Well, let's marry her and get her out of here.

I'm trying. Believe me, I am.

At the airport they'd struck me as two hapless travelers, stranded between stops. I'd driven them back over the hills to my house, and while they gave in to their jet lag and napped, I walked to the telephone *central* and called Amparo. That was when I learned about the disastrous confrontation between Señor Ferri and the *fiscal* Menendez. I was secretly thrilled that Amparo's father was about to club a priest over the head on our behalf, but concerned when I learned that he'd felt weak when he had gotten home and his wife had put him to bed. I knew how fierce she could be when it came to keeping her husband happy and calm. She was mad at everybody—Menendez, of course, for having broken his word, and us too, as was only natural, for having given her husband a reason to flare up. And she was worried about my parents, what in the world they would think.

I had to lie a little here. They don't understand, I told Amparo. They're willing to do whatever they can to help.

Claud and Ruth.

Say it the way you used to, I said.

Cloud and Root.

One way or another, we're going to be married. Keep your spirits up. Say it again.

Cloud and Root.

I laughed and then she did, to hear me relieved. Her laughter was like crystal tinkling down the line.

Where's Antonio? I asked.

He's gone out to contact his friends. He has some ideas.

I did not ask what ideas because Amparo, looking for something to take our minds off our troubles, said, You should see him in his new velvet suit. And his elevator shoes. He looks like an Edwardian prince.

It's his fault. He got this started when he was swashbuckling around the *Cristoforo Colombo* in his cape.

We chuckled some more. *Un americanito* he had brought her. Then the chuckles died out.

What can I do? I said.

Come quickly, she answered. I need you here.

Our house is cold without out you, I whispered, worried in the moment that I might have brought to mind that fruitless grinding we'd done on the bed.

But she said, *Te quiero. Te quiero mucho,* and I could hear the tears start to well.

I walked home and checked on my parents, who were both asleep, then drove to the school and told Pablo Pujol what had happened. Pujol voiced indignation, but the expression on his face was as woeful as José Luis López Vázquez at his best. He had no more names to offer. I went to my office in the school and drafted a letter to Morales Cabanas, the lawyer in Rome, asking him, in the most circuitous euphemisms I could come up with, what was the cheapest I could get an annulment for if I wanted to buy one outright, and second, what was the very fastest he could move things through the Tribunal de Rota if he had to rely on testimony from my ex-wife. I could come to Rome. I would welcome the opportunity to plead my case before the tribunal myself. I would kiss any ring that was held before me.

I did not send this letter. I drove back to the town where I lived, Bellaterra. I stopped before I got there and looked out over the "beautiful land." It was, I believe, December 12. The day was sunny and the night would be cold. The Catalans were provident and hardworking to a fault. The fields had been planted in winter wheat and the vineyards had already been plowed around the stocks. The towns were mindfully spaced, delineated by their pines. It all worked, whether the tyrant of the day was Franco or some Roman overlord. I could hear Amparo's laughter passing over it, unfreighted by anything except the pleasure she took.

The country or the woman?

The next morning was freezing, and my father, a predawn riser, wouldn't get out of bed. He barely stuck his head out from under the blanket. His hair had receded and turned gray, and his skin at the scalp line looked as brittle as parchment. He showed a sheepish grin. Rather than face the cold and a territory unlike any he'd ever traveled before, he preferred to stay in bed. I smiled. I almost cried. I was late for work, but that night, I told them, we'd talk.

But when I tried to take them through the saga of what Menendez had done to us, I had to stop. Recounted like that in one up-and-down, stop-and-start narrative, I didn't see how it could ever end; that was because when it did there was always something to nudge it into motion again, and motion—my motion circling Spain, for instance—was what it was all about. You circle some fictive center; your orbit brings you tantalizingly close, but never home. This is eternal motion. It is how Dante chose to figure illicit desire.

My mother made the obvious suggestion: Get out of Spain, bring her to the United States and marry her there in the First Presbyterian Church.

Not the College of the Bible?

My mother cocked her head.

She is Spanish, I said. It would break her heart. I didn't tell Mother it would break mine.

Then why not go to the top? she said.

We'd had an audience with the archbishop, I reminded her.

And he went to sleep, isn't that what you said? Not the archbishop. If you really want to marry her I'd go talk to that Franco, my mother urged, in the uncushioned tones of her most commonsensical advice.

Franco, I responded, was a shriveled-up little man who wouldn't wish a day's worth of happiness on his own flesh and blood. Franco was out of the question. I said I would rather put my faith in Antonio instead.

My mother couldn't claim to know, but she had heard that Franco had shaped this country up again, gotten it back on track.

As dictators went . . . I began.

While this Antonio . . . and, after glancing at her husband, she left it hanging to see what I would do with it.

I didn't take the bait. As maestros of theatrical events, Antonio and my mother would be eternal rivals, perhaps agreeing to cameo performances in each other's productions, but no more than that.

I gave my parents the palms-down tempering sign the Spanish use (they'll use the palms up to egg you on) and said, *Tranquilos.*

The next day I showed them Barcelona, which in its animation and everyday elegance brought a genuine wonder into their eyes.

The day after that, as soon as I finished work, we drove to Valencia. For the second half of the trip we had the Mediterranean to our left, never brighter and bluer, which lifted the winter right out of our spirits. I remembered the pleasure Sally had taken floating for hours in the sea when we'd gone together to Ibiza. I missed Sally. On the other hand, I didn't want her here if it was disappointment we were about to be buried beneath. We still hadn't told her that the wedding wasn't going ahead as planned. Antonio had sent her an invitation, inviting her to come be the *dama* playing chess in the forest with her knight.

At bottom, I assumed my parents had left her home so that something like that wouldn't happen. That she wouldn't meet her knight.

During the trip to Valencia, my father sat in the front seat with me, fascinated by how close the Spaniards drove to one another, how they whipped in and out of line and stuck to each other on the turns. He marveled at how much I had come to drive like them in the half year I had owned the car.

It stuck me that he was right. The *guardia civil* had once pulled me over for driving, I suppose, the way my father had taught me, as though I had weeks at my disposal and the whole breadth of a continent to cross. In Spain we didn't have that luxury of time or space. My father sensed it and marveled that I'd adapted so well.

We were at the Ferris' in Albal, just outside Valencia, before suppertime. Antonio and I served as translators. There wasn't much to say— how happy and upset everyone was at the way things stood. Everyone was complimented on their looks. *Guapa* was the word in Spanish. Tell your mother how good-looking she is. Now tell your father. I was to tell the Ferris how much Sally missed seeing them again. My mother had brought a gift, a set of his-and-her hand towels embossed with the Ferris' initials. A curious *detalle*. My mother was a big towel giver, but the Ferris were left to deduce that my sister had returned home and reported that towels were in short supply. Antonio, gay and grave as the occasion warranted, stood before my parents as the Latin charmer and the soulful Spaniard, a role that had won over his host and hostess in the United States. Amparo stood before them like nothing they'd seen before.

She hurried around doing things for them, seeing to their coats, plumping the pillows of their chairs, bringing them appetizers and drinks, but in the beauty of her enormous eyes, the rounds of her lovely cheeks and shoulders, and in the rose and honey of her flesh, they were as unequipped as I had been and would not have seen her like before.

We ate. *Sobre mesa,* the table talk that went on after supper until you went to bed, had mostly to do with contacts Antonio had made that had gone nowhere and contacts—with lawyers and minor-level politicians he'd gone to school with when he'd left the Opus Dei and studied law— still pending. Those still pending he talked up glowingly, but the point came when I spoke the unspeakable. What if none of his contacts panned out and we couldn't marry in the Catholic Church? What then? This question carried over to the next day and the *sobre mesa* after the midday meal. Señor Ferri asked me to translate. He wanted my parents to know how offended he was at his Church's behavior and how personally he took the insult that was directed, ultimately, against them, his guests. They had come to his country in an act of good faith and now his country was saying no. Therefore, he would not oppose a civil marriage and he would not oppose a marriage in a Protestant church. I happened to be looking at his wife when he let this bombshell drop, and she didn't flinch.

Amparo gasped. I assumed she had hinted to Antonio that if we couldn't marry she was capable of going off with me on her own, and, surely, Antonio had talked.

But to me it made perfect sense, even without Amparo's veiled threat. As religious as Señor Ferri knew himself to be before Christ on a cross or a statue of the Virgin being paraded down the street, he also knew himself to be a host with guests on his hands whose rights he could not honorably ignore. My parents were owed a wedding—what obligation was older than that? Señor Ferri was a bountiful Spaniard who emptied his pantry at every meal. He was a *señor en su castillo.*

It was what he and his son had in common. Castle-lovers both.

Antonio was out running down his contacts. December 26, what could be done?

Nothing, it turned out. For Amparo to marry civilly and not follow it up with a marriage in the Church, she would have to forswear her religion, a procedure that took months and began with her returning to the church she'd been baptized in and getting the priest who had administered the sacrament to sign the form that took it back. If that priest was dead you had to petition to have a successor sign for him, another procedure. A marriage in a Protestant church might allow the civil marriage to be binding, but there was no Protestant church. I went to the telephone *central* in Valencia and checked directories for Madrid and Barcelona, and all I found listed was a Methodist church in Madrid. I called and learned that it had disappeared. I made a call to the U.S. Embassy. Embassies sometimes performed marriages. In wartime, with bombs falling around them, embassies sometimes did the romantic right thing— I'd learned that in the movies. This was a sort of war. It was ways of life pitted against each other, like great clashing abstractions, with two lonely individuals caught in between. Would they marry us? Only if this *were* a movie, the embassy spokesman I spoke to replied.

I could hear my mother buzzing—we'll take it all to the States. I'll make sure somebody marries you over there. We'll even pay the Ferris' way. But Señor Ferri's honor depended on a marriage being performed in Spain so my parents could go home fulfilled. He would not be indifferent to a marriage in the States. He would just not be the same man.

I did not tell my mother, but she would be able to figure it out. It was a code of honor, a way of being, that I was marrying myself to. You don't marry just a woman . . .

·   ·   ·

THERE WAS A PERIOD of three or four days when we simply looked at each other in disbelief as our hope ran down. Then—I would put the date at December 17 or 18—Franco, the man himself, actually visited Valencia. The official occasion was the construction of a flood-control

channel that was to circumvent the city. The channel represented the fulfillment of a promise Franco had made to the city back in the mid-'50s,
when a flash flood had swept down from the mountains and overflowed
the river Turia, the same river El Cid had crossed to drive out the Moors.
That flood had killed over sixty people. Amparo had been a child then,
but Antonio had been in his Opus Dei school, and he and his classmates
had been issued shovels and sent out to attack the mud when the flood-
waters receded. If it had taken Franco fifteen years to keep his promise,
that was because it wasn't until then that American funds had become
available to begin the project. Franco had come to give the *Valencianos*
a Christmas gift, and as was customary when the *caudillo* visited provincial capitals, crowds from outlying towns were bused in to line the
streets. As chance would have it, my parents' hotel window looked down
on the motorcade's route.

Except that these things never happened by chance. Was it chance
that I had gotten on the *Cristoforo Colombo* in New York and not the
Michelangelo, which had sailed the following day? What were the
chances that Antonio would choose the same boat? And then, with all
those festive Italians whooping it up, that he'd see me standing out at the
stern? And, remember, Franco hadn't had to win the civil war, and
wouldn't have, most historians agree, if the Republican government had
armed the workers in Malaga and Seville at the outbreak of the rebellion.
Anyway, Franco should have been killed well before then in one of his
foolhardy charges against the Rif tribesmen in Morocco, back when all
he wanted to do was marry a woman for whom his father's humble birth
and philandering ways had disqualified him. But, of course, he never
had to lay eyes on this woman, at the time a mere fifteen-year-old girl by
the name of Carmen Polo, in the first place.

Try to calculate the chances.

Add into the calculations that influx of American money. And don't
forget Ike. Ike didn't have to come to Spain and embrace little Paquito

with his roly-poly paunch, as if to say, Look at what a fine little fellow we have here. Ike could have stayed home, kept his dollars to himself, and this flood-control channel would never have been built. I could have stayed at home, and almost certainly would have if LBJ and his bombing raids and Richard Nixon with his mendacity across the board had not made life intolerable for me there. What are the chances of everybody behaving as they did and of events falling out just so?

Incalculable, prohibitive, absurd.

I felt the finger of fate nudging us all along, and when Francisco Franco rode into town I told my mother, no, I would not be there to witness the event. I had had enough of higher powers. I would defy fate and walk away from this meeting decades in the making. But once she understood all the circumstances, my mother was convinced that she could persuade Franco to express his gratitude for American largesse through an act of generosity of his own. Valencia would get its flood-control channel, Franco his bused-in crowds and her son his heart's desire. Señor Ferri, poor man, would be off the hook, and the press would love it. As big a fascist as Franco might be, my mother would show him her gratitude by allowing herself to be photographed at his side. Back home, she'd supply the caption: "The day I went over there and straightened the little general out."

I wouldn't join her. I stayed in Albal and kept Amparo company. She knew all about Franco's staged visits to provincial capitals, and she probably knew this one had been months in the planning, but she couldn't keep the apprehension off her face and an anxious animation out of her eyes. I was reminded of the day we had met. The apprehension and the animation, then, had been fueled by a sort of forbidden delight; today's was about dread. I comforted her. Antonio was out running down his contacts, and they were legion, his friends. My father? Out of loyalty to me, my father wouldn't even leave the hotel room to step onto the balcony. According to mother, he said he'd wait for the circus to pass by, a comment that, in its subtle sarcasm, was unlike him. She noted it. But she had Franco in her sights now, not my father.

When the motorcade turned onto their street she went downstairs and stepped out onto the sidewalk. Did she intend to flag down Franco's car? I can almost believe she did. The day was sunny and warm, a day of shirt sleeves that only turned cool once you entered the narrow, shaded streets or the damp courtyards. Mother stood in the sun in the company of men and women from Spain's small towns who'd been paid a day's wages to come welcome their leader. They were dressed in their best finery, the women especially, their flower-printed dresses, and the men in the dark suits they wore to pay their Sunday visits, but they carried cloth sacks in which they'd packed their enormous *bocadillos* of Spanish omelet and *serrano* ham, subs the size of small clubs they would munch on for most of the day. Some were eating sardines. Mother smelled cheese and oranges and saw wineskins, which the men drank from as easily as if they were turning on a faucet. They were loud—surely residents of the same town shouting back and forth to each other—and although she couldn't understand a word, she could tell they were happy. She was listening for the first disgruntled note and just didn't hear it. Even when she forced her way up front, the crowd happily gave way, only to re-form around her, and it took reaching the curb and staking out her spot before she could collect herself and regain her sense of purpose.

Which was to get a good look at the man to see if the man was worth her trouble? She never said. She said she saw him. She said she stood right at the front of the crowd and he passed within twenty feet of her, standing in the back of an open car. The car was a convertible, as big as a Cadillac, she thought it *was* a Cadillac, cream-colored, with deluxe leather upholstery of a lighter shade of cream, and it was preceded and followed by black sedans full of plainclothes policemen, and ahead of them and bringing up the rear were uniformed policemen on motorcycles. There were no flags and no musical bands, but there was enough of what there was that it was like a small parade. And it passed by slowly. A certain reverence came over the crowd, or a questioning sort of hush, and instead of cheering wildly, or screaming *olé*'s, or whatever it was they screamed, they simply applauded. The man himself was not dressed in his general's uniform, which came as a disappointment, but in a light-brown suit, and he wore a fedora on what Mother knew to be his bald head. He did have what, at first glance, appeared to be a military bearing: He looked straight ahead and acknowledged the crowd with little abbreviated waves, resembling the half salute with which a general might dismiss a private. Then, as he came closer, she saw that he needed both hands to support himself on the seat back in front of him and that those little half salutes were all he dared permit himself. At his side sat a woman with a long pale face and a large-brimmed hat, salmon-colored, which shielded her from the sun. She appeared utterly indifferent to the occasion and might have been sitting at home, before a dresser mirror, buffing her nails. Franco himself looked very frail. He had a face eroded down to the bone, and flesh that had gone directly to his wattles, which seemed to have a palsied life all their own. He looked straight ahead because turning his head was not an easy thing to do.

Nevertheless, he turned it to look at Mother. His car slowed to a crawl, and he and my mother exchanged a long look, at which point she saw what with my twenty-eight-year perspective I have already surmised: Franco was being driven, Franco didn't drive. He didn't have the power. He probably didn't even have the power to stop the car. Mother said she might have hopped on board—the car was going that slowly—and had it out with him right there, but she took pity, which is to say, she had better things to do with her time. She let him go. But I don't entirely believe her. She had great faith in her powers of persuasion, and that willpower of hers, some of which I'd inherited, was second to none. But if she was going to take Franco on she would have had to have wanted it badly and, in her heart of hearts, I don't believe she did. I believe she

preferred that Franco kick me out of the country, like one of those im-
pecunious hippies of his, and then this little Spanish interlude would be
done. Her host's honor would be impugned, but her host would get over
it. Not that she wished a scarring sadness on me or on Amparo. I have to
believe that standing there among hundreds of Spaniards, drinking their
wine in bright arcing streams and eating their *bocadillos* a mile long, she
just wanted me home.

. . .

IN THE ARAGON TOWN OF AINSA, Amparo and I come to a similar realization that brings with it a sober relief. Ainsa is a town in a valley with
a steel-green river rushing by. The commercial center is down by the
river; the old town, within its walls, is situated well up the valley slope.
Nothing surprising there, except that the two towns have been driven
apart and there's a corridor of countryside between them. The old town—
houses built of a flat, brown-toned stone—is perfectly preserved. The
streets have been cleansed of all extraneous matter, the *plaza mayor* is
spacious and colonnaded, the church twelfth-century Romanesque; the
town is of a piece unlike any we've seen before. Signs have even been
posted on certain house fronts explaining in unflorid, informative Spanish (and three other languages) the style of the door arches, windows,
ironwork and chimneys we are seeing and the subtle ways in which the
styles have evolved. These houses are all being lived in, although the
streets are mostly empty. We can walk them at our leisure, our feet echo-
ing beyond the reach of motors, all of which are zoned off in the Ainsa
down below.

At lunch Amparo asks if I know what she wants. She wants to walk
down the main street of town wearing a crazy hat, and, as lovely as our
trip through Spain's past has been, she can't wear that kind of hat here.
Well, she *could* wear that kind of hat, but not with the pleasure she ex-

pects to take from it. I tell her I agree. It's all too closed off for its own good. The fact that this realization has hit us at exactly the same time pleases me deeply, even as it calls into question much of what we've done. Finally, these towns in their purity become monumental, and don't all monuments finally become tombs?

We enter Cataluña, in the sierra now, driving along a ridge. The flat stone is gone and a raspberry shade of sandstone I've never seen before replaces it. Whole towns are made of it. On the crest of the ridge we can see them to our right and left, and Amparo, whose fear of high narrow roads is akin to her fear of tunnels, keeps telling me not to peek. The views are grand, and it's true, if you gaze into them long enough you can go dizzy with so much seemingly so close at hand.

I'll play Thelma to your Louise.

Don't even joke about it, she says.

We head down. The towns of Coll de Nargo, Solsona, Cardoza.

Coming from the time-sealed Ainsa, Cardoza seems right to me. It's strung out along the crest of a hill. There are the remains of a sandstone castle and a *plaza mayor* built out along a precipice so you can stroll, safely behind a wall, and gaze into space. Brief tunnels or extended arches take you from one street to the next. There are few *casas señoriales;* rather there's a raggedness and a wear about the buildings that allow you to take them as they stand. We've left the monumental behind.

We run across a *hostal,* Hostal Perrico, and I suggest that we stop here for the night. Amparo surprises me. She wants to go on. She demands that we go on. Once we've driven out of town she tells me why. Cardoza has reminded her of postwar Spain, the Spain she was born into. That was a time of scarcity when very few could afford to fix up their houses. It's as if she'd forgotten it until now, but the houses and the streets of her hometown, Bocairente, smelled of it. They smelled of age. You walked by an open door and smelled the stagnation of the lives inside. Cardoza has brought it back to her.

She wonders if I've understood. Even after our President Eisenhower came to lift a sort of blockade, the misery in these towns in those times could seem permanent. You watched the whitewash flake off the houses and the doors sag on their hinges and the shutters on the windows splinter, and even the stone, the stone seemed to pulverize, and people stood there trapped, no way to go forward or back. The smell was of a steady and unspectacular and irreversible dissolution. As a girl she ran the streets and greeted the burros when they came back in the evening, loaded with firewood, fodder and mountain herbs, and told the days of the week by the aromas of the meals coming from the kitchens, but she remembers now how she could be stopped in her tracks and brought to a puzzling sadness by that smell that underlay it all. Something airless and terribly old. Someone standing there then, bathed in that smell, had his shoulders slump and his face turn gray. She's smelled that smell in Cardoza and seen more than one gray face. She doesn't want things sanitized, but just as a town like Ainsa can seem sealed in its past, a town like Cardoza can feel like a present forever deprived of a future, and she knows she couldn't wear her crazy hat there, either.

She wonders if I've understood.

I understand that that wildness of space—of water, air and rampant vegetation—might be said to have come to roost in that crazy hat of hers. And I can see how walking down the street of a Spanish town in a crazy hat might allow her to establish a moment's contact with the fearless child she'd been. A breath of freshness coming off such a hat might even be enough to bring one of these towns back to life, a town whose traditions might have remained time-sealed, inviolate, intact. I can understand that. In exchange for his services, all Sancho Panza asked of his master was an island of his own—by which he meant a little kingdom—to govern.

Do I understand?

I understand that before the day is out I have to find her a town where she can wear her crazy hat; I understand that henceforth we'll live and die by her crazy hat.

The pursuit of her happiness and, therefore, of mine.

We are close enough that we could strike out for Barcelona if we wanted to. Bellaterra is even closer. I point to it on the map. There's that little hotel that might still be on the town's main plaza. And there is the house I brought her to when we began our married life. My father froze in his bed in that house and looked up at me with the pleading truant face of our son. The morning after Amparo and I arrived from our honeymoon, I walked down the stairs with my bathrobe on and nothing underneath, and the cold came up my legs and seized me with fingers of ice. Except we got the heat going and had some good times in that house. I leave it up to her.

Smiling, she shakes her head. I nod. She has another *pueblo* in mind.

Spain is its plains and its mountain strongholds, with the Pyrenees blocking access from the north. It's easier to enter from the sea, as the Moors did in the eighth century, and as I did twenty-nine years ago. The mountain strongholds, the sierras, provide a safe if unfertile haven for those driven out of the plains, or for those who find life there too monotonous. If you figure there's a sierra for every plain, then it's not hard to understand why there's a comparable geography in the Spanish psyche and an area ideal for that unsubdued part of a Spaniard that would live in a castle and fend off the world. Amparo directs us into the Sierra of the Maestrazgo. The town is Morella. Its walls—its perimeters of defense— spiral in until you reach the castle itself, which is no longer there, reduced to rubble in the last Carlist war. The town is clean, rebuilt in all the particulars, but not transformed. Broad staircases take you from one level to another and the stone has been relaid. Retaining walls have been reconstructed. Atop the stone columns in the *calle mayor*, some of the wooden supports that shoulder the beams of the overhanging houses have been replaced. Nothing has been left unattended. Parks along the perimeter walls, drainage systems, town lights. There's an air of vigilance about the town, not so much of prosperity as of a refusal to surrender—to the elements, to time itself. I know at once why Amparo likes it so much. The town looks out over terraced valleys, the muted grays and greens of olive and almond trees. A steady, scouring wind is blowing, and she likes that, too.

That crazy hat?

She makes a tempering gesture. She smiles.

We splurge—but not by much—on a room in a Renaissance palace once owned by a certain Cardinal Ram, back when there was a renegade pope in Spain accompanied by his college of cardinals. The walls are two feet thick and the casement windows open onto that broad valley scribbled over with terrace walls. Amparo tells me we've been here before. Here? In this town? Yes, in this very hotel. Back at the start. I have no memory of it. She finds it hard to believe, and I tell her that our all-consuming efforts to get things done back then have left entire tracts of my memory blank. We came with her father, she says. The three of us came—we drove him—because he wanted to show us the town.

And we stayed in this hotel? Are you sure?

We ate here, in the restaurant downstairs. You know, one of his real pleasures was to see us eat well.

Her voice grows thick, but it's a happy association and these few tears will not lay her low. I miss her father. Amparo's tender sensibilities come from him. Two days before our visits ended and we had to fly back to the United States, he would disappear; he would actually go sleep somewhere else those two days and spare us his unmanly tears. I was able to fly to his bedside the day before he died, and he whispered what I fully expected him to: *Que detalle más bonito! Sí, señor!* Then he reciprocated. With an almost comical urgency, he told me where he had hidden a bottle of wine he had picked out expressly for me, for the next time I came. It was in a clothes closet on a back shelf and I was to retrieve it at once. *Que buenísimo!* I'd see.

That night the wind blows hard. It is not a particularly shrill wind and it does not blow in gusts. It just blows hard. It brings back some Spanish history to me. It was in this particular Sierra del Maestrazgo that the Carlists made not their last stand, because Carlists fought valiantly for Franco during the Civil War, but the stand that ended the three Carlist wars of the nineteenth century. The government beat them here and captured the town. By then their leader in the Maestrazgo, Ramón Cabrera, had emigrated to England, married and, after participating in wars that began in the 1830s, declared a separate peace. The Carlists, who took their name from their support of Don Carlos as successor to Ferdinand VII, were antirevolutionary romantics who viewed the turn to statism in the nineteenth century as a turn away from family, king and God. Even when they fought for Franco they wore large tasseled red berets and blowing capes. Cabrera, who seemed to have been little more than an ambitious young soldier at the start, acquired notoriety when the government forces captured and executed his mother. He, in turn, as the last course to a victory banquet (after coffee, perhaps, before the cognac) had captured government soldiers brought out and their throats cut. The forces of Isabel II couldn't get Cabrera out of these mountains and dubbed him El Tigre del Maestrazgo so that everyone would know what was running loose there.

The sierra was wild. Peace-loving folk would stay down on the plain.

When Amparo wakes up I tell her about my sleepless meditations on Ramón Cabrera. I tell her that spirit in the town of a militant upkeep that she responds to so strongly is the ghost of Cabrera blowing over these hills. She tells me I haven't been meditating, I've been dreaming. The Carlists were all Quixotes, and what I've done is dream myself into the biggest Quixote I could find.

She's amused by it. She's been in touch with her father, I'd bet on it, and has woken in good spirits. This town has satisfied her in ways others haven't. She starts calling me *tigre.*

We leave the Maestrazgo that morning, visiting other Carlist strongholds on the way out. The valleys broaden, the rocky terraces give way to grassy steps, and it's tempting to read a similar mollifying effect into the Carlist soul. Mirambél, where every palace on the *calle mayor* stands in elegant testimony to a better time, and Cantavieja, reposing high on a cliff, absolutely impregnable as long as belief held firm and the twentieth century, with its long-range guns and its dive-bombing airplanes, stayed away.

In Cantavieja we take a moment to stand at a *mirador* and gaze down the cliff at the valley below. On a nearby bench an old man in a beret is propped on his cane. He, too, is looking out over the valley. The cliffs are a rich iron-red streaked with gray. Birds hang in the reaches, one too large to be a hawk that might be an eagle, since vultures don't usually sail solitary like that. The old man tells us that years before he helped build that very balcony, that *mirador,* so that he would have someplace to come when he got to his present age. He didn't know it at the time, of course. When he was a young man he was off on *verbenas* courting the girls, but he must have had an inkling that the day would come when he'd prefer—and he waves his cane like a wand out toward the valley— all that instead of the girls.

Instead of Amparo, who, at fifty-two, is very much a beautiful woman? Apparently so.

I am inspired by this man, that when he was young enough to help build this balcony he would still be wise enough to make provisions for the day when he'd get his strength not from his muscles and roaring manhood but from . . . everything out there.

The arc of a life. If that was what the Carlists were telling the government to take its hands off of, I'm with them.

The old man, it turns out, is something of a real estate agent around town. I've begun to muse that if there were something available in that row of valley-fronting houses I might be persuaded to live out my life right here, and he mentions that he has a sister-in-law who owns some property on that street she might be willing to sell. He's vague about what kind of property, and I pretend not to see the crafty tightening of the lines around his eyes. Shall we take a walk with this old man to see his sister-in-law?

Well, why not? I say. Let's have a look.

And that is when my wife tells me she's still not through. She has yet another *pueblo* she wants to see. We're only sixty kilometers from Valencia, and I'd somehow convinced myself we'd come to the end.

Yes. She informs me she's been my Sancho Panza long enough. In spite of this old man and his unromantic ways, she wants to be my Dulcinea and she wants me to take her home.

Home? In that instant I have no idea where she means. With a laughing groan I almost tell her we have no home, we've been out looking for one, hasn't she at least understood that?

Toboso, she says.

El Toboso is one of the few places that anyone can locate for sure on Cervantes's map of La Mancha. Don Quixote says his Dulcinea lives there. Knights he's defeated in battle must go there and pledge their fealty to her. Where Quixote himself comes from, he's coy about, or vague. Or perhaps, like us, he just doesn't know.

You want to go to La Mancha? I say with disbelief, mostly feigned, and a sinking sense that I've known it all along.

It's the one region of the country we haven't visited. Why?

I don't know why. I give her the gesture the old in Spain give when they're up against one of life's imponderables. They extend their arms down at their sides, hands out, palms up, then hunch their shoulders and hold them until the hands begin to quiver and the question becomes absurd.

Toboso, she says. You owe me Toboso. She calls me her Don, her Tigre del Maestrazgo. It's time, she says, to get out of the mountains and down on the plains.

. . .

I WILL, you know, Amparo said. If I have to choose between what someone like Menendez says, and you, I'll choose you.

It won't be Menendez. You'll have to choose between your parents and me.

I'll choose you.

And your friends, and your girlhood, all of that.

Te quiero a tí.

Why should you have to give any of it up?

It doesn't matter.

It does.

And it mattered, I knew, because I did not want to marry a disenfranchised woman, cast adrift on the world's seven oceans, a woman without a country—who would be so ungallant as to turn a woman into that? I said, This woman I married, I never told you about her. I know her. She's a friend. If we can wait a little longer it would give her great pleasure to get our marriage annulled. To stick it to the Church, I mean. She'd probably testify we never consummated the marriage, if that's what it takes.

Amparo's eyes flashed, by which I mean they went dense and darkly bright. We had left my parents in the hotel and were sitting in the little park beside the church of San Agustín, where Amparo had once tried to teach me the Spanish I'd need to fend for myself in this country of hers.

In Franco's Spain, a married woman could not open a bank account, own property, hold a job without her husband's consent. She could not put her child on her passport. The only way she could get these privileges was if the husband declared himself dead and gave her the rights of a widow. We did not know this then. But this was the country Franco had come to town to uphold and had left me to defend.

I don't want to wait, Amparo said. She didn't want to hear anything about any consummation, or the lack of it, either.

My parents would understand. They'd come back. Antonio's suit would still fit. Your dress—

No! And she actually stamped her foot. I told my parents if we couldn't marry I'd go off with you. If you don't want me I'll go off by myself, she insisted, her eyes so bold they were black.

You told them? I assumed it was Antonio.

Don't you think I'm capable of it? Well, I am. The twenty-sixth, she made it perfectly clear.

I took her home and there with Antonio and his parents was another man, baby-faced with lively eyes, pink cheeks and a bushy black mustache. One leg was slightly shorter than the other and he walked with a jaunty limp. He was a friend of Antonio's from Onteniente, where he had returned to visit family and they had recently crossed paths. He lived in Palma de Mallorca. He and Antonio had been law students together, but whereas Antonio had gone on to become an artist with a decided medieval bent, this friend, whose name was Javier, had become a *fiscal*.

A what?

There were ecclesiastical *fiscales* and there were civil ones. Javier was of the civil sort. I wondered what the corresponding office in the States would be, but I already knew. District attorney.

Javier was Palma de Mallorca's DA. One of them. And we'd been too honest.

Well, we had, Father Menendez's civil counterpart had to agree. Out in the islands, Javier claimed, they mixed marriages together every day and no one bothered to ask. This was the twentieth century, was it not? He'd tell us what he'd do. Menendez might have the authority to block a marriage in Valencia, but if we didn't mind coming to Mallorca, we could marry there. Javier would speed things along. He'd be one of our witnesses himself. Residency was a matter of a day. His sister-in-law could become Amparo's employer, and since Amparo had already declared herself a live-in maid once, she could do so again. We could marry in the church that corresponded to our parish. We could have a chat with the parish priest and no one would ask a thing. And as long as we were there we could stay for the honeymoon. Spain might have its champions of backwardness, but in Las Baleares we like to keep abreast.

He rattled this off in a breathless voice, half laughing all the while. Every so often he would shift the weight off his bad leg. It became a little dance step that only added to his delight. The twinkling eyes and the pink cheeks and that wicked black mustache—I found I had to sit down.

Antonio went through it all again, a step at a time.

His father was up leaning on his crutch, his weight already thrown in the direction of the door. His mother sat in an armchair with a matronly bearing and that fixed smile. Both of them were used to Antonio bringing them problems and then providing solutions when their nerves were about to fray.

It seemed we were saved.

I closed my eyes, I remember, and said to myself, Sooner or later you'll learn. *Fiscal*. I never liked the word. *Fees-cal*. It hissed at you, then it dropped you flat. The Church DA. The State DA. They'll knock you back and forth between them for a while, then one of them will finish you off.

I opened my eyes and Javier—I've forgotten his last name—looked like the friendliest little fellow around, of too cheerful a disposition to be indignant over what had happened to us for long. Come over to Mallorca, he seemed to be saying, and we'll have a party.

This was a DA?

This was another of Antonio's friends.

I was about to stall for time and say I'd think about it when I realized I had no say in it whatsoever. Antonio had gotten us into this fix, now it was up to Antonio to get us out. Señor Ferri had guests whose trust he would not betray and now he wouldn't have to. Amparo had delivered an ultimatum: Get me married or watch me run off, and that ultimatum was on the way to being met. The only person as powerless as I in this affair was Señora Ferri, who had this facade of long-suffering Spanish womanhood she'd inherited from generations back to retreat behind. I didn't even have that. I can't imagine the expression on my face. Delivered and doomed. A joyous disbelief and a freezing knot of certainty that now they had gotten me for good. I'm not ashamed to admit I wanted my parents with me at that moment. My father might go wheeling off into the country for his week on the road, but my mother stayed at home.

Let's do it! I said. Let's do it before Menendez finds out and tries to pull the plug!

Pull the plug—*Quitarnos el enchufe?* I wasn't making a whole lot of sense. But Menendez they understood. Menendez *might* put out the word to all dioceses in the country to be on the alert for a marriage between a tall drawling gringo and a live-in maid.

Battle blood rose in my future father-in-law's face. He almost toppled off his crutch. *Collons!* he exploded.

His wife, who could calculate his blood pressure to the decimal point, came out of her seat. Antonio! *Cuídate!*

Papa. Amparo placed a steadying hand on his shoulder. It's all right, she murmured, *Está bien.*

I added my reassurance: Menendez is not worth it. He's a *pobrecito*, a poor pathetic creature.

Pobrecito! Nada de pobrecito! Señor Ferri shot back. There was nothing poor or pathetic about him. Did I know what Menendez had said when Señor Ferri and Antonio had sat before him? Menendez had had a stack of papers on his desk. He had said, If I allow this marriage to go through, this paper—and he held up your marriage application—in two or three years will be over on this stack. These are the petitions for annulments of those who take their sacraments with a grain of salt. Why should I want to give myself more work?

He said that? I had a hard time imagining such bitter banter coming out of Menendez's mouth.

Palabra, Antonio put in.

That I took my sacraments with a grain of salt? That because of my feckless, faithless ways, we were two or three years from another breakup?

I'd be goddamned!

I'll pack! I declared. I'll get my parents packed. I'll get tickets to Mallorca. Plane tickets, no boat. What else? Flowers. And I need something to wear.

I stopped when I saw Antonio move to the center of the room. I remembered him at his gay best directing affairs for our group on the *Cristoforo Colombo.* You take care of your parents and the tickets, he said. Get one for Amparo, too. I'll take care of the rest.

I thanked Javier. I almost saluted Antonio. I gave my future father-in-law a half hug as I passed him on the way to the door. An hour earlier I had walked in this door prepared to grind it out at the Church's pace, or watch Amparo revolt. Now, with a DA's blessing, I had a job to do and a calendar of days. It was crazy. For the moment sobered, I asked Amparo, who had come with me to the door, Do you understand what happened in there?

Sí . . . no . . . she went back and forth. She had a breathless, open-mouthed smile. A photograph Antonio had shown me on the boat had caught her like that, her head turned, mouth and eyes opened wide, an exuberant flowering of color in her cheeks, tremblingly on the brink of something grand.

We can have it all, I said.

Don't say anything, she cautioned me.

Antonio . . . I began, in praise of her brother.

Please, she pleaded with me, you know what can happen.

I did, but there was no trace of that look she'd exchanged with the traitor Menendez when she'd submitted to her Church's and country's will. Her face showed a wildness of hope now, but utterly unprovisioned. If she was casting off, there was no possibility of return. Did I understand? A voyage into the unknown, which could only get stranger and stranger, with me at her side? I kissed her. I had my parents to notify, tickets to buy, tasks to perform.

.   .   .

THE PLANE LEFT at eight the next morning, as a cold front moved in, and Amparo, my parents and I were on it. Townspeople observed us getting into a cab just before dawn, and the word spread that we had eloped, or what was more likely, that my parents and I had kidnapped Amparo, who was, after all, still a *secretarieta* at heart. Amparo had not flown before. She had not done any of the things she was doing before. I was in a foreign country, but it was she who was on foreign ground. She was merry, especially with my mother, but it was the kind of merriment I had seen take its toll on her before, merriment like a wasting of her vital energies. But she was also steeled to the task—merrily steeled to the task might be as close as I can come to describing her demeanor at that time.

I had an eye on her, another on the functionaries in the offices we had to visit, another on the parish priest who would marry us, another on my mother, whose tolerance for things foreign was dangerously low, another on my father, who in the midst of so much turmoil seemed to be drifting off, another on the man who was helping us, Javier's brother-in-law, Sergio, Amparo's ostensible employer during the past year, and another on Sergio's wife, Maite, who was glamorous in furs and all for us but clearly had something other than the sanctity of matrimony on her mind, and still another on anyone who might cross our path thinking to sabotage it all—so many eyes there was no way they would fit in the front or the back of my head.

I remember Palma as a city built in a crescent around a bay. Brown stone. Streets unwinding into broad avenues that went straight as the Roman roads they once had been. There was an international community there, an assortment of races and religions and tongues. Perhaps more prosperity than one saw on the mainland. But an island, no easy way off if you were found out and nowhere to hide. So, be aboveboard and have a good time.

But we were not tourists.

My father and I shared a room in a hotel, as did my mother and Amparo, and for three days we were petitioners. Sergio was at our disposal, a heavyset man with drooping jowls and baggy eyes and a mustache as flaccid as Javier's was pert. In fact, physically and psychologically, they seemed clear opposites. What they had in common was that they were Antonio's friends. Or Sergio was the friend of a friend, which made him a friend of ours at still another remove. Yet he drove us around. A businessman, he took time off from work to deliver us to the right desk in the right office, and after a word or two in the right ear all we had to do was sign. Amparo became a resident in his house. When we met Maite, it was as if between her and Amparo too much beauty had been packed into one small room and somebody would have to go. Then Javier arrived with his wife, Maite's sister Isabel, and Isabel contributed her part to the high vivid coloring, the dark eyes, the natural glossiness of skin. My father, when he saw the three of them together, was dazzled into a kind of boyish babble that did not sit well with my mother. I remember a single sheepish and wildly aroused look from him that said, I traveled my territory, I kept my eyes open, but there in Iowa, Indiana and Illinois, I had no idea. Where are we, son? What fabulous world is this?

We are in Franco's Spain, Father. This is what Franco has kept hidden from the eyes of the world.

I thought of my father again and again during our interview with the parish priest, Father Collosa. *Padre,* I called him—no time now for disrespect—and the first few times I found myself almost choking with a mixture of shame and sadness, for it seemed as if I were telling my own father good-bye. Father Collosa was no Menendez, no ecclesiastical authority barricaded behind his desk. He had thinning black hair and wore a cassock that made his true shape almost impossible to determine. He had small, white, utterly inoffensive hands, the most innocent hands I have ever seen. Hands ideally suited, it occurred to me, for placing the host on the faithful's tongue. The expression he wore throughout our interview was as mild and composed as we were precipitous in our need of him, and he talked to us almost entirely about our obligation to whatever children might come from our union. They were to be baptized, confirmed and educated as Catholics. We nodded that we understood. He had papers he read from in this respect, and to each of his questions, which were phrased more as foregone conclusions, we nodded yes. From me, as the alien half of this marriage, he extracted a promise. He understood I'd been baptized Presbyterian, but he couldn't presume to know how I'd been raised. He did not catechize me, but he wanted to know if I understood what was meant by raising children in a Roman Catholic household. Did I have any questions for him? I did not. His hands were clasped on his lap. They were not clenched. What he meant was that I, as the father, was to set a Christian example for my children. Yes, Father. But as the non-Catholic half of the marriage, if questions arose I was to defer to my wife. I tried to make a little chivalrous joke. I would always defer to my wife. Yes, he could see that we loved each other, but his obligation was to the children. Then he extracted his promise. Did I promise to raise the children Catholic and to defer to my wife when questions regarding their upbringing arose? And a nod here wouldn't do.

There was something in his eyes—not in those sanctified hands. Something in the very restfulness of his eyes that was wide awake and alert to a hidden advantage. Back in my Kentucky boyhood people had bargained with each other in this way; you learned to read what lay behind the pleasantness in the other's expression, not so you could call the pleasantness false and create a scene, but so you could knock a dollar or two off the asking price. In as obedient a tone as I could muster, I told Father Collosa I would be willing to sign a paper. He said that wouldn't be necessary, just a promise, from me to him.

Sí, padre, se lo prometo.

Later that same day, Javier and Sergio took us to the office in the City Hall where, as our witnesses, they would perjure themselves by swearing they knew of no impediment to our marriage, such as a previous marriage, and where our license would be issued. We had to set the date, but Amparo had already made up her mind. The second day of Christmas. The evening of December 26. That was cutting it as close as you could possibly cut it since, as things stood, her brother and parents weren't scheduled to arrive until that morning. I suggested the twenty-seventh or twenty-eighth, but the parish church was available on the evening of the twenty-sixth, Father Collosa could perform the service then and there was some justice to be had, if not triumph, in having the marriage performed on that very date. Of course, I consented. Javier, the DA, falsely swore himself with the aplomb of a bon vivant, and Sergio, the prominent businessman with the sagging face and the high-stepping wife, signed, too.

That must have been on December 23, for the next day I came down sick and spent Christmas Eve and Christmas Day in bed. We had no more offices to visit, although there was plenty left to do. Somebody had to arrange for flowers in the church, and for the wedding supper, and although the honeymoon might seem ages away, someone had to see about those reservations, too. Through all this hectic and suspenseful week, I had worried about Amparo's endurance; then I was the one who came down with a wicked cold. I took to the bed, she sat beside me holding my hand, and it was then that I told Amparo that if my reading of things was correct, Father Collosa knew our dark secret but had decided to go ahead with the marriage anyway. Did she know how I knew? Because he'd chosen to ignore the encyclical issued by the Vatican a few short months before. That encyclical, as we both remembered, had modified the mixed marriage agreement. The non-Catholic spouse, thenceforth, would have to promise only not to impede the raising of the children as Catholics, which was not the same thing as promising to raise them Catholic, come what may. But that was the promise Father Collosa had extracted from me.

She shook her head. A fine difference, she said, a splitting of hairs.

A fine difference, but why, then, even bother to issue the encyclical? And the Church was famous for splitting hairs. How many angels did it finally decide would fit on the head of a pin?

Well, Father Collosa had probably forgotten the policy had been changed.

He had the documents before him, I said. Trust me, he knows.

It was so rushed. We caught him by surprise.

He was as collected as a priest can be.

But you're not, she said. You're sick and need to get well. She felt my forehead and took my temperature. She tousled my hair. I told her not to kiss me since one of us had to be out there, maintaining our guard, but she kissed me anyway and told me I had a touch of delirium and was imagining things.

I told her we were all right as long as Father Collosa didn't have a last-minute seizure of conscience the way Menendez had. But I didn't think that would happen and I started to tell her why. It had to do with the look Collosa and I had exchanged. The look said, I know what I know, you know what you know, here's the deal. You get out there and bust your ass to raise those kids in the very Church that has taken a certain Old World pleasure in making your life miserable, and I'll pronounce the words that will send everybody home happy. A look that came down to a horse-trading glint in the eye. To go with those disarming white hands. But I didn't tell her this because Amparo suddenly turned from honey-rose to mealy-white and her eyes opened wide. *Horror!* she uttered.

I sank back in bed. I didn't want to hear this, whatever it was going to be.

Menendez . . . she breathed. The Basilica! We forgot to cancel the reservation.

Antonio probably did, I said.

Her eyes opened wider. The invitations! We forgot to tell the people! Guests will come. . . . They'll be there. The *virgen de los desamparados* . . . Antonio . . .

Antonio is bringing my wedding dress! And your tux, did you forget about that? Antonio will be bringing it, too. Antonio can't do everything!

I wondered why not. He could come as close as anybody I knew, but I didn't want to hear any more. I didn't exactly fake a swoon, but I breathed heavily and let myself go limp and left the matter of one wedding scheduled for two different places at the same time to somebody else.

Then I must have slept. When I woke up Amparo had left and my father had entered the room.

I was feeling no better, if anything worse. But when he asked I told him I was raring to go.

He was in a pensive mood, with a smile as distant as if it had crossed the Atlantic. I sure wish Sally was here, he said. I almost called her this morning and told her to get on a plane, now that we know there's going to be a wedding.

Remember, I cautioned him, there was going to be a wedding before.

I expect Amparo could use a sister right about now.

My throat was sore and I didn't really want to talk. My father would understand the deal Father Collosa had made, but I couldn't fill him in with this throat. I held up crossed fingers to him and he nodded.

A moment later he pondered, When you stop to think about it, it's like some kind of movie you've gotten us into. In the movies the good guys always win. He paused, and grinned, almost guiltily, for the question he was about to ask. We *are* the good guys, aren't we, son?

I opened my bleary eyes wide and gave him a long sigh to read.

He gave me a solemn nod, an expression of loyalty. But he knew as well as I did that we were a little band of outlaws. I sure do wish Sally was here, he reverted to his original thought. There're things Amparo can't talk about with your mother.

It turns out Amparo and Mother had gone shopping. Something new, something blue. The flowers. They had gone sightseeing. The cathedral. The fact was, they had gone off and left my father alone, and I had gotten sick, and it was only natural he'd be thinking of his daughter, the last chance *he* had for some companionship in this strange world.

You let me know if there's something I can do, he said.

I smiled and closed my eyes. I heard him leave the room. He would probably spend the remainder of the afternoon down in the hotel lobby.

An attractive but unapproachable people would stroll by, speaking in an incomprehensible language, behaving in strange ways. Christmas Eve. Then my mother was there, peering into my face, when I opened my eyes. You're exhausted, she said. You've been after this for a year and you almost made it.

I'll make it, I croaked.

If anyone deserves a rest, you do.

I'll rest when we're married.

There was just a trace of a knowing grin. To explain the facts of life my mother had waited until my father was on the road and then had sat on the side of the bed, like this, tucking me in.

We went shopping, my mother recounted. I can't tell you how many dresses Amparo tried on. I'd be embarrassed, but it seems to be something they do over here. She looks so good in everything.

I did not recall my mother making an admission like that about any other woman; certainly not about my first wife.

I wanted to buy her one, she went on. But she wouldn't let me. She said her brother buys her too many dresses as it is. I like her, my mother confided, then added, in a coy fishing tone, I hope she likes me.

Root and Cloud. I told my mother that Amparo loved them both.

After we shopped we went to the cathedral, Mother continued. Amparo said it was a small gothic cathedral, but it looked enormous to me. All that space but so few pews. And it's so dark in there. Do you know what I thought of? Father picking Mother out of the congregation in the First Christian Church in Monroe, Georgia. I doubt if he could have seen her over here.

Mother chuckled. She was chuckling and rattling on. It was her form of a pep talk.

You've got weddings on the brain, I said.

You know, I think I must. Before we left the cathedral Amparo kneeled down outside one of those dark little boxes and confessed. When she was done she looked as happy as could be, even happier than when she was trying on the dresses. I told her so.

She did what?

She confessed. Then she got up off her knees and we walked out to-gether. She took my arm. You're a pretty lucky fellow, my mother conceded. But, surely thinking of the vast cathedral and the dim space and that cramped wooden box with its sliding window, she added, It *is* strange.

I got the chills. I was either at that stage of my cold or riddled with apprehensions. When Amparo came to sit with me I committed the kind of indiscretion that Father Collosa had, perhaps, warned me against.

Mother said you went to confession. What did you confess?

My sins, she said.

What sins? I was more outraged than perplexed. You haven't committed any sins! Amparo, did you tell him about us?

Us?

I begged her not to play dumb. I pointed at my sore throat. What we're doing, I rasped. What we've done.

Mass will be said at the wedding. I had to go to confession.

Mother said you looked happier than ever.

I *am* happy.

And you feel all right?

I feel better than you.

No dizziness. None of those weak spells—you know what I mean.

I feel fine.

Just fine?

Bien. Muy bien.

And you didn't tell him, did you, Amparo?

Don't you know that priests never reveal anything they hear at confession?

Unless someone is out to hoodwink the Church.

Hoodwink?

Engañar.

Oh . . .

Or unless someone on high . . .

She laughed at me. *Cállate,* she tried to shut me up.

Please, I begged her. After we're married you can tell them I've had a wife for every day of the year, but not before. Okay?

She smiled at me, and nodded.

But I couldn't stop myself. It had been my mother's description. How does one get that happy just by kneeling before a dark and stale-smelling box? Whispering sins in an orgy of self-incrimination.

You didn't tell him, did you?

No, she said.

A lie, I knew. Another sin she would have to confess. She was telling me to get well.

But the next day, when I got up to go the bathroom, I felt weak at every joint and had to crawl back into bed. I panicked. I had all the symptoms of a common cold, but common colds did not unstring your knees and keep you from getting to the altar, if that was where your destination—and your destiny—lay.

I got on the phone and requested the downstairs desk to find me a doctor. They reminded me it was Christmas day, and I informed them that on the second day of Christmas I would either be married or buried, it was up to them. I also told them to tell the doctor when he came to bring all the medicine he had.

He came later on. How much later I could not be sure. We had already exchanged Christmas greetings with Sally on the phone. My father had gotten sentimental and a bit tongue-tied; giggling affectionately, Amparo had tried out her much-improved English; Mother had inquired about some boyfriend Sally was seeing at the time; and I had told her that Christmas without her in this distant land seemed about as unreal as the rest of it. She told me it was real, all right, and I'd better practice getting out of bed right now. She wanted to hear me get up. So I groaned out of bed, before sitting back down, which was enough for her.

When the doctor examined me he said I had a cold and prescribed warm coffee and milk, two aspirin and a shot of cognac, the standing remedy for most ailments in Spain. I asked if I could talk to this doctor alone, and my mother, father and Amparo cleared the room. Nonetheless, my voice went low as if I were about to whisper barely mentionable matters. Another confession? If Amparo could come away from it so happily shriven, why couldn't I?

What I confessed was that I knew it was no more than a cold, and that *café con leche*, aspirin and cognac would work as well as anything else. But for a year I'd been struggling for this day, and then—maudlin and sick and more confessional than I'd intended—I told this doctor that, in fact, I'd been struggling for this day for my whole life. I had crossed an ocean to get here and taken on some pretty formidable opponents, and I was one day away and didn't care how many drugs he'd have to give me to get me on my feet, I was in dire need.

A hotel doctor on Christmas day. He had maybe ten percent of his friendly bedside manner left. He had a sallow face, which the black of the eyebrows and mustache and hairline accentuated, and the black stubble of his beard added a graininess to the effect. His lips were noticeably thin and bloodless and I waited for them to smile. He said none of this would improve on his original prescription, but he'd give me enough penicillin to make me feel drugged, if that was what I wanted. It was when he was preparing the shot that he asked me if Amparo was the bride to be. When I told him she was, that was when he smiled—as he was pulling the penicillin through the needle into the syringe.

The Spanish give shots well. With a plap, plap, plap against the backside until the needle goes in with a painless prick. This doctor's shot hurt. That was what I got for presuming to marry a real Spanish beauty and then for whining about it.

I wasn't that sick, and I knew it. But now I was drugged.

So I slept. The flowers got bought, a photographer was contracted, the restaurant reservations were made. Sergio knew a small hotel by the sea that still had a room available, where an interlude that would serve as a honeymoon could be spent. I woke up to be informed of all these developments, then went back to sleep. Amparo's parents would be coming on the next morning flight, Antonio on the overnight boat. People were converging on this island. No word from anybody in the Church. If you're going to ruin a person's life—once and for all, definitively, no wiggle room left—you don't do it on the holiest day of the year.

The next day Antonio came with two boxes, and one contained a tux I was expected to wear. For the weddings I had attended in the States a dark suit had done just fine, but that was there and we were somewhere else. Once Antonio was on the scene he took charge, and went off with the other box to see what last-minute adjustments needed to be made to Amparo's dress. Before he left, we had a moment. I was groggy, in that buffer zone where the most immediate of acts can seem remote. I was taking more penicillin and a painkilling spray for my throat. Woozy and not entirely accountable—if I'd been standing at the stern of a ship an observer might have concluded I was about to throw it all up.

Antonio said, Well, monster, how do you feel?

I was propped up against the headboard, ready to rise. I told him, Like one of the figures in your paintings, half here and half somewhere else.

I thought that would please him. But he gave me the same squint-eyed look he gave his paintings when he hadn't gotten them right. Too late now to blot me out and begin again.

It's time to get up, he said. Time to get up and get well.

I got out of bed, showered and shaved. For fifteen minutes I was raring to go. Then the freshening effects of the shower wore off, and I was tempted to get back into bed. The truth was, after months of doing two or three things at once, I had nothing to do. Then I remembered to try on the tux.

I hadn't worn a tux since high school, when my mother had actually bought one for me, along with the cummerbund, suspenders, studs, cuff links and bow tie, so that I could attend the proms, freshman through senior years. They had always made me feel more military than sociable. But Antonio knew my measurements from the suit he'd had made for me, and the tux he'd rented fit. A black cummerbund and suspenders were included, and a bow tie. There were no studs and no cufflinks because there was no shirt.

I did not own a white dress shirt. Antonio had not thought to buy me one. My mother had dressed me once, but I was not about to step back into those times. I went through my father's suitcase, as I had as a boy, looking for those small gifts he'd bring me from the road, and discovered that he had one white shirt, the one he planned to wear that night. And my father, now that I'd become such a hulking figure (among the fine-boned Spanish), was a much smaller man.

I called the desk. Stores were as closed on the second day of Christmas as they were on the first. I dressed and went down to the desk so that I could make them understand.

The day was cold and clear (a record cold was on the way) and the sky a glassy blue. I was not so much foreign to the Spanish as I was foreign to the healthy, walking around in my penicillin-spun cocoon. Among the many people milling around in the lobby or standing beside their bags, I didn't see my father, or the Ferris, for that matter. I wasn't even sure the Ferris had arrived. The desk clerk was happy that the doctor had been able to put me back on my feet, and, yes, he knew what was in the works, a wedding, wedding parties were daily fare in their very popular hotel. Not that brides like mine, he managed to insinuate with a wink, came along every day.

He wore a maroon blazer himself, and his shirt was white, but he was a smaller man than my father.

I repeated what I needed. I appealed to the Spaniards' theatrical nature. A wedding that had hinged on so many things at one time or another now hinged on a white shirt.

If not a men's store that was open, a store that rented costumes, or a tailor who worked quickly, a tailor who specialized in shirt fronts, he could forget the back. Or, it occurred to me, a theater and the rack of stuff it'd have in wardrobe.

I started to laugh. I had no idea where Amparo was in that moment, but I caught myself casting wild glances around the hotel lobby in hopes that she was there, and I think what I had in mind was to make a run for it. I would grab her by the hand, we would get up a head of speed, and make a run for it right off this island and that backward peninsula and that Old World continent with its age-old strictures and labyrinthine ways, and we'd keep going until we'd come to a place so carefree and eager to please that we'd really have to work at it to find a custom, law or divine command to be in violation of.

I remembered Amparo, as she had been that first day, laughing and bounding ahead of me up some palace stairs.

In a place such as I had in mind all palace stairs would lead to connubial sanctuaries.

In such a place all weddings would be shirtless affairs.

I continued to laugh, and the desk clerk stepped out from behind his counter. I thought he meant to send me back to bed. But he looked me over from shoulder to shoulder, then up and down. He sent a bell boy after someone called Pedro, then told him to bring Eduardo, too. He positioned Pedro on one side of me, Eduardo on the other. I wondered if they were about to strong-arm me back to bed or, perhaps, out of the hotel entirely. But the desk clerk gave the two of them the same sizing up he'd given me, and then, with a dip of the head and a pull at the mouth that indicated better than nothing, he told Pedro to go take the shirt off his back and give it to me.

Pedro's shirt was white, but I agreed with Pedro: It was a permanently discolored off-white and the collar was frayed, which Pedro was reluctant to admit, since he had come to work in it. But he had a better shirt at home. He would take me there. And before he could be stopped he'd gotten on the phone and told his mother to iron the shirt he had in his chest of drawers.

I rode with him, in his 600-model Seat, the smallest car Seat makes. Pedro was my size—the reason the desk clerk had thought of him. In fact, he was a little heavier in the shoulders and neck, the reason the desk clerk had made that less-than-satisfied expression. My drug cocoon had enlarged to include Pedro and his tiny car. He lived on the outskirts of the city in one of those apartment-block complexes that make the drive in to any center-city in Spain, where the historic buildings are located, such a tasteless ordeal. My story was my upcoming marriage, and on the way Pedro told me his. His apartment was new. When he had it furnished down to the last ashtray he would marry his *novia* and they would move in. The mother? His mother would . . . move over. Pedro didn't mind moving his mother in before the last ashtray was in place, but he could never bring his bride there. *Hombre!* Who could? I thought of the cold, spartanly furnished house I was bringing Amparo to. Pedro's engagement had been going on eight years. I thought of what I'd been going through strung out for that long. His *novia* lived with her parents and a brother—Pedro was inviting these comparisons. But he didn't know. He was innocent, typical—a typical, innocent Spaniard bred to progress at a generational pace—and he was zipping across Palma in his cockpit-sized car so that he could help get me outfitted and then get back to work.

His mother was ironing every hint of a wrinkle out of that shirt on the dining-room table when we walked in. The apartment was spotless and as cold as its shiny tiles. It was heated by a single butane heater that they rolled from room to room. The artwork was devotional and most of the pieces were no larger than dessert plates—*Ave Marías,* pressed-tin depictions of the Virgin. There was one Christ hanging on a cross, a large mirror in an ornate frame and a small television snuggled in a corner. It was the only thing snuggled anywhere. Pedro's mother, a round indefatigable woman who would probably live another forty years, insisted I try the shirt on, as if she were prepared to do alterations on the spot.

I stood in front of the mirror in Pedro's shirt. Pedro stood behind me, his mother did too, but they were both included in the frame. Pedro's shirt was too big in the neck and chest. In it I looked sicker—gaunter— than I was or felt. Who would marry me? I shifted my gaze to Pedro and his mother, who for the time I'd been standing there seemed to be holding their breath. It was one of those moments you don't forget. I didn't know who those people were or how they had gotten into my frame. The apartment was a mostly unfurnished, generic noplace. I recognized this pale, glassy-eyed version of myself, but was unconvinced. A blink of the eyes, or a half step aside, and I could make it all go away.

I summoned a vision of my wife-to-be in a last-ditch attempt to make any of this real. If all our efforts were finally going to end in farce, I wanted her to tell me so, or at least I wanted to go down with her face in my mind's eye, not the faces of Pedro and his mother. Instead of the woman I knew I got Amparo as I'd seen her in another of Antonio's photographs. She had eyes round as Roman coins, black as olives. She wore an accountable-to-no-one, utterly unprincipled smirk. The face I saw beside mine in the mirror belonged to a fearless little provocateur known as the *secretarieta*.

Bien, bien, I gave in, and Pedro's mother bustled up to me, tugging the shirt straight, running her finger around the loose collar, making little *ayyy*'s of alarm and disapproval to herself. For a moment I let her. Then I collected myself. *Sí, está bien,* I insisted. Pedro's mother and I went back and forth—*sí, no, sí, no*—until Pedro himself intervened, *Está bien, Mama. Sirve.*

She turned on her son. *Sirve? Para casarse?* She was asking with incredulous indignation who would possibly say that that shirt was good enough to go off and get married in?

Bueno . . . Pedro temporized.

Alguien que no quiere casarse de verdad, she retorted, but this was meant for Pedro, not for me. Pedro might not really want to get married, and might be putting it and the siring of grandchildren off until the last ashtray was in place, but not I. I thanked the woman. In gratitude I gave her a big swelling smile, expanding my chest, too, until the shirt fit. I coughed and took the shirt off. Pedro took me back to the hotel. When we got there what I remember him saying was *Ves?*—you see, you see what I'm up against?—and I told him I did.

. . .

LA MANCHA—we stand in it, and the difference between it and Old Castile is clear. La Mancha is New Castile, it is the Spanish Wild West; as the Moors were beaten back into their Andalucian strongholds, settlers poured in and took over towns or laid out new ones. The battle of Navas de Tolosa in 1212 gave La Mancha to the Castilians for good. We stand in a field outside the town of Consuegra. I hang back and Amparo walks on beside a vineyard. Ahead of us is the wall-enclosed, cypress-shadowed cemetery of the town, but a man with cemeteries on his mind might look at these grape stocks and see grave markers in their rows. I go up and grip one around its shaggy girth and give it a shake. But it doesn't shake. It's as deeply rooted as a tree. Above Consuegra a row of portly windmills mounts the hill, cylindrical in shape and in color a glimmering nocturnal white, their great oaring blades still. The windmills constitute a key difference between New and Old Castile. Here, on any elevation above the town, you're likely to find windmills, not castles. Another difference is the width of the streets. In *manchegan* towns, streets run straight and wide out onto the plains. That is, as straight as streets can ever be said to run in Spain, for there will always be a curving white wall to break up the grid. There is more space here—the towns spread into it, the clustering isn't as dense. And there are fewer towns. In Tierra Campo above Valladolid, from almost any given point, four or five are visible, but here in La Mancha you see wheat fields, vineyards, olive groves and then, and this is crucial, at the horizon a low wrinkling of hills. You pivot around. The space is Western in its expanse, but it *is* enclosed. In Old Castile it is spotted with hamlets, with their castles and churches and *palomares*, but at the horizon it extends in a blur. In La Mancha, at any turn you'll see at a distance those low encircling hills. That makes La Mancha a theater, a theater in the round. Old Castile is more like a tabletop, crowded from time immemorial, but in La Mancha, in spite of that great expanse, you're always on stage.

Quixote, who had a feel for the land, knew it. Panza plodded on.

I call out to Amparo to look around her, to see what a theatrical moment this is, but a brisk wind blows my voice back to me. It doesn't matter. She's looking around on her own, aware of what we're surrounded by and that wherever we stand we're center stage. I think of the old definition of God that I first read in Pascal: God is that circle whose center is everywhere and whose circumference is nowhere. I realize that to be in God's eye at the center of the stage is to be Quixote.

I call out to her again. She turns. Dulcinea she wanted to be.

She wears jeans, a loose-fitting pale blouse that the wind wraps around her. The evening sun spreads gold over her cheek. She closes her eyes as she waits for me and takes the warmth, and the flickering eyelids, with their long lashes, which I can't see, I can remember very well. Sleep, I would tell her, and stand over her, waiting for the eyelids to go still. Some of my happier moments came when they did—when the flickering of those veined lids ceased—and I knew she would have a good day ahead.

She waits for me. Every quest goes in two directions at once in this theater in the round, in this roundness. I waited for her at the altar, but now, in Quixote country, she's forged ahead and waits for me to team up.

What is this town? she asks.

Consuegra?

In the *Quixote*.

I don't remember. It's mentioned. Puerto Lapice is the next town over, and that may or may not be where it all began.

I thought it all began in El Toboso.

I mean where a certain gentleman named Quexana transformed himself into Quixote and had his first adventure. His inspiration came from a farm girl named Aldonza Lorenzo, whom he transformed into his Dulcinea. Do you know the title he gave her?

Tell me.

Lady of My Thoughts.

Claro, she says, as her schoolgirl's reading of the classic comes back to her.

The key is, I go on, once they're transformed they stay transformed. No one remembers Quexana or Lorenzo anymore.

You did.

I'm not native to it, I explain. I have to approach it as a pedant would, I'm afraid.

Pobre. She stretches up to kiss me on the cheek. She squeezes my hand. Look at us here, twenty-nine years later, she says in a marveling voice. If she's Panza she's caught a bit of her master's spirit. She's been bitten by the bug. We're Lamar and Amparo, but as long as we're standing here we can become somebody else. We're on hallowed ground.

Twenty-nine years ago I did become somebody else. Maybe you did, too. I'm not sure how many transformations we're entitled to.

One more, she says, giving my hand a playful tug.

Remember how the *Quixote* ends, I caution her.

How?

In disillusion and death.

She makes a mock grimace, accompanied by a mock groan.

Then her face turns serious, reflective, as the evening sun falls on it. The playfulness is not gone, she's just put it in its most meaningful frame. It's not exactly a "long and mournful countenance," but it is the thoughtful countenance that allows her to keep the child alive.

Well, until then, she says.

Until then?

Until it ends in disillusion and death. Then she adds something that surprises me and endears her to me even more, if that is possible. She says it in a child's tone of wonderment and intimate companionship: Are you afraid?

I am.

Of what?

Of what happened to Quixote. He woke up, it all turned drab on him, he recanted his madness and died.

She won't let me get too somber, now that she's brought us here to La Mancha. Will I turn drab on you? she asks. She's fishing, baiting me with her eyes.

Never, I say.

You'll tell me when the poetry's over.

I won't have to, I say. It won't happen.

When it does.

No.

So . . . she casts a glance around her at the extent of our stage. Swallows are darting over the wheat fields, the cypress tips are bending in the wind. The windmills glimmer like prehistoric relics above the town, in their big barrel-like girth, on the point of being converted into phantoms. . . . Who do you want to be?

I can't improve on Cervantes, I tell her. You are Dulcinea, the Lady of My Thoughts.

Who do *you* want to be?

Your champion.

With a stormy little pout she gives up on me and stalks ahead. I catch up with her. That night I take her to bed in Consuegra, and the next day I take her to Toboso.

It's a clean town of wide streets and squared stone, *señorial*, Amparo calls it, by which she means it's a town of taste and refinement worthy of being inhabited by gentlemen and gentlewomen. Signs—silhouettes of Quixote and Sancho—tracing the route of the *Quixote* over La Mancha have led us here, and once we are walking Toboso's streets other signs lead us to the "palace" of Dulcinea. These latter signs are plaques containing quotes from *Quixote* fixed to the walls of prominent buildings. We come upon one fixed to the wall of the church. *Con la iglesia hemos dado, Sancho*, it says, and I seem to remember that that was what Quixote said to his squire when they came upon the church in the night, hoping that such a magnificent structure might prove to be the palace they were seeking. But, Quixote says, we've arrived at the church, Sancho, and not at my lady's palace.

My father said that, Amparo recalls.

What?

That we'd run into the Church. *Con la iglesia hemos topado, Sancho.*

That's not how Cervantes puts it. He says *dado*. We've reached the church, Sancho.

My father said, *topado*—he meant run into, collided with. He said it after he came back from his meeting with that traitorous *fiscal*. What was his name?

Menendez . . . or something like it. Your father said that? After he tried to clobber him with his crutch?

Yes. I'd forgotten.

I wish you hadn't. I wish you'd told me.

So you could have had my father quoting Quixote in the heat of the battle?

Yes. Misquoting. But it would have been a nice effect. Quixote wouldn't have minded, although I'm not too sure about Cervantes. Remember, Cervantes was devout. He made that pilgrimage to the shine of Guadalupe. He climbed up that hill and left his leg irons there. But Quixote regarded all that stood in the way of Romance as his enemy.

Topado, she muses, in memory of her father, who fought the good fight. *Iglesia* with a big I. Church with a big C.

Versus Romance, with a big R, I chime in.

We let the signs lead us to Dulcinea's palace, the palace that Quixote and Sancho never found but that the town authorities have seen fit to give them, nonetheless. It is a self-sufficient little complex of buildings enclosed within its whitewashed walls. There's a mill inside, a grape press, a *palomar*. It has its own chapel. A gentlewoman owned it, plus considerable adjoining terrain. If Quixote hadn't been crazy or so enamored of transforming farm girls into something they weren't, she would have been a woman worth serving. Then Sancho wouldn't have had to worry so. And Cervantes wouldn't have had to have his Don come crashing down at the end.

But Quixote was crazy. He didn't love an accomplished woman. He loved what feats could be accomplished in the name of love. He loved turning a dish-faced, barnyard-scented farm girl into a queen.

We walk the town some more. There are more of these wall-enclosed complexes and there's a Dulcinea museum we don't go into. The Tourism Ministry knows what it has and has struck a nice balance between the amenities tourists expect and Toboso as a living town. Kids kick a soccer ball against the wall of the church, and an unmuffled motorbike makes the sound of a ratcheted-up hoof beat down the resonant streets. But Amparo and I were on more familiar ground out on that plain.

Where to now? I ask her.

I think, she says, since it's on the way, I'd like to go home.

You're no longer Dulcinea, are you?

No.

But someone nearly as fabulous.

That's for you to say.

Special, then.

I'll give you that.

Who said, One never forgets the places one ran as a child?

I don't know.

But you did have the run of the town.

You could say that.

And they called you *la secretarieta* because you were a little law unto yourself.

She laughs at me then—clear, musical, the music a fountain makes as it sprays high into the air.

In a manner of speaking, you were your own crazy hat, weren't you?

She cocks her head, gives me a puzzling frown. In what manner of speaking?

You had a special license. You did what you wanted. You were beyond canons of taste and decorum. You had the liberty to blend in or stick out.

I was spoiled, she admits.

No, you both belonged and you led the way.

Is that really what you think?

You were in your element. That is to say, the elements were all in you.

A curious way to put it. I believe you've just paid me a *piropo*. Or is that something Don Quixote said to his Dulcinea?

No, it's something I said to you.

Ahh . . .

She sends her voice low. Down out of the watery air, rising from the warmth of the earth. Take me there, she issues her command. Last town, I promise.

We saddle up burro and steed and proceed to her hometown of Bocairente.

.   .   .

SHE WAS TWENTY MINUTES LATE. Instead of eight o'clock she arrived on the arm of her brother at the church door at eight-twenty. Antonio and I had been at the church earlier to see what would take the place of the Basilica of the *desamparados*, where, it turned out, Antonio had not canceled our reservation. Perhaps Menendez himself had. Guests whom we had invited did arrive, and I like to think they saw another wedding, a proxy for ours. The church we were about to be married in did not suit Antonio's taste, and, to be honest, as a church, it didn't suit mine. The nave was gothic, its vaulted ceiling groined. But the altarpiece, the *retablo*, was baroque, and when I stood before Father Collosa, or when we kneeled on the velvet-padded *reclinatorio* to pray, I saw sunbursts and angels and gold-plated cherubs erupting from a wall. Earlier Antonio had stepped off to one side of that *retablo* to speak with Father Collosa privately. I'd seen him kneel, and although my parents were there, too, and I was paying attention to them, I couldn't keep my eyes off Antonio. Forget the box with its small sliding window. He'd stepped off to the side to confess. Father Collosa bent down to hear him. I kept waiting for him to glance up at me, the second Antonio confessed to what he had done to cover up my sin. But Father Collosa was good. He devoted his attention to this *alma en pena,* this suffering soul, before him. With no change of expression he chastised, forgave, and absolved Antonio, then made the sign of the cross above him, returning him to us as relieved of his sins and as happy as Amparo was said to have been.

Maybe Collosa hadn't known all along, but if Antonio had told him our secret, he had eliminated the middle man. It would no longer take Amparo's confessor in the cathedral to walk this classified information over to Collosa in his parish church. Father Collosa could be in the middle of the ceremony and about to pronounce the words and then find his conscience seizing up on him as Menendez's was said to have done.

Confession, both as a sacrament and as a psychological phenomenon, defied my understanding. I was sick and suggestible and dying to have all this done. I wore another man's shirt, which hung on me like stiffened flab, and an ownerless tux whose tails reached past my knees, and I was prepared to believe that sins were never absolved. Rather, they were like little indestructible units of matter that got passed around. Amparo and Antonio might walk around shriven, but I got loaded down.

There came a moment when I simply gave in. Sometime during those twenty minutes that I stood at the altar waiting for my bride, I surrendered to the forces that be—or were—which is another way of saying I placed my fate in the hands of God. Mother, dressed in an elegant pink gown, a hotter pink than she was accustomed to wearing, stood with me for a while. Then she said her feet were hurting and sat down. She invited me to sit, too, reminding me that I wasn't well and implying that we might have a long wait on our hands. I insisted on standing. The wedding guests were our witnesses, Javier and his wife, Sergio and his. And then Señor and Señora Ferri, who had arrived tired and looked even more tired and solemn-faced now. The church was cold. All of the women wore furs. Thanks to the medicine I was taking, I wore a fur-like insulation of my own. Once I caught my father's eye, and he was a humble enough man not to be offering advice now. What could he say? Hang tight, son? Perhaps in Indiana, Iowa and Illinois. He smiled limply, as frank a communication as would ever pass between us, and sometime around then I let myself go.

If she didn't come, if these were the first twenty minutes of the rest of my life without Amparo, so be it. Twenty minutes might become two hours, and while everyone else despaired I would still be there. In my passivity, I felt strangely safe. What could they do to me—walk up and usher me off the stage? Well, somebody had ushered me on. I stood there with Father Collosa waiting for him either to pull the plug or to accept a fait accompli and absolve me of my sins on the spot.

What sins? They accused me of robbing Spain of a national treasure, and the fathers with eligible sons stepped forward with patriotic fervor to cry foul. The country or the woman? The country *and* the woman. I wanted it all. National honor demanded that someone put a stop to me.

I had nothing else to do as I stood there but give in to my delirium. When Amparo appeared in the church door with her brother at twenty after eight, I had talked myself into believing it was because I deserved her and she deserved me.

Antonio wore his black velvet Edwardian suit, which I had not seen, only heard about, a white shirt with ruffles, and elevator shoes. Since Amparo was in heels, the shoes barely kept him at her height. He walked gingerly in them, and I got the impression he was testing his footing every step of the way. His expression was sobered and his complexion pale to the point that he might have considered wearing makeup. But he'd had no way of knowing what this moment, which began on a boat in the high seas, would do to him. He kept his eyes raised to that gaudy *retablo* behind us, which meant, since I knew what he thought of that *retablo* as a work of art, that he had his eyes turned back inside his head.

But he'd gotten a last chance and had dressed his sister well. It may have been my sickly eyesight, but there in the back of the church the white of her dress had a ghostly silvered sheen—he'd trimmed the neck and the

hem in white fur, in subtle contrast to the airy evanescence of the veil—
and as she proceeded up the aisle it was as if she were gathering into flesh
before my eyes. She began as a lovely wraith; she arrived at my side
as lovelier flesh and bone. This, of course, was how Antonio the artist
worked, but on this one occasion, by the time he'd brought her to me, he'd
misted his sister into something solid, bountiful and warm to the touch.

Actually, I felt a deep sympathy for Antonio. The shakiness of his
step was truly heroic. Show me the man who could walk this woman up
the aisle—a woman taking on heat, weight and a wildness of blood with
each stride—and not shake. Thank you, Antonio. You may hand her
over now. I sent another mental note to my mother, who had stood up
with me, that it was time for her also to stand aside. The moment had arrived. Father Collosa had a job to do. You could raise a Romanesque
vault to gothic heights, throw on some baroque and whip it up to a ro-
coco froth, you could issue encyclical after encyclical and split papal
hairs, you could canonize and demote saints by the score, you could play
footsie with Franco and institute an Inquisition of the mind, but the day
would come when a woman stood at the altar demanding to be married,
and there was nothing you could do. Except do it.

Marry her to me.

I, of course, was the wraith now. Long before we were to kneel on
the *reclinatorio* to pray and hear the Mass, I had to reach out and steady
myself. Amparo stood at my side, cradling a bouquet of orchids, whose
scent was as strong to my nose as smelling salts, and I had to hold on. A
photographer was taking pictures and, unbeknownst to me, somebody
was making a super-8 film. It was during this time that they caught me at
my pious best, my eyes raised and apparently trained on that *retablo*, too.
With so much gold and so many angels ascending into heaven, it would
have been hard not to look that way, but the photograph that delighted
the children was of me in the role of some El Greco apostle gazing toward the hereafter while Amparo looked distractedly off to the side, the

same look she wore when we'd all gone on a trip and she wasn't sure if she'd turned off the stove. How, the children wanted to know, could I look so enraptured and their mother so pestered by daily affairs when she was the Catholic and I was the . . . what?

The true believer. With an American-sized willingness to believe. With a Quixote-sized capacity for belief. Not worshipping God, per se. Rather Romance, with a capital R.

If the children really want to know.

But this is not about the children. This is about before the children came and after they'd gone.

Father Collosa, either a true innocent, a sharp-eyed horse trader or a closet worshipper of Romance himself, married us. He got us both to say *Sí,* then held out a small silver tray with our golden wedding rings on it. With our rings in place, he signaled me to lift the veil and reveal Amparo's face. With her face revealed, he indicated I was free to kiss her. With her lips freshly kissed, he proceeded to say Mass and to place the host on her tongue, while I knelt beside her. Then he left us and stepped down to the aisle to administer communion to the other Catholics in attendance, which included worshippers who didn't know us from Adam and Eve. With communion administered, he returned to where we knelt and said the benediction. He hadn't served the host to me, of course, but he had given me a smile that I could take as a sacramental blessing or read as a deal well struck. My choice. I smiled back.

This is not about the children, Father Collosa.

That's what you think, young man.

Somebody was playing the organ, and there must have been a wedding march as I escorted Amparo back down the aisle. I don't remember it. I remember a shattering sound, like the gates of heaven crashing open, or maybe just the church doors, and then stepping onto the street with my wife, where there was no one to throw rice—the rice throwers, presumably, were all gathered outside the Basilica in Valencia—but where we heard the rattling and honking and bass-thudding music of the city, and beyond it the tug-horns from the harbor and the foghorns from out at sea, and beyond them the sea, the cold wind of the terrible cold front blowing in and the inaudible but vastly present sound of the water moving around that those who live on islands must never stop hearing, and that those who marry on them hear as a sobering reminder that they are alone now as never before with a long way to go if they hope to get back to the mainland.

What mainland? Any mainland.

But we had a wedding supper to go to first.

It isn't very clear to me at all. I think I must have timed myself to make it through the wedding—knowing when the Church did them, it did them indissolubly—after which I allowed my drugged consciousness to sink. I don't know whether we took a taxi or Sergio or someone else drove us to the restaurant. In my mind's eye I see a small, low restaurant you step down into, a restaurant like an outpost somewhere on this island, a restaurant, I suppose now, like a bunker to protect us against all our enemies, but I know not to trust my memory to such a dramatic extent. I could ask Amparo. She lies behind me, sleeping in and reclaiming her strength, as I write this. Or she rides beside me in the car if it's the images without the words I'm considering. The restaurant had photographs of celebrities of some sort—actors, politicians, bullfighters—in rows along the wall. Celebrities who had sat where we sat, eaten where we ate. What we ate? Turkey *à la catalán* seems likely. With pine nuts and raisins. At some point someone at another table stood up and toasted us. I see that man's face. Swarthy and handsome, with the complexion of a too richly tanned boater or a movie actor with his makeup still on, he eyed Amparo with a smoldering glance and raised his glass to the big R. I see very little of us. My mother and Antonio. Antonio, voluble in his

English, and my mother ready to jump in and take over the instant he faltered. Javier, the DA, as I proceed to drink the wine someone has poured me and Javier cautions me not to drink too much. His face, the sparkling eyes, the red in his cheeks and lips, the sporting mustache—no DA, as I know them. A boyhood friend of a friend. With a relishing click at the corner of his mouth, he's reminding me I have to conserve my strength for the night ahead. My father, finally swamped under so much Spanish language and so much Spanish beauty, going down with a smile on his face. My father-in-law taking me aside with tears in his eyes to tell me something, something prescribed, traditional at this moment, threatening only in the sense that it carries the weight of history behind it—but I don't remember what. My mother-in-law fighting a grimace behind her pleasant-faced mask, as if the food or her son-in-law were not to her liking. It would be years before she warmed up. I don't see Amparo at all at that festive table. Perhaps she was sitting too close to me, *pegada como una lapa,* as the Spanish say. Stuck like a barnacle.

She's drowsing in bed behind me now, or riding along in this small rented car. I tell her I'm having trouble making any chronology stick for that wedding supper of ours, and minutes go by before she answers. Or kilometers do. When she does answer it's with a laugh that has her amused and amazed, it seems, to equal degrees.

I think about that wedding now, she says, and I don't know how we did it. I don't think I could do it again. How did we?

See it through?

Get to that altar. Get that priest to marry us and not denounce us instead. If you ask me what I remember, it's standing there wondering: What brought me here? How in the world did I do everything I had to do to be standing at this altar in this wedding dress? And I remember thinking something picked me up and dropped me there. I wasn't capable of getting there myself.

It wasn't the force of destiny, I tell her, if that's what you're suggesting. It's tempting, I agree. I get on the next day's boat and I never meet Antonio. But that wasn't what it was. It was us.

I still don't believe it. I was the *nena*. I didn't know anything. You remember how innocent I was.

Maybe *because* you were innocent you wouldn't give up. Maybe because I was I wouldn't either. I was as innocent as you, just in a different way.

You were *more* innocent, she claims. Anybody who knew anything would know better than to get involved in all that. You went off to Tarragona, and I said to myself, If he's got any sense he won't come back.

That was all show.

What was?

That trip to Tarragona. I knew I was coming back.

I hoped you wouldn't.

No, you didn't.

Yes, I did. I said to myself, If he comes back I'm about to be changed into something I'm not, and I'm not ready for that yet.

You were twenty-two. Franco was pushing eighty at the time. It all had to change soon.

I'm not talking about Franco! And I'm not talking about Spain! Me!

You *were* Spain for me. And Franco had you in thrall. We had to refight the war—and win it this time!

Is that what we did?

One of the things. I had Franco up on the end of my lance, didn't you know that? Of course they had to marry us.

It *was* a little like a war, wasn't it? Dodging around from city to city. And then just a few of us huddled in that cold church.

And that restaurant. I remember it being half underground, like a bunker.

It was intimate, if that's what you mean. There were candles. I believe there was a fire.

What else?

Turkey.

Yes, I remember that.

My mother had her corset on too tight. I had to help her loosen it.

So that's what accounted for it.

What?

The expression on her face.

Mother accounts for the expressions on her face.

And your father?

He took you aside. He talked to you.

Yes. Do you know about what?

He probably told you to be good to me or he'd hit you with his crutch.

He was crying.

He always cries.

You're not going to cry now, are you?

If I didn't cry then, why would I cry now?

That's right, now that you mention it, you didn't cry then. I don't remember you crying at all.

It was all so new—and strange. I never cry when something's new. Don't you know that about me by now? I cry when it's old. When there's no way out. When it's the same old thing.

Twenty-eight years, this marriage is twenty-eight years old, and you're not crying now. You're not, are you?

Not yet.

And we were finally alone, weren't we?

Yes.

No chaperone. No *carabina*.

No. Not even Antonio.

And it was cold, wasn't it?

They said the coldest day in fifty years.

But we weren't.

No.

Anything else you remember?

She smiles. She holds my gaze. In a range that only husbands and wives of twenty-eight years can hear, she whispers, Oh, yes. I remember a lot.

Our history. Hers and mine.

. . .

I TAKE HER BACK. I set her down on the streets of her hometown and watch her run. After traveling the small towns of Spain, this town of Bocairente, where Amparo grew up, is no less magical for me. It's half looped round by a river, which has all but dried up. Its ocher houses grow up out of rock. Its ocher church sits like a citadel on top. And rising above it, on an adjoining hill, a cypress-marked *via crucis* takes you to the chapel of Santo Cristo, which has been painted white.

Up there, under an olive tree, perhaps surrounded by *margaritas* but probably not, I kissed her for the first time. We'd escaped to get away from three little girls—ages nine, eight and five—who followed us around town as though we were gods. Townspeople dressed as *cristianos* were pursing *moros* through the streets. In the process they passed over the Roman bridge that still stood and led into the convoluted streets of the old town. The history lover in me dies hard. If a town, at any given moment, could be a history of the country in miniature, why couldn't a woman?

I return her to those streets. It's so little to ask. People stop her at every turn, wondering if it can be so. The *secretarieta*, Don Antonio and Doña Delia's little daughter, the little town secretary, that little law unto herself. Her reputation hasn't diminished, it's grown. TVs, VCRs, home computers and the Internet—Spain is as electronically up to date as the rest of Europe, and so is this town—but people still sit around their *mesas camillas* and treat themselves to the nuns' pastries and warm themselves with *herbero*, that liqueur steeped in seven local herbs, and they tell stories and, for better or worse, they do not forget. Towns like this are in need of a special personage to carry them from one generation to the next. Amparo has satisfied that need. Pretty, tireless, unbounded, mindful and sweet. They remember her. They come out of their houses and stores to greet her. On the *plaza mayor* we sit beside the fountain and she is on display. On the margin of the light she casts, I am marginally memorable myself. Our children, if they were here, would be, too.

Add twenty-nine to nine, eight and five, and those three little sisters, Fina Mari, Marita and Maria Rosa, are grown married women now. I am tremendously fond of them all, but more attached to Fina Mari than the others, not because she is the oldest but because she had an engagement that lasted for more than ten years, and then one night, sitting beside the very café on the *plaza mayor* that her fiancé and his brothers ran, we had a talk, and the next year she married. We couldn't attend the wedding, but Fina and her husband spent their honeymoon with us in the United States. What did I tell her? I really can't recall. And I'm not claiming I was the decisive voice. But what I remembered was the man nicknamed Flor, who had once taken Amparo and me aside in this very town and in drunken, rhapsodic tones pronounced us in love.

I was taking Flor's place. I was doing my part to keep the big R big.

Fina has worked in the same pharmacy—the only pharmacy in town—since she was sixteen. She is known as the *chica de la farmacia*. She knows everybody's ailment in town, just as her husband, Chimo, as innkeeper, knows many of their dark, gossipy secrets. What do they do with this knowledge? Without an ounce of malice—Chimo is as round-faced as a choirboy and Fina has the light coloring and soft modeling of features that puts everybody at ease—they pass it on to me. And what do I do with it?

Nothing. I sit before Casa Chimo at a table I have reserved and watch the people pass by. Amparo sits with me, or she goes off to visit schoolgirl friends still in town. Fina sits there, too, or one of her sisters and their husbands. The sisters' parents, Rosa and Pepe, don't get out quite as much as they used to, but they might happen by. Then there are the aunts and uncles. There's an ever-widening spiraling out of family members, followed by a spiraling back in to a point, which, because the Spanish are such ceremonial food- and drink-takers, is usually a table.

The plaza fountain isn't much. But since the plaza is wedged into the side of a hill there is a curving wall seven stories high across the way from me, three of those stories belonging to residences on the plaza itself but the top four to the backs of houses located on the street above. Since in times past the basement of any given house frequently served as the stable, it was not unusual, I've been told, to sit where I'm sitting and see a burro, say, poke his head out a window four stories up.

A Quixote might sit here looking halfway up that wall of windows waiting for a burro to appear. So that he could transform it into . . . what? Some fabulous beast? A unicorn? A griffin? A poet's winged Pegasus of a horse?

At this time and place, or, as the Spanish say, *a estas alturas,* a burro would be fabulous enough.

So when Fina and her family ask me why I like to sit at this table so long, musing on the plaza, I'm likely to tell them I'm waiting for a burro to appear. They are all masters of *detalles,* and Chimo especially has the wherewithal and the puckish sense of humor to pull off such a stunt, so I've pretty much convinced myself that if I sit here long enough a burro *will* stick its head out and bray at me. It would mean convincing someone in this day and age that someone else lives in the hope that such a thing will still happen; then it would mean finding a burro and dragging it across someone's living room and hoping it doesn't shit on the floor; then it would mean coaxing that burro up to that square of a window and getting it to poke its sweet muzzle of a head outside and bray a greeting down to that man seated in the plaza below. Of all the people I know, perhaps only the Spanish are still capable of staging such an event, but I won't hold it against them if they don't. Or, put another way, I very much believe in them; they might not believe in me quite as much.

But I have brought their *secretarieta* back, so I should expect something in return.

Is this the town we're looking for? It's Amparo's, not mine, but could I inherit it from her? Should we take advantage of the soaring dollar and buy one of those houses four stories up, and should I lead a burro in to look down on me?

I don't put it in those terms, but one evening when Fina and I are sitting there alone I begin to tell her of our search for the perfect *pueblo*, and before I'm done I've taken us back through all the regions of Spain. Andalucia, with its *pueblos blancos;* Extremadura, more rugged, less sightly, somehow more real. The fishing villages of the *rías bajas* in Galicia; the great hegemonic reach of the high plains of Old Castile. The mountainous cow towns of the Asturias; Cantabria, with its aging seaside resorts. The Basques, nursing their grievances in their green valleys and closed stone towns. The Pyrenees mountain towns of Aragon and Cataluna; the fought-over sierra towns of the Maestrazgo. La Mancha, the wind-blown stage for it all. When a cold wind blew into this small mountain town of Bocairente, where Fina and I now sit, it was known as a *manchegan* wind, and the townspeople threw those blankets they manufactured around their shoulders. When you plot our route out that way, it all comes home here, with that wind sluicing in from Quixote country, carrying the invigorating scent of herbs down out of the sierra, but also carrying, for those with the ear for it, the distant rumor of old histories, which were never not the histories of old loves and old wars.

Come live with us, Fina says.

And wait for my burro to appear? I'll become an old, old man, I say.

Two English families live down in the *barrio medieval*. A French family has a house, too, but they only come during the summer. We don't have an *americano*.

Do you need one?

Doesn't every town? she says and covers my hand. The mayor is a friend of ours. He'll help you find the right house.

It's Amparo's town, I tell her. We'll have to talk to her.

What was it that my wife said back at the start? That in towns like this, one, two, three or four generations sit around their *mesa camilla* at night and they tell their stories and they don't forget. When life turns bitter their memories do, too. I don't tell Fina that. She knows it anyway. I wait for Amparo to walk up.

When she does she says, No burro? and sits down.

Not yet.

Chimo's come out to bring her her favorite drink from this region, *horchata*, vanilla-tasting and made from the *chufa* bean and served cold. Fina enlists her husband to help convince us to buy a house here, and Chimo, who's seen some of the world, but, finally, is bound to his bar, widens one eye skeptically. It's a look—sardonic and playful—directed to his wife and asking her not to bother his customers.

The fact is, I can't remember the last time I paid for a drink at this table.

I say, You can believe this or not, but a case can be made that it's all right here in this plaza.

Gracias, Chimo says.

For what?

For allowing me to believe it or not. For not robbing me of the hope that there are better places on this planet than this.

Chimo sits down with us.

I said a case *can* be made.

We are halfway into May. The days are long but the evening is coming on. Those seven stories across the plaza face west and measure the diminishing light. The light level is up to the fifth story now. Forget the burros. Not a single human being steps out onto a balcony up there, either. That curving white wall is as blank as an old Cinemascope movie screen, and we are sitting down in the well waiting for the movie to start.

A cool breeze is blowing, not a cold one.

The plaza is filling with people out for a walk, or out to sit, like us, at other tables scattered about. The cars have been routed somewhere else. Occasionally motorbikes cruise down to circle the fountain, but after they've looked us over they either cut the motor to stay a while, or they depart.

Fina's sister Marita shows up with her husband, Vicente, and their two children, one a toddler. Marita's habitual look is startled and pleased, Vicente's shrewd and amused. Their five-year-old son, Jordi, has round black eyes he points at you and fires—what my father would have called "a pistol."

The third sister, Maria Rosa, is the tallest and most regal-looking of the three. Her husband, Juan, drives a truck and is currently out on the road, hauling a load of melons into France and waiting to see if the French will stop his truck and dump the melons out as they have with other Spanish shipments of fruit and vegetables. When Maria Rosa walks up, the talk turns to Juan and his perils and the incorrigibleness of the French, but it soon turns back.

It's such a pleasant evening that even the sisters' parents, Rosa and Pepe, are out, and when they join us at our table the talk turns to just how long we think we can get away with not coming to their house for dinner. Rosa is an implacable font of good-intentioned energy and Pepe a man who's learned to dodge out of the way, with the startled and often speechless look of his second-oldest daughter.

Rosa plunks herself down, and after bullying us into a promise to eat with her tomorrow, she wants to know it all. Not so much where we've been as what we've left behind. How our children are, Amparo's mother,

Antonio, and more distantly removed kin. When it gets too distant, Rosa takes over and begins to tell her stories, which take us back through the first appearance Amparo and I made as a couple in the town, when Rosa's daughters were so dazzled. Then Rosa jettisons me and centers on Amparo. *La secretarieta, la chiquita, el tesoro del pueblo*—and the epithets go on. Amparo running the streets, leading her band, climbing the hills, ranging along the river at the bottom of the gorge—this indefatigable and ubiquitous little girl. But Amparo also in church, to be confirmed, to be confessed, to be served the holy communion, and when each August fifteenth the Virgin was taken out and paraded through the streets before ascending to heaven to be reunited with her son, Amparo in her pristine and virginal beauty to be asked to lead the way.

Que maravilla! Que preciosidad! Que cosa más . . . Rosa goes on, but, finally, words won't do.

I say, A case could be made.

I get up to stretch my legs and walk away and leave them there at that table on the *plaza mayor*. But now that I think of it, the *plaza mayor* in Bocairente is called the *plaza del ayuntamiento*, for the town hall is located at one end. And it was on her way across the plaza to the town hall that my wife as a child was most visible and memorable; she'd been sent to lead her one-legged father home to lunch. Everybody saw her then, and everybody left their kitchens or dinner tables to come to their doors to greet the town secretary, Don Antonio, and his little girl as they passed. The nickname most people knew her by came from those walks, and, of course, in the mind of someone as fierce in her enthusiasms as Rosa, they are walks that have never ceased, not to this day.

Or tomorrow, when we'll eat lunch there and hear about them all again.

A case could be made.